Keystone

NUMBER SIX
Foreign Relations and the Presidency
H. W. Brands, General Editor

Keystone

Texas A&M University Press, College Station

The American Occupation of Okinawa
and U.S.-Japanese Relations

Nicholas Evan Sarantakes

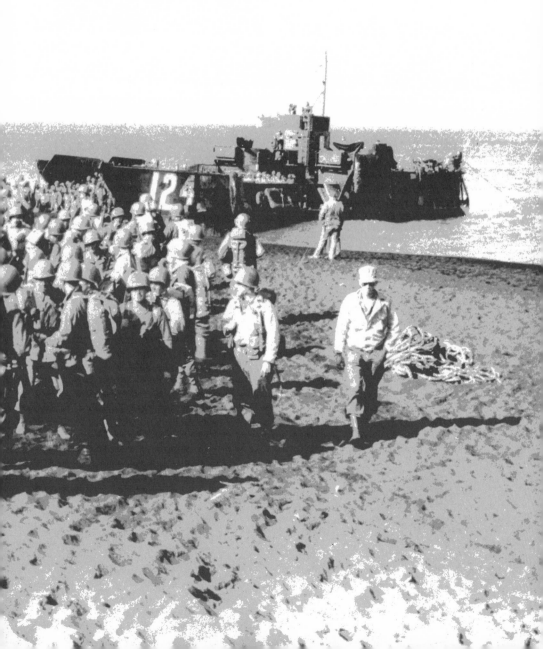

The paper used in this book meets the minimum requirements of the
American National Standard for Permanence of Paper for Printed
Library Materials, z39.48-1984.
Binding materials have been chosen for durability.

In association with
The Center for Presidential Studies
George Bush School of Government and Public Service

Library of Congress Cataloging-in-Publication Data

Sarantakes, Nicholas Evan, 1966–
    Keystone : the American occupation of Okinawa and U.S.-
Japanese relations / Nicholas Evan Sarantakes.
        p.   cm.—(Foreign relations and the presidency ; no. 6)
    Includes bibliographical references and index.
    ISBN 0-89096-969-8
    1. Japan—History—Allied occupation, 1945–1952.
2. Japan—Military relations—United States.   3. United States—
Military relations—Japan.   4. Okinawa-ken (Japan)—History.
I. Title.   II. Series.
DS889.16.S26   2001
952'.29404—dc21   00-044340

In memory of

Edward Thompson
(1900–1986)

Martha Heléne Thompson
(1910–1996)

Evanggelos Sarantakes
(1893–1976)

Ourania Sarantakes
(1903–1993)

&

Mary Sarantakes
(1942–1983)

Contents

Illustrations

Maps

Acknowledgments

The process involved in writing a work of nonfiction is an odd one. It is an amazingly solitary pursuit, yet no author can proceed without the support and assistance of others. This study is no different.

First, Roger Dingman supervised the initial development of this book as a dissertation at the University of Southern California. His advice, criticism, and observations deflated my ego, but they also made this a better, more readable work. Gordon Berger, a member of my dissertation committee, always answered questions about Japanese politics and made sure that I never exceeded the factual foundation of the documents.

Robert A. Divine read an earlier version of chapter 9, and George Herring did the same for chapter 4. Michael Barnhart made some useful comments on a conference paper based on chapters 9 and 10. Michael Schaller, Gordon Chang, and H. W. Brands graciously agreed to read the entire text in its almost final form. I gained much from their comments.

Many individuals and institutions helped with financing the development of this study. Professors Dingman, Herring, and Berger, along with Frank Mitchell, the late William Lammers, and Walt Rostow wrote letters in support of various funding requests, and I am grateful to each of them for their correspondence on my behalf. A number of foundations provided sorely needed research grants and fellowships, without which I would not have been able to do the research as quickly as I did. The General Douglas MacArthur Foundation, the Truman Library Institute, and the Johnson Library Foundation provided research grants. The U.S. Marine Corps Historical Foundation provided a dissertation fellowship that allowed me to spend the second half of 1995 on the road traveling to various archives, doing research. My family also came through in difficult financial moments. I want specifically to thank my grandmother, who did not live to see the completion of this project, and my father for their help.

As I traveled across America, many people provided me lodging for a few days to several weeks. A graduate school colleague, Rachel Standish, and her husband, Mark, gave me a wonderful place to stay when I was in Palo Alto, California. Henrietta Helm and her bed and breakfast in Independence, Missouri, made me feel welcome at the Truman Library. During my two weeks in Boston, Massachusetts, Doug Koen, an old friend from our days in Scouting, gave me a sofa to sleep on and the largest library of films on videotape that I have ever seen. (I spent most of my time in Boston viewing this collection during the 1995 U.S. government shutdown). The house of the Crist family (David, my cousin Heather, and their daughter Caitlin) became an important way station for me during my travels. Most importantly, my uncle and aunt, David and Peggy Thompson, housed me for two-and-a-half weeks while I did research at the U.S. Army Military History Institute, Carlisle Barracks, Carlisle, Pennsylvania. In my opinion, this stay in Pennsylvania was the most productive part of my journey across America. My sister Katie helped me find a copyeditor that I could afford with my meager resources.

I also had a considerable amount of help as I did my research. Bill Scott and Robert Marr, undergraduates at the University of California, Los Angeles, served as research assistants. At the Eisenhower Library, archivists Jim Lyerzapf and David Haight guided me through the paper trail in expert fashion. Mike Parrish did the same at the Johnson Library, as did Elizabeth Safly, Sam Rushay, and Dennis Bilger at the Truman Library. Edward Nagouchi, a researcher for the Japanese television network, NHK, shared some of his findings with me. Leonard Downie, executive editor of *The Washington Post*, helped me find two series on Okinawa his paper ran in the mid-1960s before it was indexed. Bob Wampler, director of the U.S.-Japan Project at the National Security Archive, was key in obtaining the declassification of several Nixon-era documents. Donna Alvah, a graduate student at the University of California, Davis, provided me with copies of documents. Randy Papadopoulos of George Washington University provided me with citations to relevant literature. Aaron Foresberg, a fellow Longhorn, acquired and translated copies of Sato Eisaku's diary for me under a short deadline.

Finally, the good people at Texas A&M University Press have been wonderful to work with. Series editor H. W. Brands and the staff at the press have been supportive of this effort, offering suggestions that were always constructive and made this work better than it otherwise would have been. This book is my first, but I have had enough experience with the academic publishing process to appreciate supportive efforts. This praise of an Aggie institution should count all the more coming as it does from a proud graduate of the University of Texas.

The old saying is that with this type of assistance, I alone bear responsibility for whatever faults remain. It is true.

Finally, I would like to point out that macrons do not appear over any of the Japanese words in this text. Because this book appears in English and is intended for an American audience, I believe that the use of such diacritics would be a distraction to the reader.

NES
Commerce, Texas
Austin, Texas
Los Angeles, Texas
Summer, 2000

Introduction

In 1972 the United States returned the prefecture of Okinawa to Japanese administration, ending twenty-seven years of American rule. This island was the strategic keystone of the postwar American base system of double containment in the Pacific and the only spot in that chain that American officials insisted on governing. Administrative control and the geographic location of Okinawa made it possible for U.S. forces stationed on the island to strike at almost every strategic target of importance in the Pacific and East Asia without having to consult with any foreign power. Under the legal cover of "residual sovereignty," Americans had ruled the Ryukyu Islands as a colony in everything but name since the end of World War II.

The account that follows seeks to address the reason for this odd distinction. Specifically, two questions must be answered to explain the American occupation of Okinawa: First, why would the United States insist on administering an entire province of a country that it otherwise called an ally? Second, why did the Americans return Okinawa when they did? The answers to these questions serve as the thesis of this work.

American leaders believed they faced two sets of potential enemies in the Pacific: the Communists in Soviet Russia (and later China) on the one hand and the Japanese on the other. Historical documents clearly show that U.S. policymakers had considerable doubts about the dependability of the Japanese. American officials viewed Japan in some ways as a latent threat to the American presence in the Pacific for a number of years after the war and then worried that the Japanese might adopt a policy of neutrality during the Cold War, abandoning the struggle against communism. Returning Okinawa was an important retreat from this viewpoint, but the United States only agreed to do so after Okinawans made their feelings and nationalism clear at the ballot box in 1968, warning the Americans that continued occupation put the security relationship with Japan and the regional political order based on that partnership at risk.

Previous considerations of postwar diplomacy between these two countries have largely ignored the issue of Okinawa, concentrating primarily on the occupation of Japan. These accounts fall into three categories. The first group argued that the occupation of Japan was an unqualified success. Americans and Japanese quickly put away the hatred of war and went about the business of peace. General of the Army Douglas MacArthur and other Americans nobly and selflessly purged Japan of the corrupt institutions and evil individuals that had brought the nation to its greatest disgrace. Rejecting a harsh and vindictive peace, the United States also helped Japan rebuild economically from the destruction of war. MacArthur, his admirers, participant-historians, the general's biographers, and (for a variety of reasons) his enemies, advanced this interpretation.[1]

Beginning in the 1970s, a wide assortment of historians began a frontal assault on this view as documents became available through the declassification process. Scholars quickly challenged and dismissed the idea that the occupation was an endeavor exclusive to the United States, noting the influence on occupation policy and the presence of troops from the wartime allies that had defeated Japan.[2] Other writers argued that occupation policies might have helped the Japanese but were primarily designed to further U.S. policies and objectives in the Cold War. Japanese figures supported American efforts out of self-interest.[3] At other times, though, the Japanese challenged and diluted U.S. actions. A number of historians also argued that the initial emphasis on political and economic reforms gave way in 1947–48 to a focus on economic recovery, a change that became known as the "reverse course." Historian John Dower, a leading expert on the occupation, defined this phenomenon as "the shift of occupation priorities from democratization of a former enemy to reconstruction of a future cold war ally."[4]

A more extreme version of this second interpretation viewed the occupation and the San Francisco peace and security treaties as the basis of a political order that reduced Japan to an American client state. Thereafter, Japan had no independent foreign policy and was made into an important forward base for the United States as the Cold War came to Asia. These actions often ran counter to the expressed desires of the Japanese public.[5]

Until recently, no major work has made an extended examination of U.S.-Japanese relations since the end of the occupation. In 1997 two well-known and established historians published studies that examined this period and offered explanations as to how two very different nations could become and remain allies. In *Altered States* Michael Schaller asserted that "a coherent strategy in East Asia designed to deny Japan's industrial potential to the Communist powers" was the driving force behind foreign policy in the region. This policy was largely successful, but the American general public came to regret it when Japan turned into a major economic rival in the 1980s and 1990s. Although significant, Okinawa clearly played a secondary role in this depiction of the bilateral relationship. Walter LaFeber in *The Clash*, a study of diplomatic relations between the two countries since their first contact in 1853, argued that the United States and Japan have repeatedly confronted each other because each believed in and practiced different forms of capitalism. The two nations eventually went to war when these systems challenged one another in China. In remission during the 1950s, this fundamental conflict reemerged when Japan resumed its commerce and trade with China in the 1960s.[6]

Like these works, an examination of the American occupation of Okinawa could address the larger issue of U.S.-Japanese relations, but other than the battle histories there have been few studies about the island.[7] (The best-known book about Okinawa is actually a novel, *The Teahouse of the August Moon.*)[8] Political scientist Watanabe Akio examined the formation of Japanese attitudes in his impressive study *The Okinawa Problem*. Writing during the reversion negotiations, he argued that reversion was a "measure of the 'maturity' of the new alliance on the one hand and the re-emergence of the defeated nation on the other."[9] Another political scientist, Frederick Shiels, explored the American decision-making process on this issue in a collection of case studies.[10] Morton D. Morris and Arnold G. Fisch, Jr., have offered works on the occupation of Okinawa. Morris's book is part memoir, part op-ed piece, and as was so typical of the expatriate community on Okinawa, he used emotion more than logic to make the point that the Okinawans neither needed nor wanted reversion. Fisch, in the official U.S. Army history of the military-government phase of the occupation, argued that Americans set out to transform the Ryukyus.[11] Higa Mikio's study of postwar Okinawan politics was an important study from the Okinawan perspective and has remained useful in explaining public opinion on the island.[12] The idea that Okinawans were victimized first by the Japanese during the war and then by the Americans during the occupation has nearly become an article of faith in the prefecture, and many American writers have taken this position as well.[13]

This study offers an analysis that differs to a large degree in both focus and finding from these previous works on U.S.-Japanese relations and Okinawa. The past always affects planning for the future, and generals always prepare for the last war; Americans in the 1940s and 1950s were no different. The United States had no guarantee regarding the foreign policies Japan would pursue after the occupation ended. Preventing Japan from returning to an expansionist foreign policy was a major element of the San Francisco peace and security treaties of 1951. At the same time, the Cold War created new concerns. American planners needed a base structure that could function against two entirely different sets of enemies. As time passed, it became clear to American decision makers that Japan had renounced its old ways and would not be a threat itself. Japan's dependability as an ally was another matter. American politicians, diplomats, and generals constantly feared that Japan would waver in its commitment to fight in the Cold War crusade. Americans constantly worried that Japan would go neutral as they watched "pro-American" leaders barely holding on to power. In a time when neutrality was seen as serving only the interests of the enemy, something had to be done about Japan. Keeping Okinawa was that something. Americans were using the island to hedge their bets on Japan.

Three recurring themes appear in this account. First, Okinawa was a colony—Americans used the term freely, although policymakers did so mainly in private—because U.S. military forces stationed on the island had a dual mission in the double-containment system. The strategic location of the island was the primary reason for the existence of the colony. Given their location along Japan's southern flank, American forces on Okinawa could check any advance the Japanese tried to make along the Chinese coast. Planners in the U.S. Air Force, Marine Corps, and Army used the island's proximity to the Asian mainland to develop plans that allowed them to project American power onto the continent against a Communist foe. The air force could, and did, hit a number of important targets on the Eurasian landmass from airfields in the Ryukyus. The Marine Corps used the island as a forward base for rapid deployment. The army based its logistical and supply operations in the Pacific on Okinawa. The fact that three service branches used the island made it that much more valuable. Other than military utility, however, there were few reasons for an American presence. The United States gained nothing economically from ruling Okinawa. In fact, the Ryukyus were a drain on American resources; most Okinawans bought Japanese goods.

Second, the colony existed and continued to exist, despite the efforts of many important figures, because partisan politics drove the issue in Japan and Okinawa while bureaucratic confrontations shaped the official position of the U.S. government. There were sharp and distinct differences between Japanese political parties on the propriety of an alliance with the United States. Subtle differences also existed among the various factions of the governing Liberal Democratic Party (LDP), which controlled the government. The debilitating effects of this debate kept the Japanese government from developing a comprehensive policy regarding Okinawa. On the other side of the Pacific, bureaucratic rivalries in Washington shaped American policy toward the island. The leadership of the military, particularly those in uniform, demanded that the United States retain the Ryukyus even after the occupation of Japan ended. The Joint Chiefs of Staff wanted a base from which to operate without having to suffer political restrictions. Interservice rivalries and disputes between the civilian and uniformed leadership of the military complicated the policy positions of the Defense Department. American diplomats took a different view. Although they supported the strategic function the base served, representatives of the State Department had reservations about American administration for two reasons: First, ruling the prefecture would be an expensive proposition. This argument was advanced in the 1940s as the U.S. government was attempting to decide the fate of the island. Second, individuals in the State Department were concerned later that continued American rule put the larger relationship with Japan at risk. In bureaucratic conferences some suggested that prolonged American rule of a populated foreign land ran counter to traditional American policies of self-determination, anticolonialism, and democratic government. The military feared these arguments and worked to restrict media access to the island as well as limit congressional involvement lest the American public or their representatives become outraged at these violations of U.S. principles and force the return of the archipelago. The military, primarily the army, was successful in this endeavor. Congress rarely became involved in matters about the Ryukyus, serving mainly as a policy-making, rather than as a political, institution when it did. Okinawa was never a vote-getting issue. These different approaches to the Okinawa issue in Washington and Tokyo were important. American officials had the tactical advantage of well-defined positions and could deflect issues on a short-term basis, but the Japanese had the weight of public interest at the national level behind them and in the long run were able to overcome the resistance of U.S. bureaucrats, who had no broad support to sustain their views.

Finally, Americans needed and obtained local consent, or at least acquiescence, to rule this colony and use it as a base for military operations. In the early 1950s the United States helped rebuild the island, which was a major reason for Okinawan tolerance of American administration. Local labor and construction firms helped build the bases. The island became one of the fastest-growing economies in Asia because of the businesses that serviced the American military. The U.S. government also instituted a number of programs that met the local needs Okinawans defined as necessities: for example, massive school construction in the 1950s, the establishment of the first university on the island, and a study-in-America program. Whatever the shortcomings of American rule, and there were many, it also had a constructive element. When the Okinawans objected to American decisions, they challenged the policy and often forced modifications or reversals. The population of the island was not helpless and weak. The agency of the Okinawan people was an important factor in the American administration. This fact in itself helped undermine claims that the United States needed to continue its administration of the archipelago.

A word about expectations is in order. What follows is primarily a study of U.S. foreign policy. This study does not pretend to offer a comprehensive examination of American-Okinawan social interaction during the years of occupation, the impact the foreign presence had on the residents of the Ryukyus, or a full analysis of Japanese politics relating to the prefecture. These topics are no less important than the diplomatic relationship and should receive their due attention after the archives in Japan become accessible. (Most books about Okinawa written in Japanese are mainly contemporary in nature, produced without access to documents or the detachment and perspective of time.) To the extent that this volume explores these issues, it represents an effort to put American actions and decisions into an international perspective—events abroad often affected the range of options available to policymakers in Washington.

The narrative begins with an account of the battle for Okinawa. The commander of the invading American Army, Lt. Gen. Simon Bolivar Buckner, Jr., came to Okinawa with definite ideas on how to fight the Japanese and what to do with the island after the battle and the war. He recognized the vital strategic location of the island and thought the United States should keep it as a prize of war. He also had well-formed ideas on the legal mechanisms the United States should use to sanction this act.

The third chapter examines the policy debates about the fate of Okinawa that began in Washington during 1945. The Joint Chiefs of Staff wanted the United States to assume sovereignty over the island. The State Department opposed this, initially arguing that administration of the island would be excessively expensive. President Harry S. Truman avoided a decision on the matter and let the issue drift. This nondecision had a devastating effect on social conditions for both the indigenous population and the American soldiers later stationed on Okinawa.

Chapter 4 focuses on the events that led to a firm decision to keep Okinawa and the negotiations of the Japanese peace treaty, which gave the occupation of the island legal sanction. The settlement John Foster Dulles negotiated with Japan and America's wartime allies came to resemble the vision Buckner had held for postwar Okinawa. The United States kept the island under the legal cover of "residual sovereignty," which gave the Japanese a basis for their claims to the island in future years.

The development of the island in the first half of the 1950s is the subject of the next chapter. With the support of Okinawan labor, the United States initiated a number of building projects that changed the face of the island. The Korean War slowed down construction, even though the air force used Okinawan airfields to bomb North Korean targets.

Chapter 6 considers the troubles that wracked the American administration of Okinawa and, as a result, U.S.-Japanese relations. Problems ranged from disputes over the proper amount and form of rental payment for private land used by United States bases to the election and removal of a Communist as mayor of the largest city on the island. The collective weight of these problems led the American ambassador in Tokyo, Douglas MacArthur II, to recommend that the United States return Okinawa to Japanese administration. Secretary of State John Foster Dulles and Pres. Dwight D. Eisenhower were equally concerned and began exploring such an option. The military, however, viewed the problems the nation faced with Japan as a clear sign that the Japanese were an uncertain ally of questionable dependability. In the end, the Japanese did little to push their claims to the Ryukyu Islands, which allowed the Pentagon to block action during the negotiation of a new security treaty.

The conflict between the military and the diplomats intensified, and chapter 7 examines the rivalry between Edwin Reischauer, MacArthur's successor in Tokyo, and Lt. Gen. Paul Caraway, the high commissioner of the Ryukyu Islands. Reischauer went to Tokyo determined to do something about Okinawa, which he considered an international issue waiting to explode. Caraway believed that the American presence in Okinawa was in the best interests of both the Okinawans and the Japanese. He fought and bested Reischauer in a bureaucratic contest to control policy, and his victory assured that little would change.

Chapter 8 looks at developments in Tokyo and Okinawa that moved the United States and Japan closer to reversion. The new Japanese prime minister, Sato Eisaku, although a strong supporter of the alliance with the United States, became an ardent advocate for reversion once in office. In doing so, he channeled a widespread national consensus supporting reversion in a direction that would not undermine Japanese ties with the United States. In 1966 a new U.S. ambassador arrived in Tokyo and a new American high commissioner took charge in Okinawa. These two men were determined to work together and understood that changing political conditions in both Japan and Okinawa would soon require reversion.

The next chapter concentrates on the diplomatic negotiations that led to the agreement between Sato and Pres. Richard M. Nixon to return Okinawa to Japan. American and Japanese diplomats wanted an agreement that would preserve the security alliance between their two countries. Reversion removed a dangerous source of discontent and achieved the goals both countries desired. U. Alexis Johnson was a key player in these negotiations, first as U.S. ambassador in Tokyo and later as undersecretary of state in the Nixon administration.

The final chapter follows the difficult final negotiations and the ratification process in both countries. There were groups in Japan, Okinawa, and the United States that opposed reversion. Some Americans still worried that Japan would adopt a policy of neutrality in the Cold War. Many to the left of the political center in Okinawa and Japan wanted to do just that and hoped to use reversion to end the American alliance. Frustrated when Sato produced an agreement that thwarted this desire, anti-American activists took to the streets in protest in a last-ditch effort to block ratification. They failed.

The story that unfolds on the following pages is a drama of the first order. It is the story of mobs rioting, prostitutes plying their trade, diplomats navigating the treacherous corridors of power in two countries, and clever politicians taking high-risk gambles. The narrative moves from the dingy, rubble-filled streets of Naha to the majesty of the Oval Office. But it begins at a sandy beach on a temperate Easter Sunday in the last year of World War II.

Keystone

CHAPTER 1

The Battle, 1945

On April 1, 1945, American amphibious assault vehicles cut through a calm sea in a mass of even lines as they approached Okinawa. A light breeze and a slight overcast made the morning cool, but the soldiers and marines in the boats were of no mind to notice the weather. These troops expected to suffer casualties of 80–85 percent when they stormed the beach. They had feasted on steak and eggs that morning. The food was good, though too good. More than one wondered if this was their last meal, and for some it was. The men rode to the island with a tense atmosphere of fear and apprehension surrounding them. As they neared the landing site, they slowly realized the Japanese were not firing at them. Some marines stormed the beach and hit the ground before they realized there was no enemy fire. "What's going on?" one asked. Columnist Ernie Pyle, in the seventh wave, expected to see mangled bodies when he arrived, and reluctantly looked around. "And then like a man in the movies who looks and looks away and then suddenly looks back unbelieving, I realized there were no bodies anywhere—and no wounded."

Men in later waves were actually singing when they arrived on the island. This uncontested landing left the commander of the Tenth Army befuddled. As the army and marine units under his command advanced inland standing up, Lt. Gen. Simon Bolivar Buckner, Jr., later recorded in his diary: "The Japs have missed their best opportunity on the ground and in the air."[1] Thus began the American presence in Okinawa.[2]

Buckner was a major proponent of this presence. He had fought hard to get the American military to agree to the invasion of Okinawa and had definite ideas on the postwar future of the island. Although he tried to avoid interservice rivalries, his decisions and failure to appreciate the differences in tactics and doctrine between the army and marine units under his command actually enflamed the disputes between these services. Buckner's mistakes contributed to high casualty rates that seemed remote at the end of that first day, making American military leaders determined to hold the island after the war. While Americans could have done better in the ensuing battle, the main reason it became a bloody meat grinder was the determined and capable Japanese defense. This resistance also removed the strongest advocate of a postwar American presence on the island, which complicated the administration of Okinawa in many ways during the immediate postwar years.

In 1944, when Buckner assumed command of the newly formed Tenth Army, he was in his late fifties. Other than the graying of his thick hair, his features showed little sign of age. His solid physique reflected the amazingly good athletic condition in which he kept himself. A naturalist and a party animal of the first rank, Buckner had a jutting jaw and dark, blazing eyes, his appearance marred only by a hawklike nose (which makes it easy to understand his success as a womanizer).

Buckner's early career was average at best. For most of his life, he lived in the shadow of his father. The original Simon Bolivar Buckner was a graduate of West Point who became a lieutenant general during the Civil War. Having earned his rank in the Confederate Army, though, his military career ended with the war. The elder Buckner entered politics afterward, becoming governor of Kentucky and the vice presidential nominee of the Gold Democratic ticket in 1896.

Simon, Jr., graduated from West Point in 1908, to which his father had secured an appointment for him from none other than the president of the United States, Theodore Roosevelt. He saw no combat in World War I, spending most of the interwar period in U.S. Army schools as either student or instructor. He was the commandant of cadets at West Point in the 1930s, a position roughly equivalent to dean of students (in their works, James and William Belote and George Feifer confused this position with superintendent, which is comparable to university president). In these training and educational posts, Buckner absorbed and then disseminated the U.S. Army doctrine that accorded artillery the decisive role in determining the outcome of an engagement. When world war came a second time, Buckner spent most of it in Alaska, an area of secondary importance. He had numerous clashes with the naval commander for the northern Pacific, and this almost ended his career. He learned from the experience, though. When he assumed command of the Tenth Army in 1944, it was under the theater command of Adm. Chester W. Nimitz, commander in chief, Pacific Ocean Areas, and Buckner did his utmost to avoid any interservice confrontations. "Buckner is playing the Navy," Gen. Joseph Stilwell noted in his diary during an inspection trip toward the end of the battle for Okinawa. "It is all rather nauseating."[3]

Interservice rivalries were almost unavoidable during the invasion of the island. The Tenth Army that Buckner commanded was the product of two different military services, each with distinctly different approaches to fighting. The III Marine Amphibious Corps and the XXIV Corps of the U.S. Army were the main combat units in Buckner's field army. According to army doctrine, the proper way to destroy an enemy was through the use of overwhelming firepower in a headon confrontation. The mission of the infantry was to find and hold the adversary, and the artillery would then destroy him. These tactics required material superiority for success and did not win much respect. In Europe, German generals held the U.S. infantry in contempt, respecting only the American artillery. British and French officers in North Africa called the Americans "our Italians."[4]

The marines, on the other hand, had made amphibious assault their specialization during the interwar period. Marine doctrine called for combined arms assault. Naval gunfire would soften up enemy coastal fortifications, and aerial support would cover advancing ground troops. Marine tactics stressed maneuver on short supply lines. Training emphasized esprit de corps and discipline to an extent far greater than did the army.[5]

The objective for the Tenth Army remained in dispute. Buckner spent the summer of 1944 putting together a staff, creating the new field army, and preparing for an invasion. Buckner favored an attack on Okinawa. He not only believed this island was the best location from which to stage an invasion of Japan, but also that after the war "Okinawa should be retained by us as a means of access to the China sea." American bases on the island could serve as "a check against further aggression by Japan and as an outpost to prevent Russia from expansion into the Pacific from Chinese ports that she might acquire at the end of the war by occupying them under the pretext of helping us against Japan." He also wanted the United States to find some legal device that would avoid giving Okinawans U.S. citizenship in order to avoid complicating American race relations. A number of admirals, however, preferred an attack on Formosa. The issue came to a head on September 2, 1944. Vice Adm. Raymond Spruance questioned the wisdom of an attack on Okinawa. Using vague language to protect security, Buckner wrote in his diary that "Adm. Nimitz said that unless our project went through we would be tied to a southern project that would make the war last another year." Nimitz's view ended the debate between Okinawa and Formosa, but the invasion of Okinawa remained in doubt for several more weeks as staff officers resolved supply, manpower, and logistical problems.[6]

Problems started during the planning of this joint operation. The Tenth Army staff planned the invasion but ignored the operational differences between the U.S. Army and Marine Corps, writing a plan that emphasized army tactics and assigning similar missions to both army and marine divisions. At the same time, the staff of Adm. Chester Nimitz expected that preliminary air and naval operations would give U.S. forces command of the air and sea, but they also anticipated strong Japanese counterattacks from Formosa and southern Japan. As a result, these naval planners emphasized mobility and combined arms operations for a rapid conquest of the island that would reduce the exposure of navy ships. To accomplish this task, the staff of the Tenth Army decided to stage the landing on the west coast, just below the neck of the island. The marine III Amphibious Corps would take the northern section of the island while the army's XXIV Corps marched south.[7]

Although Buckner did exceptional work to prevent interservice slights and rivalries and developed a good working relationship with his main marine subordinate, he did little to alleviate the difference in doctrine and tactical expectations between the services' units, treating them as if they were the same. Buckner was a firm believer in U.S. Army doctrine.

During the battle, he explained his strategy for winning to a group of reporters: "We're relying on our tremendous fire power and trying to crush them by weight of weapons."[8]

Japanese defensive fortifications complicated matters for Buckner. The Japanese goal was to disrupt "the enemy's plans by inflicting maximum losses on him, and, even when the situation is hopeless, holding out in strong positions for as long as possible." The Thirty-second Army under the command of Lt. Gen. Ushijima Mitsuru was assigned to meet this objective. Tall, physically imposing, and sporting a short mustache, Ushijima's main strength was the serenity he radiated, a quiet dignity that inspired his men. He left most of the details to his staff, of which the two most important members were Lt. Gen. Cho Isamu, the chief of staff, and Col. Yahara Hiromichi, senior officer in charge of operations. Cho was an energetic, fiery individual, while Yahara was a measured, dispassionate military intellectual. Although they would clash over tactics, they remained friendly. After a careful analysis of Okinawan geography, Yahara accurately predicted both the landing site and size of the American invasion force. In a memo to Ushijima and Cho, he argued that the Thirty-second Army lacked the strength to defend the beaches and suggested that the army defend only the militarily valuable southern half of the island, conceding the landing and the unpopulated north to the Americans. The mountainous geography of that region made it impossible to build airfields and thus limited its military importance. Ushijima and Cho agreed with Yahara and adopted his proposed strategy. This decision effectively sealed the fate of the island and determined the outcome of the battle. The contest would be a bloody siege of attrition that the Americans would win if they were willing to pay the cost in casualties.[9]

Ushijima quickly ordered the construction of defensive fortifications. The Japanese established three lines of defense using an interconnected system of tunnels, blockhouses, pillboxes, trenches, caves, and Okinawan tombs. These structures channeled American attackers into prepared lines of fire and impact zones, and many of the positions overlapped. The Thirty-second Army also had more artillery than any other Japanese force the United States had encountered in the war, including a six-month supply of ammunition. Japanese and Okinawan workers fortified the reverse and forward slopes of hills, thus neutralizing the potential effectiveness of American artillery.[10]

Contrary to standard opinion in the prefecture, which holds that the residents of the island were innocent bystanders, Okinawans gave active and voluntary support to the Japanese war effort.[11] Okinawans contributed roughly twenty thousand combat troops of their Home Guard to the Thirty-second Army. Okinawan conscripts might have accounted for up to one-third of Japanese defenders. A battalion commander in the 24th Division noted that these local troops were an asset: the Okinawans fought well, and their knowledge of local terrain helped his unit during night actions.[12]

These efforts, however, were not in play as the marines made a rapid and almost painless advance to the north. The 1st Marine Division raced across the island, enjoying the temperate, dry weather and reaching the eastern coast on April 4—sailors aboard the USS *Tennessee* joked that the marines had already made contact with the Russians coming from the other side. The marines marching north sucked on sugar cane, and one recalled that the advance was "more like maneuvers than combat; we didn't even dig foxholes." Admiral Spruance, the task force commander for the Central Pacific who also had authority over the Tenth Army, put pressure on Buckner to change plans in order to reduce the time his ships were exposed to Japanese attack. Securing the northern half of the island to prevent any reinforcements from augmenting the Japanese forces in the south quickly became the priority. The only area where there was strong resistance was on the Motobu Peninsula on the northwest side of island. The Japanese defended the peninsula because heavy guns there could fire on and control airfields on Ie Shima, a small island off Okinawa. A veteran of this rapid American advance recorded a general sentiment in his memoirs: "Everyone was asking the same question: 'Where the hell are the Nips?'" His commanding officer had no idea. "Don't ask me why we haven't had more opposition," Maj. Gen. Roy S. Geiger, commanding the III Amphibious Corps, told a *New York Times* reporter. "I don't understand it." The marines reached the northern tip of Okinawa on April 13 and secured the Motobu Peninsula on April 20.[13]

The uncontested landing and rapid conquest of the northern half of the island put a greater than expected emphasis on logistical efforts. Quartermaster units were able to land supplies on the beaches without much difficulty and operated around-the-clock, although stormy weather and kamikaze attacks occasionally brought this process to a halt. The poor

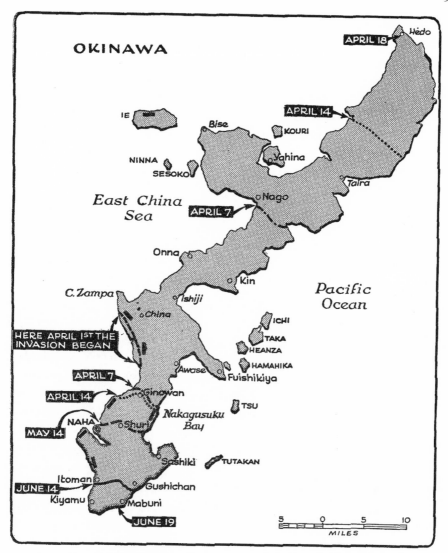

MAP 1. *This map from* The New York Times *shows the progress of the battle to take Okinawa in 1945. From* The War in Maps: An Atlas of the New York Times Maps, Fourth Edition *by Francis Brown, copyright 1941, 1946 by the* New York Times. *Used by permission of Oxford University Press, Inc.*

quality of Okinawan roads and bridges was a significant problem that slowed down supply efforts. The roads were narrow and unsurfaced dirt paths. In dry weather, American trucks kicked up thick clouds of dust that reduced visibility to the length of a truck hood. Following rain showers on April 4–5 and 10–11, convoys sank into these churned-up, muddy paths. Engineers had to widen the roads and surface them using coral, limestone, and the rubble from destroyed villages. These construction units also replaced weak and narrow bridges with ones that could support American trucks and tanks. Supply shortages plagued army units, with their heavy logistical tail, far more than the marines.[14]

While the early combat operations on Okinawa were tepid and mild, events transpiring off the Okinawan coast were quite different. The 77th Division, an army unit, took Ie Shima after a brief, but intense, three-day fight that included street-to-street combat in the main town on the island. "The last three days of this fighting were the bitterest I ever witnessed," declared the division commander. The capture of Ie Shima, however, is better remembered for Ernie Pyle's death.[15]

A bloody battle had also started at sea. As Nimitz later wrote, "This was not a battle by vast opposing forces, but an unending series of small fights." Japanese kamikaze planes hit American ships hard. The navy established a circle of radar pickets around the island to provide early warning of an incoming attack. The destroyers in these pickets took the brunt of the Japanese attack. The ships would twist and turn to evade their attackers as their own guns turned the sky gray and spent shells shot up geysers as they hit the sea. The USS *Laffey* suffered twenty-two separate attacks in one eighty-minute period; the radio operator reported seeing fifty planes in the air. Four bombs, six kamikazes, and strafing fire hit the ship. Samuel Eliot Morison, the Harvard University historian, observed that "no ship has ever survived an attack of the intensity that she experienced." Weary sailors at one station placed an arrow-shaped sign on their ship that read: "Carriers this way." Japanese pilots were seeking aircraft carriers and battleships, but most were inexperienced and mistook the destroyers on picket duty for capital ships. The erroneous radio reports of pilots convinced the Japanese that the kamikazes were achieving results. The commander of the Fifth Air Fleet, Adm. Ugaki Matome, brushed in his diary that the "operation is developing extremely in favor of our side. The enemy received a heavy blow this time, and odds are apparently leaning to our side. Some even think that victory will be ours with one more push." Morison witnessed firsthand much of this April carnage from the deck of the *Tennessee.* "For the Navy it was one of the toughest months in the entire Pacific War," he wrote.[16]

As Japanese attacks continued, Admiral Nimitz tried to speed up the ground operations. According to the admiral's biographer, Nimitz blamed the intense air attacks not on the Japanese but on the slow progress of U.S. Army units in the south. Admiral Spruance shared this view. In a conference with Buckner on April 23, Nimitz reportedly said, "I'm losing a ship and a half a day. So if this line isn't moving within five days, we'll get someone here to move it so we can all get out from under these stupid air attacks." Buckner, however, made no mention of any such warning in his diary. According to him, the major thrust of the meeting was his effort to convince Nimitz about the importance and postwar utility of retaining the island. The admiral did give Buckner a bottle of liquor. The general said he would open the bottle when all organized resistance ended. "I am getting thirsty," he told his wife. The next day he wrote, "Adm. Nimitz left this morning, apparently well pleased."[17]

Nimitz was reportedly upset because the XXIV Corps was bogged down in the south, while the III Amphibious Corps quickly took the north. On April 4, the same day the marines reached the eastern coast of Okinawa, elements of the XXIV Corps made contact with the first of three Japanese defensive lines. From April 9 through 12, the Japanese first blunted and then turned back the 96th Division, which was advancing on the west side of the corps' front line. Maj. Gen. John Hodge, commanding the XXIV Corps, decided to use artillery to break the Japanese defensive positions. Hodge waited six days for enough ammunition to reach his guns, only to see the Japanese withstand the barrage. The evening after Nimitz met with Buckner, the Japanese retreated as their strength ebbed to the breaking point, using an artillery barrage of their own to provide cover.[18]

The second defensive line fell more easily, mainly due to Japanese mistakes. Buckner used the III Amphibious Corps and the 77th Division, fresh from its conquest of Ie Shima, to relieve the battered divisions of the XXIV Corps. General Cho helped the Americans when he convinced Ushijima to launch a counterattack against the recommendations of Colonel Yahara. On May 4, Japanese units launched their attack, mainly against army divisions. American guns caught Japanese troops in the open and turned them into "artillery meat." The Japanese continued to attack for another day before the offensive ended. Buckner described the

Japanese counteroffensive as "one of the best coordinated attacks I have ever seen. The enemy means business, but he had waited too long and he didn't have what it took." According to James and William Belote, the attacks on May 4–5 were the "only serious Japanese mistakes of the Okinawa campaign." Ushijima knew this when he called Yahara into his office and told the colonel he was right. "I am ready to fight, but from now on I leave everything up to you," he said in tears. "My instructions to you are to do whatever you feel is necessary." Yahara was outraged. The futile offensive had wasted men and resources that the Thirty-second Army could have used to prolong the battle and bleed the Americans even further. "It was now too late to accomplish anything. I was not only frustrated, I was furious."[19]

Despite American success, a controversy broke out over Buckner's use of the marines. Maj. Gen. Andrew Bruce, commanding the 77th Division, suggested that the Tenth Army stage a second landing in the south, using his unit and the III Amphibious Corps. Some marines wholeheartedly endorsed this view, while others on the Tenth Army staff, as well as III Amphibious Corps commander Maj. Gen. Roy S. Geiger, opposed the idea. Buckner looked at his supply lines—which reflected his grounding in army doctrine—and decided against this plan. He told the authors of the army's official history of the battle that a second landing would be "another Anzio, but worse." (Anzio was the site of a disastrous Allied amphibious assault in Italy.) The issue hardly registered in Buckner's diary.[20]

As the battle continued, this decision became controversial. Homer Bigart, war correspondent for the *New York Herald Tribune,* filed a story critical of Buckner's decision about a second landing. Bigart correctly observed that the Japanese were fighting a battle of attrition in the southern half of the island. He also accurately noted that the marines took the northern half of Okinawa quickly because the Japanese made little effort to defend that section of the island. Once the III Amphibious Corps finished taking the north, Buckner deployed them in the south, using what Bigart called "ultra-conservative" tactics. "A landing on southern Okinawa would have hastened the encirclement of Shuri. Instead of an end run, we persisted in frontal attacks," he wrote. "It was hey-diddle-diddle straight down the middle." Syndicated columnist David Lawerence used this dispatch as the basis for two columns criticizing Buckner's strategy and interservice leadership. In his first column, Lawerence claimed an amphibious assault would have worked and saved American lives.

He noted that Buckner had no combat experience and wondered why Nimitz had not ordered a second assault. A week later he started another column about Okinawa with a loaded sentence: "Why is the truth about the military fiasco at Okinawa being hushed up?" He said the truth was beginning to leak out with the high casualty figures. He called the battle a "fiasco" and blamed Buckner and the army for conservative tactics. In a deliberate distortion of the facts, Lawerence wrote that the rapid marine conquest of the north was ample proof that they used sound tactics. He demanded an immediate investigation into Buckner's decision. When Buckner saw these editorials, he poured his outrage into his diary. "The enemy should be pleased by his services for them."[21]

Buckner was not one to take criticism of this nature lightly, and he responded forcefully at a press conference on June 15. In his diary the general noted that he had tried to put the entire campaign into a strategic context and to give credit to the units that had made major advances against the Japanese. The only publication that gave extended coverage to this conference was the *New York Herald Tribune*, and according to the account in this paper, strategy and American progress on the island were the major focus of the general's presentation. The purpose of taking the island, Buckner said, was to use its airfields to bomb Japan and develop it as a base for the invasion of the Japanese home islands. He explained that the geography of southern Okinawa ruled against a second landing. Reefs would have made an amphibious assault difficult and the hilly terrain would have made it easy for the Japanese to contain American forces on the beach. "If we'd scattered our forces we might have got licked, or it might have unduly prolonged the campaign; or we might have been forced to call on additional troops, which we did not want to do." Buckner said that he needed to control the number of service personnel on the island because the congestion of more units would have slowed down construction of the airfields. "We didn't need to rush forward, because we had secured enough airfields to execute our development mission."[22]

Buckner also had defenders in both the navy and the press. When Nimitz read the Lawerence columns, he responded with a statement that attacked the journalist and defended Buckner. "The article, which has been widely reprinted shows that the author has been badly misinformed, so badly as to give the impression that he has been made use of for purposes which are not in the best interest of the United States," Nimitz charged. While the criticism might seem reasonable in the United States, he explained, the invasion of the island was planned, and his staff had considered a number of different options. "During the operation each service took losses and each service inflicted great damage to the enemy. Comparisons between services are out of place and ill-advised." A reporter for the Associated Press characterized the admiral's statement as "rare" in its bluntness, while Richard Kluger noted in his history of the *New York Herald Tribune* that Nimitz carefully avoided criticizing Bigart's reporting.[23] Adm. William V. Pratt, a retired chief of Naval Operations and military affairs columnist for *Newsweek,* also defended Buckner's decision. He rhetorically asked if Lawerence had the expertise to comment on amphibious landings: "Does the source of the criticism, coming from an excellent reporter but one who, nevertheless, is not thoroughly versed in the art of war, insure its complete reliability?" Pratt then went on to explain in detail the geography of southern Okinawa, noting that it had narrow beaches that were in front of hills. This terrain would make it easy for the Japanese to defend against a second landing. Anzio, he observed, had better features for an amphibious assault. A correspondent for *Time* magazine also commented on the controversy: "Hair-trigger critics might profitably bear in mind that the U.S. forces' real troubles on Okinawa came not from the errors of friends buy from the implacable resistance of a fanatical enemy."[24]

Lawerence responded to Nimitz, saying the admiral was "grossly misinformed." He said he had based his comments totally on Bigart's dispatches. Bigart and the *Herald Tribune,* however, retreated from their earlier criticisms of Buckner, denying Lawerence any cover: "This correspondent still believes that a landing on the south coast of Okinawa would have been a better employment of the Marines. But to call the campaign a fiasco is absurd. The writer covered the Italian campaign during the Anzio and Cassino actions and he knows what a fiasco is." The editorial board of the *Herald Tribune* later noted that Bigart's report "did not on its face, warrant the conclusions Mr. Lawerence drew." As a result, Bigart's comments "would seem to leave Mr. Lawerence open to merited rebuke."[25]

While the newspaper controversy developed, the Japanese continued to bloody the navy. On May 3, kamikazes hit and severely damaged every ship at Picket Station 10 to the southwest of Okinawa. These Japanese pilots also began to score hits on the big ships. On May 11 a kamikaze struck the aircraft carrier *Bunker Hill,* and a giant ball of fire instantly replaced the ship on the horizon. Vice Adm. Marc Mitscher transferred his flag to the *Enterprise.* The next day another plane crashed into the battleship *New Mexico,* forcing the ship to retreat to Guam for repairs. The day after that attack, Mitscher watched another kamikaze plunge straight down into the flight deck of the *Enterprise.* A giant pillar of smoke and debris shot up into the air, but there was little damage or loss of life. There was, however, a giant hole in the flight deck, thus ending the carrier's combat effectiveness. Attacks like these helped make Okinawa the bloodiest battle in the history of the United States Navy. Kamikazes damaged roughly a quarter of the fleet surrounding the island, sinking thirty-four ships, killing five thousand sailors, and injuring another five thousand men.[26]

Under pressure from admirals worried about the beating their ships were taking, Buckner ordered an offensive for May 11 to take the third defensive line. By the time Buckner ordered this action, he had both of his corps at the front, the marines to the west and the army divisions east. The anchor for the Japanese in the west was Sugar Loaf Hill, a slope about one hundred yards in length with a nice, gentle grade that reached about forty feet in height. Horseshoe and Half-Moon were two other hills to the side of Sugar Loaf. Together, these three hills protected the entrances into the capital city of Naha and Shuri Castle, the Thirty-second Army's headquarters. The hills were heavily fortified and the area soon reeked of death. The odor of decaying bodies, burnt vegetation, and spent artillery rounds overwhelmed one veteran. "You could smell the front long before you saw it; it was one vast cesspool." The Japanese on and in these hills held out against the better part of the 6th Marine Division for a week despite the valiant efforts of some Americans. On the first day of the attack, Maj. Harry A. Courtney led a charge of about forty marines, who had been stuck at the base of the hill, in what they called "a banzai charge of our own." Courtney and about twenty others made it to the crest of the hill. "Keep coming—there's a mess of them down there!" was the last thing he said before a shell exploded at his feet. (He was posthumously awarded the Medal of Honor.) Cpl. Donald "Rusty" Golar was one of the remaining marines on top. He emptied his Browning light machine gun into Japanese positions, drew his pistol and fired off a clip, and then started throwing hand grenades down the reverse slope. Running out of hand grenades, he grabbed a Browning automatic rifle and fired until the weapon jammed on him. He then turned to help remove a

wounded marine, only to take a fatal bullet himself. Despite these hero-
ics, the Japanese retook the hill after only twelve hours.[27]

Repeated attempts to take the hills failed. As one marine marched with
his unit toward the fighting, he noticed the haggard faces and expres-
sionless eyes of the men marching away. "Where's the rest of your battalion?" he asked a man he recognized. "This isn't a battalion. These are
the survivors of a battalion," the man replied. The first marine turned a
corner and saw corpse after corpse "stacked as you would stack cord-
wood." Ponchos covered the dead, leaving only their legs visible. The
marine looked at his own feet and understood. In the midst of the bloody
fighting, the Japanese and Americans observed what future Pulitzer Prize
winner William Manchester so eloquently called the "Truce of the
Fucking Dogs." Both sides held their fire in amazement as one dog
mounted another in the middle of the battlefield. The marines finally
took the hills on May 21, using a combination of tanks and infantry as-
saults, and entered Naha on May 24. Lt. Col. Victor Krulak of the 6th
Marine Division staff informed Maj. Anthony Walker that the division
commander had assigned the defense of the city to his unit. Krulak also
named the major acting mayor of Naha. He told Walker to collect his
pay from the imperial treasury.[28]

As the Tenth Army turned the flank of the Thirty-second Army's defensive line, the Japanese began withdrawing from the front. Heavy rain
that started to fall on May 21 turned the battlefield into a thick bog that
slowed the American advance and covered the Japanese retreat. Yahara
organized a plan for what he called "retreat and attack," basing his plan
on Napoleon's actions at the battle of Marengo and the French counterattack on the Marne in World War I. "Our general retreat policy . . . was
aimed at a total retreat toward fortifications."[29]

Yahara counted on the weather to neutralize U.S. tanks and air power.
The rain continued to pour well into June and turned the battlefield, already stripped of vegetation, into a mud slick. "All movements during
most of May and early June were physically exhausting and utterly ex-
asperating because of the mud," a marine recalled. Manchester observed:
"There is one massive difference between peacetime mud and wartime
mud. In peacetime it is usually avoidable. You can step around it, or take
another route. In combat you fight in the mud, sleep in it, void in it, bleed
in it, and sometimes die in it."[30]

American interservice rivalries nearly took a tragic turn at this time.

Wanting the glory of capturing Shuri and headquarters of the Thirty-second Army, the 1st Marine Division crossed into the zone of the 77th Division and seized the citadel on May 29. Maj. Gen. Andrew Bruce, commander of the 77th Division, worked frantically to call off a scheduled artillery strike after the marines informed him they had taken the old castle.[31]

Buckner was excited and optimistic about the events of late May. He was also woefully ignorant of conditions at the front. He had never understood the tactics of his opponent and had even publicly admitted as much at the beginning of the week. While his men slogged through the rain and accompanying mud, he entertained other generals with "old fashioned cocktails"; Buckner improvised, using "Okinawan raspberries for cherries." As Yahara arranged the retreat of the Thirty-second Army, Buckner, ever the womanizer, had a few navy nurses over for dinner and dancing "to the accompaniment of Radio Tokyo and artillery fire." Two days after the Japanese had finished withdrawing, Buckner recorded in his diary, "The entire enemy line appears to be crumbling."[32]

During the newspaper controversy, Buckner had to worry about a critic far more influential than any journalist. Gen. Joseph Stilwell, the former U.S. advisor to Chiang Kai-shek in China, was on an inspection trip of the Pacific and arrived on the island unannounced. He visited a number of command posts and the frontlines. Stilwell was disgusted with Buckner's conduct, releasing his venom into his diary. "There is NO tactical thinking," he wrote. "Buckner laughs at Bruce for having crazy ideas. It might be a good thing to listen to him." Stilwell was stunned when he got the same treatment. "Buckner is tiresome. I tried to tell him what I had seen, but he knew it all. Keeps repeating his wise-cracks. 'The Lord said let there be mud,' etc. etc." The only mention of Stilwell that Buckner made in his diary, other than his itinerary for the day, was: "At press conference, Stilwell said press had under publicized and failed to appreciate this campaign either in hardship overcome [or] ferocity of fighting." When Stilwell returned to Manila, he met with Gen. Douglas MacArthur and told him what he had seen. Buckner and MacArthur had clashed before on manpower and supplies, issues that had developed because the Tenth Army fell under the theater command of MacArthur's rival, Nimitz. When the U.S. invaded Japan, the Tenth Army would be under MacArthur's command, and he had no intention of keeping Buckner in this assignment. In a meeting with Stilwell, MacArthur asked him if he would be willing to lead the army during the invasion. MacArthur was clearly planning to get rid of Buckner, and the only question remaining was who would replace him. Stilwell was no fool; he understood what MacArthur intended and said he would accept any assignment he received.[33]

The Japanese established what would be their last line of defense on a sharp, four-mile-long cliff wall that American troops would have to climb. On June 10 Buckner had a letter to Ushijima dropped behind Japanese lines. In the letter he carefully praised Ushijima's accomplishments and invited him to enter into negotiations for surrender. Buckner made the offer "with little hope of results but largely at the behest of psychological 'experts.'" Nevertheless, the effort impressed the press; a reporter for the *New York Journal-American* called the gesture "without precedent in the Pacific War." The message took a week to reach Thirty-second Army Headquarters. After reading Buckner's letter, Ushijima said with a forlorn smile, "The enemy has made me an expert on infantry warfare." He rejected the offer, which the Americans had expected.[34]

The quality and quantity of combat troops available to the Thirty-second Army was the greatest problem the Japanese had in forming the new line. Their army had about eleven thousand troops left, about the size of an American division, and most of them were service and support soldiers filling in as infantrymen. All of them were exhausted from two and a half months of fighting, and the Americans quickly breached the line with tanks and flamethrowers. "Looks as though the enemy were at the end of their rope so far as organized defense is concerned," Buckner wrote in his diary. Coordinated resistance and the Thirty-second Army died on June 15.[35]

Buckner soon followed. He had always made a habit of visiting the frontlines of his units. He occasionally did a little shooting during these trips, and on at least one occasion, observers with binoculars reported seeing Japanese soldiers dragging away the dead that Buckner had shot. The general's troops, however, were less then pleased when he came to visit, because his presence often attracted Japanese fire. He arrived in a jeep flying the three stars of his rank, accompanied by a large band of staff officers. Instead of wearing subdued insignia on these visits, Buckner prominently wore three silver stars on his helmet. His rank was highly visible, and a marine officer recalled that they provoked artillery barrages as the Japanese attempted to kill this high-ranking officer. This shelling normally started just after the general left.[36]

On June 18 he decided to visit the 1st Marine Division. Climbing a hill to a forward observation post, the general expressed concern about the plight of Okinawan civilians. Marines at the post saw Buckner's helmet with its three shiny stars and asked him to remove it and wear one that was less conspicuous. Buckner declined, telling the marines he was not afraid of the Japanese and was not going to hide. Minutes later, a battalion command post on a nearby hill radioed a warning that Buckner's stars were clearly visible to them. The general removed his helmet, placed it on a rock to his left, and put on another that had no rank insignia, but it was too late. A Japanese artillery unit had already seen Buckner and was busy targeting his position. As the general stood just beyond the crest of the hill with his arms akimbo and looking toward the enemy, the Japanese fired one round, the shell exploding on the rock next to Buckner. Fragments tore a hole in the left side of his chest. Officers standing three feet behind him got up unhurt but saw Buckner lying on the ground, bloody, with mud splattered in his hair. "General Buckner has been hit!" a radio operator yelled into his mike. The marines carried him off the hill on a poncho. Buckner asked if anyone else was hurt and seemed relieved when told no one else was harmed. He died a few minutes later at a battalion aid station while a marine private held his hand and kept repeating, "You are going home, General; you are homeward bound." Silence gripped the small crowd surrounding the general until someone began reciting the Twenty-third Psalm: "Yea, though I walk through the valley of the shadow of death, I will fear no evil: for thou art with me. . . ."[37]

Buckner's death was front-page news in the United States, and obituaries appearing in American newspapers were laudatory, indicating that the newspaper controversy the week before had done little to discredit him.[38] Robert B. Atwood, the publisher and editor of the *Anchorage Times,* wrote, "General Buckner was tops in everything that he did and represented." Atwood also noted, "His fighting was consistent with his living and with his thinking—hard, sincere, and thorough." A *New York Times* reporter on the island gave him the titles "defender of Alaska, liberator of the Aleutians," and "conqueror of Okinawa." The article concluded with quotes from Nimitz, Secretary of War Henry Stimson, Secretary of the Navy James Forrestal, and Fleet Admiral Ernest J. King, all praising Buckner's ability and leadership. No marines were quoted, although Forrestal observed that he was "held in high regard in the Navy and Marine Corps." The *New York Herald Tribune* ran an extremely flattering obitu-

ary, which included a section on the battle of Okinawa. Some journalists used Buckner's death as an opportunity to renew their defense of
the general against his critics. Editorials in the *Honolulu Star-Bulletin* and
the Portland *Oregonian* argued that the pending defeat of the Japanese
undercut the validity of the charges made against him. Even the Washington *Evening Star,* which ran Lawerence's column in the District of
Columbia, retreated a bit from his criticisms of Buckner in an editorial
noting the general's death.[39] On the floor of the U.S. Senate, Senators
Happy Chandler and Alban Barkley, both from Buckner's native state of
Kentucky, praised the fallen commander. "It was the will to win that characterized Simon Bolivar Buckner as he met his death on Okinawa,"
Chandler stated. "A man who attacked life aggressively, he never asked
the men under his command to do a job he would not do himself." Barkley
reflected on his long admiration for Buckner's father and his association
with the general when he was assigned to a post in Washington. "By his
gentlemanly qualities and his personality, his sincerity and his devotion,
he endeared himself to all people who came in contact with him." He
was quickly buried the next day in a "funeral that was stirring in its sim-
plicity," according to a reporter for the *New York Journal-American*.[40]

Buckner was not forgotten in the months and years that followed.
Nakagusuku Bay was renamed Buckner Bay on July 4, and three days
later the army posthumously decorated him with the Distinguished Service Cross—the navy followed suit in October, giving him the Distinguished Service Medal. Three and a half years after his death, Buckner
was reburied in Kentucky at the foot of his father's grave with 1,800
people in attendance, including the chief of staff of the U.S. Army, Gen.
Omar Bradley. In 1954 Congress posthumously promoted Buckner to the
rank of general.[41]

The naming of a new commander for the Tenth Army provoked an
army-marine confrontation. Maj. Gen. Roy S. Geiger of the III Amphibious Corps assumed command of the army, as Buckner had wished, and
shortly thereafter was promoted to the rank of lieutenant general.
Geiger became the only marine officer to command a unit the size of an
army in combat. "We then witnessed the War Department break all
records in flying General Joseph Stilwell from the United States to take
over the command to avoid having the world see a Marine in command
of a field army of six divisions," Victor Krulak of the 6th Marine Division
noted bitterly.[42]

What Krulak did not know, could not have known, and did not receive much notice was that Stilwell's appointment resolved a difficult command problem. Geiger was not the senior general in the Tenth Army. A major general commanded each of the three subordinate units of the Tenth Army: Geiger, Hodge of the XXIV Corps, and Fred Wallace of the Island Command, the logistical and support elements. Although all three held the same rank, Wallace had seniority and, according to regulations, command. Wallace was a West Point graduate who had hurt his leg in an accident while playing polo in the early 1920s. Never fully recovering from this injury, he served in a series of staff assignments during the war. Even though the wartime expansion of the army resulted in rapid promotions for career officers, Wallace still held the same rank that he had when the war started. He was one of the twenty division commanders that Gen. George C. Marshall, the U.S. Army chief of staff, had removed after the service conducted a series of maneuvers in Louisiana in 1941. In the U.S. military there is a correlation between unit size and the rank of its commander; if an officer assumes command of a unit that corresponds to a higher rank, a promotion might accompany the new position. Command of an army was an assignment for a lieutenant general, and if Wallace succeeded Buckner, he still might yet receive a third star. Leading the Tenth Army to victory was a moment of glory and achievement that Wallace wanted. He, Geiger, and Hodge met in conference after Buckner's death. Wallace cited regulations and formally assumed command—at least on paper. Hodge and Geiger were not about to hand over command of a field army to a desk general, however. Since they commanded the combat elements of the Tenth Army, Hodge and Geiger just ignored Wallace. Geiger's promotion did little to resolve the issue, since there was bureaucratic quibbling about regulations prohibiting a marine officer from assuming the administrative versus tactical command of an army. The Tenth Army remained divided for four days, with two commanders, until Stilwell resolved the matter with his four stars. His assumption of command was front-page news in the United States, drawing extensive and positive press.[43]

The battle for Okinawa technically ended before Stilwell arrived on the island. Geiger declared the island officially secured on June 21 when marines reached the southern coast. "When it is said that an island is secured, that means that there are no more organized lines of resistance, there is just fighting all over the damn place," remarked a naval officer assigned to military government operations.[44]

Japanese actions conceded the island to the Americans. The army minister sent a telegram to Ushijima, offering praise that implicitly acknowledged Japanese defeat. "Your troops struggled hard, preparing superbly for decisive battle." The Thirty-second Army also learned from this telegram that Buckner had died in battle. Cho was ecstatic at this coup, but Ushijima seemed to lament the death of a fellow commander. Conceding defeat, Ushijima decided to take his life in the traditional way. The general had a lavish dinner with his staff. Then the group followed Ushijima to a ledge overlooking the sea. First Ushijima, then Cho, committed hara-kiri at 4:30 A.M. on June 23. In his book, Feifer attempted to challenge this version of their suicide, but eyewitness accounts leave little reason to doubt this account. The next day Imperial General Headquarters announced the end of the Okinawa operation.[45]

There were a number of small bands of Japanese soldiers who refused to accept defeat and fought on as guerrillas. On June 23 the Tenth Army formed a giant skirmish line across the island and marched north. Seven days later this mop-up operation came to a close. Over eleven thousand Japanese troops were killed or captured in this effort. Stragglers would continue to be a problem well into the fall, but Stilwell announced the end of the Ryukyus campaign on July 2.[46]

America had the island, but Okinawa was devastated. A veteran of the First World War, Stilwell walked through the rubble of Shuri and recorded in his diary: "SHURI—a mess. Much like Verdun."[47]

What to do with the island became a major issue after the general Japanese surrender six weeks later. The U.S. military wanted to retain control of Okinawa. The high number of casualties suffered in taking the archipelago virtually required such a position. Okinawa was the bloodiest battle in the history of the U.S. Navy. The Tenth Army suffered 39,000 casualties, equaling 20 percent of American ground forces. (In comparison, these numbers approximate casualties for both armies at the battle of Gettysburg during the American Civil War.)[48] Lester J. Foltos, in an award-winning article, showed that the Joint Chiefs of Staff and their planning staff were determined to retain control of the Pacific islands so "that American troops would never have to repeat this grizzly task."[49] The stubborn defense of Okinawa and Buckner's failure to appreciate the nature of this defense and the operational differences between the army and marine units under his command had contributed to these high numbers. Much as had been the case during the battle, internal differences between the Americans played a significant role in determining the fate of the Ryukyu Islands. The debate on Okinawa was fought along lines of bureaucratic competition within the U.S. government rather than those of partisan politics or ideologies. The U.S. government would muddle through this issue in part because Buckner, a major proponent of retention, was dead. He had a clear vision and rationale for keeping the island. The United States would expend a considerable amount of time and energy before it deciding on terms largely similar to those Buckner had proposed.

CHAPTER 2

Occupation in a Vacuum, 1945–47

America's mission in Okinawa was clear to Col. Wainright Purdy III: "My job is to teach these natives the meaning of democracy, and they're going to learn democracy if I have to shoot every one of them." That line always "gets a huge laugh everywhere," remarked John Patrick, author of the stage and screen versions of *The Teahouse of the August Moon*.[1] This fictional account of life in Okinawa is the best-known depiction of the early occupation period, but it credits Americans with a greater sense of purpose than they actually had. The United States was unsure of what to do with Okinawa, and Pres. Harry S. Truman let the situation drift. This uncertainty had a devastating effect on the Americans and Okinawans living on the island.[2]

Debate about Okinawa's future started before the end of the war. Buckner told Nimitz during a visit that the United States should establish bases on Okinawa and retain administration, using some legal mechanism that would avoid assuming sovereignty and giving Okinawans U.S. citizenship. "We will be wise," Buckner wrote in a letter summarizing a meeting with Nimitz, "to hold this island after the war under conditions that will permit us to have military control without incorporating the Okinawans into our population as civilians free to enter the U.S."[3] He made similar comments to the *Anchorage Times:* "I hope that we keep this island after the war, since it is a vital strategic base to use for preventing trouble from any Asiatic power. It looks right down Japan's throat, gives access to the China Sea and the Asiatic coast, cuts north-and-south traffic by sea in the western Pacific and gives our fleet and air forces an operating base connected by Iwo Jima and the Marianas with a line of bases that cannot well be broken or isolated." The editor of the newspaper endorsed this position.[4]

Japanese leaders also worried about the future of the Ryukyu Islands. These officials feared that the island chain might become a disputed province between itself and China or the United States. Two days after the surrender ceremonies on the USS *Missouri,* Stilwell wrote in his diary: "Gen. Honai wrote to me asking help to prevent Ryukyus from becoming another Alsace-Lorraine."[5]

The comparison between Okinawa and Alsace-Lorraine, the region over which France and Germany had contested for much of the last century, was a reasonable one. The Ryukyu archipelago had existed as an independent state for hundreds of years, though under the shifting domination of either China or Japan for most of that time. In 1879 Japan formally incorporated the islands, making Okinawa a *ken,* or prefecture, rather than a colony. Although Okinawans often suffered discrimination at the hands of metropolitan Japanese, they were more a part of Japan than not. Americans, however, focusing on the late date of incorporation and the discrimination, had difficulty in understanding the Okinawan desire to be part of Japan.[6]

Stilwell was the wrong man to approach for help on this matter. He had the nickname "Vinegar Joe" for a reason. He could be a hard and cruel man on occasion, and he had no sympathy for the Japanese. Consider his description of Kawasaki, Japan, while on a tour just before the surrender ceremonies on the *Missouri:* "The place is *ruined.* Completely gutted. Soul-satisfying sight." Stilwell, however, would leave Okinawa in a few weeks and would be dead from cancer a year later. Even if he had been of a mind to speak out on Okinawa, he would have had little time to do so.[7]

Had Buckner lived he might have saved the Joint Chiefs of Staff (JCS) a considerable amount of grief. The JCS wanted an outright annexation of the Ryukyu Islands, but this idea had little support outside of the military.[8] Annexation directly challenged Pres. Franklin Roosevelt's wartime pledge that the United States would take no territory as a result of the war, but Buckner's ideas about the island nicely skirted the issue. Since Truman and Secretary of State James F. Byrnes were unwilling to abandon Roosevelt's promise, the annexation proposal made no progress.[9]

In February, 1946, Nimitz, in his new position as the chief of Naval Operations, adopted Buckner's views on Okinawa and made a suggestion that he thought would resolve the problem. Naval interest in the island had declined in recent months after a typhoon the previous fall convinced strategists within the service that developing ports on the island was no longer wise, thus making it easier for the admiral to make his proposal. Nimitz recommended a trusteeship for Okinawa and annexation for the Japanese Mandated Islands. Trusteeship implied that the governing power administered the territory for a limited time with a specific purpose and under some form of legal warrant. Trusteeship also avoided the unpleasant odor of colonialism. The reason for this differentiation between the Ryukyus and the Mandated Islands was the population. According to the JCS planning staff, "The Nansei Shoto and Nanpo Shoto have fairly large heterogeneous and more advanced populations. In accord with the position of moral leadership which the U.S. has taken in the United Nations, we should offer these areas for trusteeship."[10]

Four months later, planners in the State Department responded, disagreeing with the proposal. "The Ryukyu Islands should be regarded as minor islands to be retained by Japan and demilitarized." Unlike the military, the diplomats thought the presence of a large civilian population required the return of the islands to Japan. "The Okinawans who inhabit these islands are closely related to the Japanese in language and culture and the islands have been administered as an integral part of Japan for more than six decades." If these facts were not enough to necessitate return, there were also economic reasons. "Control of the Ryukyus by the United States would in all probability require a considerable financial outlay by the United States for the support and development of the islands and would involve the United States in the thankless task of governing three-quarters of a million people of totally alien culture and outlook."[11]

The Joint Chiefs responded, stressing the price paid for Okinawa and the danger of trusting Japan. "The United States currently possesses strategic control of the Pacific by reason of our necessary and extremely costly conquest of the island areas in question. This control can be relinquished, weakened, or in any way jeopardized only at the expense of our security."[12]

The chiefs sensed they were losing the debate on Okinawa. Adm. William Leahy, the president's military chief of staff and the senior member of the JCS, knew the Japanese were going to lose control of the Mandated Islands; the Potsdam Declaration, issued in July, 1945, said so. He decided to separate the two issues. On September 10 he sent a letter to the president: "It would appear that a decision on this question could and should be reached apart from consideration of the general degree of political control to be exercised by the United States over other Pacific Islands." Once the United States assumed control of the Mandated Islands, it would be easier to persuade the White House and the State Department that the United States should also take Okinawa. Army chief of staff Dwight Eisenhower also recognized that the military was losing the debate. On September 20, at a luncheon meeting of the chiefs, he recommended retreat on the issue. The military should state American base requirements and let the State Department handle the business of securing political and legal control.[13]

The Joint Chiefs approved a compromise, adopting the position Nimitz suggested. In a memo the chiefs sent to the State-War-Navy Coordinating Committee, they gracelessly backed off from the demand for outright annexation and said they were willing to compromise and would accept a trusteeship. The next day, the chiefs sent a letter to the president over Leahy's signature, explaining why they would accept trusteeship in the Ryukyus but not in the Mandates. In a ten-page presentation, which made snide remarks about the failure of the Washington Conference and the foreign policy of the Harding administration (which no doubt pleased Truman's partisan heart), the JCS made it clear that they would prefer exclusive control over all areas in question, but that they were moderating their requirements because the Ryukyus had a large population and were a little less vital to U.S. strategy in the Pacific than the Mandates. Even with this concession, the military leaders knew their views and those of their counterparts in the State Department were still 180 degrees apart. "In SWNCC 59/1 it is concluded that the Ryukyus (Nansei

Shoto) are unnecessary for our base system and that, therefore, they should be demilitarized and returned to Japan," the letter read. "The Joint Chiefs of Staff consider that the conclusion classifying the Ryukyus (Nansei Shoto) as unnecessary and minor is unsound. They strongly reiterate that exclusive strategic control of the Nansei Shoto . . . is, from the military point of view, vital to our future security interests." A forward line of defense would prevent a future enemy from penetrating the Western Hemisphere and keep combat operations away from American shores. These considerations worried the chiefs since they expected future technological innovations that would allow an enemy to project its power over increasingly longer distances than was currently possible. The military claimed their advice would ensure American security for generations. "The Joint Chiefs of Staff are not thinking solely in terms of the present but in terms of the future, the next twenty-five, fifty, one hundred years and beyond."[14]

President Truman and his White House staff were of a mind to follow the advice Leahy offered in his first letter and to ignore the second. "Let it ride," Clark Clifford, the president's advisor and confidant, told staff members. Truman wanted to let the issue "coast." George Elsey informed Clifford that the president had to make a decision before his scheduled speech in front of the United Nations General Assembly.[15]

Truman settled half the issue on October 22. In an Oval Office meeting with the Secretaries of State, War, and the Navy, Truman decided the United States would request trusteeships for the "Japanese Islands." The Mandates were the territory in question. This was an easy issue. The wartime allies had already made their position clear with the Potsdam Declaration—Japan was going to lose control of these islands. Okinawa was a much more difficult matter: Were the Ryukyus actually a part of Japan proper? Should the U.S. keep the islands or return them to Japan? Truman had no pressing reason to answer these questions and held off from making any decision on Okinawa.[16]

Truman's nondecision had a devastating effect on Okinawa. Military government personnel were uncertain about their mission and purpose, and morale dropped. Since the military was unsure how long it would stay on the island, it did little to repair the damages of war or to build permanent buildings that would stand up to the typhoons that regularly visited the area. Three and four years after the war, the capital city of Naha was still a field of rubble. Okinawa quickly developed a reputation as an assignment to avoid and became a dumping ground for incompetents.

Up to this nondecision, troops assigned occupation duty had good spirits and more importantly a clear mission "to prevent civilians from interfering with military operations." This mission actually started during the battle and translated into securing rear areas, putting civilians into detention camps for their own safety, and preventing the island's population from harboring Japanese stragglers.[17]

The man assigned this task was the military governor, Brig. Gen. William E. Crist. A 1920 graduate of West Point, Crist had taught ROTC at Cornell University and had studied Chinese as a language officer between the wars. Although commissioned as an infantry officer, Crist was an exceptional staff officer. In Hawaii, during the planning stages for the invasion of Okinawa, Crist took over an inefficient military-government unit. Organization and morale improved dramatically after he assumed command. While a good manager of paper, Crist was a mediocre leader of men. He set a poor example for his personnel on Okinawa: He went souvenir hunting in defiance of orders. When it started to rain, Crist instructed that the canvas tents his men slept in should have wooden floors with no preferences shown toward officers; he then insisted that his tent be floored first. Inexperienced in combat, he disgusted many of the enlisted men when he dove into his personal air raid shelter as U.S. planes approached after Crist had just given a lecture on air-raid and enemy-plane-recognition procedures. Crist micromanaged; he insisted on initialing every paragraph of every memo written in his command. He also ordered a major to inspect the fingernails of the unit's cooks, an action resented by both the major and the cooks. Finally, he made racially charged comments about the intelligence and dependability of the Japanese in front of his Japanese-American translators. "Don't trust these people," he said. Contempt for Crist unified his officers and men. Novelist Vern Snieder, then a military government officer on Okinawa, enjoyed a measure of revenge by using Crist as the model for the buffoonish Colonel Purdy in *The Teahouse of the August Moon*.[18]

During the battle, the biggest concern of those assigned to military-government units was the reaction of the Okinawans. Would the civilians fight fanatically to the bitter end, or would they accept the American conquest? After his first month on the island, Crist reported, "Experience to date has confirmed the rosiest expectations of the most confirmed optimists." Another concern was the reaction of the Americans to the Okinawans. How would American troops act among enemy civilians? In his study of the battle, George Feifer argued that Americans committed numerous atrocities. While U.S. troops were guilty of violating the laws of war—there are always depraved acts in combat—Feifer's argument was overstated. As one veteran wrote in his own account: "Feifer misleads. In reality, there was less hate and more dignity, less terror and more grinding duty, more kindness and rationality, fewer guts, brains and maggots than he suggests." The memoir literature provides clear evidence that American troops were disgusted when they saw the bodies of women and children killed in combat. If nothing else, the killing of these unarmed noncombatants threatened to undermine the righteousness of the American war effort.[19]

Overcrowding and food shortages were the major problems for military-government units during the fighting. The detention camps and villages used to house Okinawan civilians were at ten times their capacities. Historians James and William Belote have identified the housing shortage as the greatest problem facing the military units. After an inspection of a camp, General Stilwell entered into his diary "crowded, all healthy looking & well fed. (2 K rations & 1 C each day!)." The translators, however, reported that the Okinawans constantly complained that they were hungry. There was plenty of food on the island; the problem was transportation. The same mud-slicked roads that slowed down combat operations also made getting supplies to the camps difficult.[20]

When combat operations on Okinawa ended, the mission of military-government units changed ever so slightly. With the battle over, their combat role of keeping "civilians from interfering with military operations" changed from securing rear areas to developing the island as a staging area for the invasion of Japan. With a modified new mission came a new commander, Col. Charles I. Murray, USMC. Murray brought strong credentials to the job. Commissioned in 1917, he fought in France with the 6th Marine Division and earned the Distinguished Service Cross, Purple Heart, Bronze Star, and the Navy Cross (second only to the Congressional Medal of Honor). He returned to the United States as a captain and served as an aide-de-camp, first to Pres. Woodrow Wilson and then to the commandant of the Marine Corps. During the interwar period, Murray served with the marines in Haiti. Before arriving on Okinawa, he was the military governor of Guam.[21]

Murray had a straightforward mission. The battle had essentially destroyed Okinawan society. An army officer recorded in his journal that only one building in Naha was still intact and none of the streets were passable. A month into the battle, a marine unit returned through a village it had stayed in shortly after the landing. An officer in that unit wrote that the town, the buildings, even the terrain had vanished. "There was not a trace of the village or the fertile green slopes that surrounded it." He estimated that the two armies destroyed 90 percent of the buildings on the island during combat operations. Banks, centers of commerce, shelter, industry, governmental records, schools, and sources of food had vanished. Okinawan society disappeared during the battle. There was little the Okinawans could do to support themselves, much less oppose their American conquerors.[22]

Since the Okinawans were unable to provide for themselves, controlling them was a simple but expensive endeavor. The Americans had to provide everything from food to clothing. The price, Murray told a visiting congressional delegation, was well-worth paying. Okinawa had twenty-two airstrips for use in the coming invasion of Japan. The value of the island increased as outlying islands proved unsuitable. In the summer of 1945, the military claimed roughly 85 percent of the land for base development.[23]

The island served two different purposes in the invasion of Japan. First, Okinawa and other islands in the Ryukyus were forward air bases for bombing Japan in Operation OLYMPIC, the invasion of the southernmost main Japanese island of Kyushu. In his detailed study of the planning for the invasion, historian John Ray Skates stated that air planners considered the airfields in these islands "ideal." Plans called to place 48½ air groups in the islands by November. This number did not include Royal Air Force squadrons that were in transit when the war ended.[24]

Okinawa also served as a staging area for Tenth Army ground troops in Operation CORONET, the assault on the main Japanese island of Honshu. The ultimate assignment of this force, however, was an issue that was unresolved when the war ended. Early plans that MacArthur's staff wrote were based on the idea that the invasion force would consist of the First, Eighth, and Tenth Armies. Buckner's death and Stilwell's appointment to lead the Tenth Army seemed to resolve the command crisis MacArthur had faced earlier. The only problem remaining was the status of the unit. During the invasion of Okinawa, the army was in Nimitz's theater command. The admiral was supposed to relinquish the army to MacArthur when the battle ended. In July the Joint Chiefs had to send a radiogram to Nimitz to get him to comply with this agreement. Yet he still found a way to delay surrender of the Tenth. "Ambiguous radio[gram]," Stilwell recorded in his diary. "The whole thing is snarled up." Fearing that Nimitz would demand a role in the postwar occupation, MacArthur had the CORONET plans revised. Planners eliminated the Tenth Army from the attack and assigned its combat elements, the XXIV Corps and the III Amphibious Corps, to the First Army, an action MacArthur had threatened as early as June. The situation remained confused even after the war ended. Stilwell noted in his diary that his staff was working on plans for a landing in Korea, codenamed Operation BLACKLIST. The entries in his diary, however, make it clear that Stilwell remained uncertain about his ultimate assignment, if any.[25]

The end of the war and the policy debate that broke out in Washington left the Americans on Okinawa uncertain about their mission and the length of the American occupation of the island. A confusing series of flip-flops between the army and navy on responsibility for governing Okinawa ensued. This lasted from the middle of 1945 until well into the spring of 1946. Rumors spread among the bored men about the return of Crist and other plans for the island. The military continued to delay construction of permanent buildings until this policy debate reached a resolution. Thus officers and men remained sheltered in tents and lightweight Quonset huts that offered only minimal protection from the rain and wind of the typhoons. Morale suffered terribly.[26]

No recreational facilities were available. The boredom was stifling. American service personnel had to find or create their own entertainment. A naval officer under Murray's command noted in his diary that he was *"junketing about the island on missions that sometimes have no point other than to help relieve the boredom of my men some of whom I always take along."* Many took up the manly art of poker. The main purpose of the game was to inject some excitement into the otherwise numbing routine of life on Okinawa. Players sat in the sweltering heat of the island in cut-off uniform shirts and shorts trading rough talk. With little else to do, many mastered the game and developed the talent to read their opponents. The challenge of competition and the thrill of victory, rather than economic profit, were the chief motivations for playing the game. Money had little value on the island since there was little to spend it on.

In fact, the Americans chose to gamble with checks rather than cash or military script. Occasionally, units would manage to get a film for viewing. Such opportunities, however, were few and far between. Murray reported that the primary interest of the men in his command was getting a discharge and going home.[27]

The military administration of Okinawa quickly boiled down to Murray and a small cadre of ensigns and lieutenant commanders, most of whom had formerly taught at universities. The colonel was fond of saying, "The trouble with this outfit is we've got too many damn college professors." Murray, however, knew he needed these dedicated men. He even made a special note of his manpower resources in his final report: "The personnel situation for Military Government was a serious problem and would have been much more so had not a small nucleus of trained officers, who were familiar with the operation through all its periods and phases, voluntarily elected to remain." A reporter for *The Christian Science Monitor* observed, "What most strikes the visitor is the manner in which young officers in the field can be at the same time kindly but firm in handling the extremely delicate political, cultural, and economic problems which daily confront them." When Murray relinquished command in July, 1946, there were less than 250 officers and men under him.[28]

The main reason these field-grade officers agreed to stay was a plan proposed by one of their own, John Caldwell. A future president in the University of North Carolina System and chancellor of North Carolina State University, Caldwell on his own initiative wrote a memo in which he proposed to make their low numbers a strength. He suggested that the United States begin developing local government. "The Okinawans have demonstrated convincingly that they possess sufficient indigenous leadership to manage their own affairs in much larger degree than is allowed them at present," he wrote. Although Okinawa would remain a controlled economy, "the minimum controls which must be exercised can be performed by a civilian government under overall Military Government control of policy." The U.S. Navy would establish only the broadest of parameters but leave the responsibility of implementation to the Okinawans.[29]

A few days later, Murray called the young naval officer into his office to explain the ideas in the memo. Caldwell said that current operations were unwieldy and expensive, but this could be easily rectified. The mission of the U.S. military government should focus on developing local autonomy, releasing land for farming, and rehabilitating the economy. This effort would actually reduce the burden the Americans would have to carry. The colonel was a hard-charging, hard-drinking marine with a bad temper. On one occasion Murray had an officer reassigned when he discovered the man had appropriated an Okinawan house that was larger and better furnished than the one he had confiscated. This time, however, he kept his temper in check and told Caldwell to continue. Murray said he was interested in the plan, but only if Caldwell would stay and help implement the program. Caldwell agreed to this condition after speaking to a number of officers, finding them eager and receptive as well.[30]

Lt. Comdr. James T. Watkins IV, one of those who stayed, recorded in his diary his reasons for supporting Caldwell's program and remaining on Okinawa. *"As I see it, the salvation of the Okinawans depends upon themselves. Therein lies my hope. But we must give them the needed organs of government if they are to be able to help themselves."*[31]

A key element in this plan was the appointment of a civilian governor. The Americans selected Shikiya Koshin, a leading educator, to serve as governor of the island. On April 25, 1946, Murray stood at his desk with his officers flanking him while Shikiya and his future staff stood on the other side. The marine commander read a document "in a clear voice, slowly and with suitable emphasis" appointing Shikiya governor. In a short speech, Shikiya said, "With thankfulness for the kind intentions of Military Government, we Okinawans are filled with hope that, in striving to build a better Okinawa than before, we will achieve the golden age for Okinawa with our own hands." Shikiya would serve a full term as governor. In 1950 he would became the first president of the University of the Ryukyus and held this post at the time of his death; the school named its library after him.[32]

Shikiya's appointment was the high-water mark for the Caldwell plan. Back in Washington, Nimitz and Eisenhower agreed that the army should assume responsibility for governing Okinawa. The navy wanted out of Okinawa. Port facilities had proven disappointing. A typhoon that struck Okinawa back in October, in which navy cooks rode out the storm in a large walk-in refrigerator, convinced a number of admirals that the island was unsuitable for naval use. Control of the island would do little to help the navy block an enemy from advancing into the Pacific; the air force or army could make better use of the position. The navy agreed to transfer authority over Okinawa to the army. In this new administrative arrangement, MacArthur ruled the island in his capacity as the commander of U.S. Army forces in the Pacific. His responsibility for Okinawa, however, was separate from his authority as the commander for allied personnel in Japan. One of the lieutenant commanders Caldwell convinced to stay wrote his wife about the incoming army administration: "I am afraid that they will be a sorry crew. Whatever the Army did in other theaters, in this one they put into Military Government the officers they could most readily dispense with."[33]

The transfer to army control initiated events that ended Murray's career. Army inspectors discovered that over half the food rations for Okinawan consumption were spoiled. Murray immediately placed the Okinawans on half-rations and reported this development to the commander in chief, U.S. Pacific Fleet and Pacific Ocean Areas. A subsequent investigation held Murray responsible for failing to provide adequate security, storage, inspection, and supervision of the food stores. The commander of the Pacific Fleet placed a letter of reprimand in his personnel file, reading "You are hereby reprimanded for the negligent performance of duty outlined above." In the U.S. military, this type of letter is a permanent mark against the officer in question and stays in his file permanently, essentially eliminating any chance of promotion or meaningful duty. For all practical purposes, Murray's career was over. Less than a year before, his immediate superior, Maj. Gen. Fred Wallace, with the support of the commanding general of Pacific Fleet Marines, had recommended Murray for promotion to brigadier general. "I have always felt that the big shots—that is the brass back in Pearl let me down," he wrote in retirement. "In other words, they sold us down the river."[34] Murray's bitterness is understandable but unfounded. The destruction of his career had nothing to do with the transfer of authority to the army. His command was found deficient in the function of one its main missions, and as the commander, Murray bore responsibility for this failure.

Murray still had friends within the service. He lasted for another three years in the Marine Corps before he retired, and, in a naval tradition inherited from the British, he was promoted one rank his last day in uniform leaving the service with the flag, rank, and retirement pay of a general. Observers had also noticed and appreciated the hard work of Murray and his naval officers. Americans of Okinawan heritage started a relief organization; their newspaper praised these naval officers for their contributions, noting that their low number was their greatest limitation.[35] Okinawans lost their most ardent advocates when these naval officers left the island.

The departing naval personnel put on a brave show, however. A crowd estimated at five hundred watched the transfer-of-command ceremony on July 1. At 0900 hours (9:00 A.M.), standing upon a stage covered in red, white, and blue bunting, Murray made a few remarks. His successor, Col. William H. Craig, U.S. Army, gave a few comments afterward. Finally, Shikiya stood in front of the flowers and American flags decorating the stage and, in the words of one naval officer, "stole the show" with a simple, eloquent speech. Americans in the crowd nodded with approval. "We agreed that the Chiji's [governor] speech had done more than any other single act since the invasion to win respect for the Okinawans from their conquerors," Commander Watkins entered into his diary three days later. "It was a great occasion."[36]

Army administration brought no major changes to the island. The United States governed Okinawa as part of Japan, which required that the Japanese pay for any improvements. Japan simply lacked the economic resources to fund any construction. Until the president made a decision on the island's future, the army was no more willing than the navy had been to spend its money on construction projects that it might lose quickly thereafter. No one took any action to rebuild the island's infrastructure. Okinawa had no running water, no electricity, no sewers, and no roads other than those built for the military. A Foreign Service officer sent to the island on routine business returned with a report on the social conditions in which the American troops and indigenous population lived, which the American consul general called "absolutely appalling." One of the few American reporters to visit Okinawa described the city of Naha as "a mass of ruins on either side of a military highway." He also observed that "hundreds of thousands of natives are living in shacks not fit for human habitation." A few months later, a report sent from MacArthur's headquarters to the secretary of war admitted this assessment was correct. Americans had built less than twenty thousand of a needed seventy thousand homes. What the report failed to mention was that all the construction had taken place while the navy governed Okinawa. The army had done no building in the year it had administered the Ryukyus.[37]

Facilities for Americans were not much better. Troops continued to live in tents and Quonset huts, which peeled apart in typhoons. The main problem the U.S. military faced on the island remained stifling boredom for the men. Morton Morris, in his book on occupation life, wrote that there were plenty of recreational opportunities available, but many of the activities he then cites were simple means to while away the time. The most significant reason for boredom was the lack of facilities on Okinawa. Unit commanders tried to combat monotony as much as possible. The Red Cross organized car tours of the island. Units sponsored movies, picnics, and sporting events, which were the major forms of recreation. Enlisted men competed in interunit baseball and football leagues and officers served as coaches. Boxing matches were another popular form of entertainment. "I never saw a bad bout," Morris recalled. In fact, when Eisenhower visited the island in 1946, the entertainment for his stay was a boxing tournament.[38]

Sex, however, was officially forbidden—at least for enlisted personnel. There were few American women on the island, and most were either officers or the wives of officers. Regulations prohibited enlisted men from having relations with these women. American servicemen were more than willing to seek pleasure with Okinawan women, but a nonfraternization rule barred any contact. Americans were enormously wealthy compared to the Okinawans, and there was little doubt that determined soldiers could buy their way around that regulation and pay Okinawan women to service them. Morris reported that prostitution had official sanction. Unit commanders arranged to have buses travel to the prostitution districts of local towns. This arrangement came to an end when the chaplains learned that the military was supporting this behavior. The result, Morris argued, was an increase in rapes and venereal disease rates.[39]

Actually, the American sexual exploitation of the Okinawans, rape in particular, had been a problem long before the army assumed control. Murray reported that the biggest problem in American-Okinawan relations was "the constant preoccupation of large numbers of American soldiers abroad with creation of opportunity for illicit sexual relations." In a folksy column, a writer for the *Daily Okinawan*, the military newspaper, made a telling observation about the actions of U.S. servicemen. "Up to now us Americans ain't give them no reason to be sure that a general movin' inter to their villages by wud be a good thing. Whenever we convince 'em that a free association atwixt us wud be beneficil to them it won't be long till we got it." Okinawan leaders, however, focused the blame for the rapes on black servicemen and asked Murray to keep the nonfraternization rule in place for their protection. This request found a receptive audience among the American rulers. Watkins sent Murray a memo recommending the removal of all black units. Murray agreed and made this suggestion in his final report, blaming black servicemen for most of the rapes while being careful to state that not all blacks were rapists. Arnold Fisch, in his study of military government in Okinawa, showed that black servicemen were not the worst offenders and that the departure of black units did little to reduce the number of rapes. Filipino troops earned the distinction of being the most frequent rapists. Seeing no difference between the Okinawans and the metropolitan Japanese that had occupied the Philippines, these soldiers avenged their homeland on Okinawan women.[40]

The army made no more effort to spread American values than it did to rebuild the island. The new army administration essentially discarded the ambitious goals of the Caldwell plan. Those most active in an effort to spread American values and rebuild the island were religious missionaries and chaplains. In the United States a number of clergymen who had served on Okinawa created a relief organization called "Friends of Okinawa."[41]

There were some challenges to this neglect, though. The total disregard the military police showed for the civil rights of the Okinawans disgusted Paul Skuse, a former patrolman in the Boston Police Department and a naval officer who stayed on Okinawa in a civil service position. The military police constantly raided Okinawan villages to confiscate stolen U.S. property. At the time, however, most Okinawan possessions, including clothing, came from the Americans. Skuse had enough of the MPs and wrote a memo to the military governor, complaining about their actions. "To conduct mass raids of native villages and to confiscate all such properties regardless of how they were acquired is an abuse of police powers that is characteristic of the OCPU, NKVD, Kempei-tai, and other feared organizations of fascist and communistic states." After reading the memo, Brig. Gen. F. L. Hayden called Skuse into his office and told him that Americans earned the Bill of Rights through revolution and war. Skuse asked the general if that was what the Okinawans had to do. The response infuriated Hayden. He threw Skuse out of his office and considered firing him. He soon realized that Skuse was right, and his last official act on Okinawa was to promote him one civil service grade. As Hayden was boarding his plane to leave Okinawa, he saw Skuse, turned around, and came down the ramp to thank him. The raids continued, though. Skuse observed that a new flurry of activity occurred shortly after the arrival of a new military police commander on the island. Then, in 1952, the MPs made the mistake of bursting into a Naha restaurant and conducting body searches on a number of officers on a general's staff who were entertaining visiting Japanese dignitaries. The raids came to a permanent end soon thereafter.[42]

Disease reduction was the only major achievement of army military government. The biggest health problem for Okinawans when the army took over was malaria. There were slightly more than twenty-three thousand cases a month. In two years this rate dropped 75 percent. By September, 1949, there were only five hundred cases.[43]

The overall situation in Okinawa during the mid-1940s was "bad." The worst fears of the naval officers who first administered the island were coming true. Okinawa had the reputation in the army as an assignment to avoid. In March of 1949, Maj. Gen. L. A. Craig, inspector general of the U.S. Army, toured the island. "The Inspector General's report showed that troop training, living conditions, and recreational facilitates were far below accepted Army standards," the unit history of the Ryukyus command recorded in understated language. Chairman of the Joint Chiefs of Staff Omar Bradley was more blunt. "Slums" was the word he used to describe dependent housing during a JCS inspection of the island.[44]

This poverty was a result of the unresolved policy debate on Okinawa. Indecision in Washington resulted in a similar policy of inaction on the island. The United States did little to rebuild after the devastating destruction of the battle. Changing international circumstances, however, and the squalid conditions on Okinawa would soon combine to force action.

CHAPTER 3

Debate, Decision, and Diplomacy, 1947–51

On January 12, 1950, Secretary of State Dean Acheson appeared before the National Press Club in Washington and gave the most controversial speech of his life. What got him into trouble was his mention of an American line of defense in Asia. "This defensive perimeter runs along the Aleutians to Japan and then goes to the Ryukyus," he said. "The defensive perimeter runs from the Ryukyus to the Philippine Islands." Acheson got in trouble for what he failed to mention: Korea. After war broke out, critics argued that the omission of the peninsula from this line was a green light to the North Koreans to launch their attack on the South. Most ignored his comments about Okinawa: "We hold important defense positions in the Ryukyu Islands, and those we will continue to hold. They are essential parts of the defensive perimeter of the Pacific, and they must and will be held."[1] This passage signaled that the U.S. government had reached a decision about Okinawa's future and that the debate of the late 1940s about America's role in the Pacific was over. The United States would retain Okinawa after the occupation of Japan ended and use the island as a military base with the dual mission of defending Japan and protecting other nations from the Japanese.[2]

MacArthur reopened the issue of Okinawa at an interesting time. In 1947 he was at the height of his influence and power. His vision was that an American-controlled Okinawa would allow Japan to pursue a foreign policy of neutrality. The Truman administration would agree, but for reasons of its own that were quite different than what MacArthur had in mind. The civil war in China had started, but its resolution and the start of the Cold War in Asia were still two and a half years away. The concern in Washington at the time focused on the Soviets and resurgent Japanese militarism rather than the Chinese Communists. The location of the island made it a useful base for one strategy based on the defense of strong points and another based on a defensive perimeter.[3]

On March 19 MacArthur surprised the foreign correspondents association when he accepted a long-standing invitation to attend a luncheon, and then while there he called for a Japanese peace treaty. "The time is now approaching when we must talk peace with Japan," the general said, after announcing that he was speaking on the record. Reporters were searching for their pencils and pads. Responding to a question, MacArthur said he wanted to sign a treaty "as soon as possible." In another lunch meeting, this one with visiting Foreign Service officers, he suggested that a peace conference gather in Tokyo that summer. Opposition from China and the Soviet Union scuttled this idea in short order.[4]

On the other side of the azure-colored Pacific, MacArthur's initiative forced the bureaucracy in Washington to begin considering the Okinawa issue again. Foreign-policy specialists had ignored the matter until then. The Joint Chiefs of Staff still considered Japan a danger lying dormant and insisted that the United States retain Okinawa. In several memos, Eisenhower, still army chief of staff, also suggested the creation of an anti-Japanese security alliance. Secretary of War Robert Patterson, however, objected to the retention of Okinawa, expressing "grave misgivings." Making the island a permanent base and assuming responsibility for the population would be expensive, he argued. Eisenhower responded, explaining the thinking of the JCS. "It will be necessary, when the occupation of Japan has been terminated, to retain Okinawan bases for the purpose of assisting in our surveillance of Japan, in order to complete our Pacific peripheral base system, and in order to provide in case of need for the projection of U.S. power against the Asiatic mainland." Eisenhower, however, acknowledged to his staff that Patterson had a point. "While the strategic value of Okinawan bases must be considered great, there can be no doubt that the Ryukyus, economically, politically, and socially, would be a liability to the U.S." At the bottom of Patterson's memo he wrote, "Would it be possible to take any special portion or section—isolated from population?" In his response to Patterson, Eisenhower suggested enclaves. This solution would allow the United States to keep naval and air facilities in the south and return the rest of the island to Japan, avoiding the responsibility of civil administration. Patterson dismissed the idea as unworkable, noting that most of the population lived in the southern third of the island.[5] Eisenhower remained wedded to the concept and would favor an enclave solution long after he left the army.

While the civilian and uniformed leadership of the army remained divided on the fate of the island, the State Department was in a precarious situation. Given the huge distance and the complications of bureaucratic rivalries with the Pentagon, American diplomats had little accurate information on actual conditions in Japan. (William J. Sebald, the senior State Department representative in Japan, owed his appointment to MacArthur following the death of Sebald's predecessor, which put him in a difficult bureaucratic position. He had to send his telegrams to the State Department though army channels, and his responsibilities amounted to serving as both the general's personal foreign minister and the U.S. ambassador to MacArthur.) Someone from Washington needed to consult with MacArthur on a peace treaty. The task of meeting with the American shogun fell upon George F. Kennan, the director of the policy planning staff in the State Department. Kennan, at the time a major voice in Washington policy-making circles, had an ambivalent attitude toward the Ryukyus. He had no sharp views about retention one way or the other and was in no hurry to discuss the matter.[6] Kennan, however, had serious doubts about a treaty. He wondered if a formal peace agreement might not be premature. He worried that occupation reforms had left Japan weakened and susceptible to communist pressure. Kennan considered Japan the only great military-industrial power in Asia, and the war in the Pacific had shown how dangerous a hostile Japan could be. With these concerns in mind, he set out for Japan in late February, 1948.[7]

After thirty hours and an unheated flight, Kennan and his party arrived in the Tokyo in the middle of a snowstorm. Kennan and his military companion, Maj. Gen. Cortlandt Schuyler, had lunch with MacArthur despite having gone without sleep for forty-eight hours. MacArthur ignored Kennan, speaking solely to Schuyler. After several days of briefings, Kennan asked to meet alone with MacArthur. The general agreed, and the two spent most of the evening of March 5 talking about the occupation and foreign policy. A good deal of conversation centered on Okinawa. The general told Kennan that the United States should secure a defensive line stretching from the Philippines to the Aleutians. "Okinawa was the most advanced and vital point in this structure." MacArthur had two reasons for this view. First, Okinawa was the one place from which U.S. forces "could easily control every one of the ports of northern Asia from which an amphibious operation could conceivably be launched." Second, "with adequate force at Okinawa, we would not require the Japanese home islands for the purpose of preventing the projection of amphibious power from the Asiatic mainland." Permanent American administration would also be best for the Okinawans. The Japanese discriminated against them, and the Americans would be able to provide them with a higher standard of living. Indecision, MacArthur said, was killing the morale of the troops on the island.[8]

These arguments apparently convinced Kennan, at least about Okinawa. When he returned to Washington, he argued that it was still too early for a peace treaty. The Ryukyus, however, were a different matter for two reasons. First, he believed the Soviet Union had no intention of attacking Japan, and second, he expected that American troops would become a divisive issue in Japanese politics. "The United States Government should make up its mind at this point that it intends to retain permanently the facilities at Okinawa, and the base there should be developed accordingly." Politically, the islands were better suited for American bases than the Philippines, especially if Japan lost sovereignty. The United States would be the only administering power. Both Kennan and MacArthur wanted to keep U.S. bases out of postoccupation Japan, and Okinawa offered the best way to do so.[9]

Kennan's position on Okinawa represented a fundamental shift in State Department thinking. In 1948 Kennan spoke with the power of the "long-telegram" and the "X-article." He had also just spoken with MacArthur, which gave his views even more influence. If there was any doubt about his authority, it ended when he sent his paper to the Far Eastern division, and it came back with only minor revisions.[10]

The MacArthur-Kennan view began gathering support within the bureaucracy. Later in the year, the Central Intelligence Agency (CIA) endorsed this position in a report sent to the White House that remained classified for thirty years. Keeping Okinawa served two purposes. First, the island was a good base for positioning American forces in the defense of Japan. Second, controlling Okinawa would "give the US a position from which to discourage any revival of military aggression on the part of the Japanese."[11]

Meeting in the West Wing of the White House on October 7, 1948, the National Security Council (NSC) approved NSC 13/2, a report based on Kennan's paper. The NSC agreed that a Japanese peace treaty was premature, but the United States should begin making preparations. The NSC report differed from Kennan's paper in two major ways. First, the navy insisted on retaining its Yokosuka Naval Base in Japan. Second, the Joint Chiefs of Staff asked the NSC to withhold final judgment on Okinawa. The chiefs wanted an explicit statement that the United States would retain control of the Ryukyus. The State Department's position was now the same as that of the JCS, but Undersecretary of State Robert A. Lovett replied with a legalistic view that no authoritative and final decision would be reached until the United States signed a peace treaty with Japan. Even though it was obvious what the policy of the U.S. government would be, the chiefs took a legalistic position of their own and were unwilling to commit to any construction and development without an irrevocable commitment. Until such a guarantee was forthcoming, they asked that the matter be dropped.[12]

A bureaucratic deadlock over legal interpretations prolonged Truman's policy of indecision, even though all parties agreed to the retention of the archipelago. As a result, the squalor on the islands remained unchanged. A correspondent from the *New York Herald Tribune* who managed to visit the Ryukyus reported, "Very little has been done for the occupation personnel in the last four years beyond trying to keep wartime installations from blowing away in periodic typhoons and little for the Okinawans beyond supplementing the local food supply."[13]

Ironically, the civilian leadership of the army used this poverty first to break the deadlock and then to initiate base development. In late 1948 Secretary of the Army Kenneth C. Royall proposed new language to the

National Security Council that both the State Department and Joint Chiefs could accept. To meet the JCS requirement about a firm assurance regarding America's future on the island, he removed qualifying language from the disputed passage on Okinawa, so that it now read, "The US government intends to retain on a long-term basis the facilities at or near Okinawa and military bases there should be developed accordingly." To satisfy State Department concerns, he added a paragraph that the United States would keep this decision secret but would obtain legal sanction in the near future.[14]

The civilian leadership of the army made it clear that they wanted a resolution of the issue so they could do something to alleviate the massive poverty on the island. Royall explicitly stated as much in his proposal to the NSC. Undersecretary of the Army William H. Draper, Jr., explained that the army could do nothing for the Ryukyus as long as they were part of Japan. The islands were an occupied area, and policy prohibited the army from spending funds on nonmilitary improvements. The Japanese were responsible for paying the costs of the occupation, and it was clear they had little to spend for expenses in Japan proper, much less Okinawa. "The Department of State might wish to enunciate a policy statement clearly separating the Ryukyus Islands from Japan proper," Draper told Charles E. Saltzman, an assistant secretary of state. "The Department of the Army would then be glad to ascertain the legality of implementing this policy by reimbursing Japan for Japanese materials and labor properly utilized for the benefit of the Ryukyus Islands with dollars appropriated for rehabilitation and/or relief requirements of the civilian economy for the Ryukyus."[15]

The NSC approved the Royall compromise. The U.S. government still wanted to wait before beginning negotiations, but when the time came, the document would separate Okinawa from the home islands. Except for the addition and subtraction of a few nouns, the new report was identical to the proposal Royall made. On May 6, 1949, the National Security Council approved NSC 13/3; yet nothing happened.[16]

Then, on July 23, Typhoon Gloria ripped through the Ryukyus and conditions changed. The storm lasted eight hours, whisked away sandbags, ripped metal siding off disintegrating buildings, and turned day into night. "Water was everywhere, falling from the heavens, blown in heavy sheets by the wind, and sucked up out of the boiling seas," one serviceman recounted. The storm destroyed half of the buildings on the island, and airfields were flooded and unusable. Undersecretary of the Army Tracy Voorhees visited the island a few weeks later. Okinawa concerned him even before the typhoon hit. Douglas Oliver of the Office of Far Eastern Affairs in the State Department had just authored a report that was circulating in Washington. He was critical of American conduct on Okinawa and recommended a reconsideration of the NSC decision. Voorhees had Oliver brief him before he left but was still "shocked" when he arrived. Naha had an open sewer system and no running water. A reporter from *Life* magazine accompanying Voorhees found "an ugly, cluttered graveyard of rotting material" and American troops that were "depressed and sullen."[17]

Voorhees reacted to the destruction and poverty with speed and force. The pending Communist victory in the Chinese Civil War—Mao Tse-tung announced the founding of the Peoples' Republic of China on October 1— made it quite easy for him to overcome legislative and bureaucratic resistance. Voorhees arranged to have the military engineering district on Okinawa placed under MacArthur's command. He requested seventy-three million dollars for construction from Congress and personally lobbied individual members for the funding. His efforts produced the desired effect: Congress approved a fifty-million-dollar appropriation after only a month of consideration in a speed not normally associated with that institution. Heads rolled. The military governor was relieved of his command before the month ended. The new governor was Maj. Gen. Josef R. Sheetz, a capable, if not ironic, choice. Sheetz had played a large role in tearing up the island as artillery commander for the XXIV Corps during the battle of Okinawa. Before returning to Okinawa, he held a military-government assignment in Korea. Described as "breezy" and a "convivial hustler" in a *Time* magazine article, he quickly and energetically turned matters around. Within two months he reported a dramatic jump in spirit and morale to MacArthur. When Sheetz retired in 1951, Mac-Arthur awarded him the Legion of Merit, a prestigious decoration given for distinguished achievement in high office and not normally conferred as a retirement medal.[18]

Voorhees also sent two separate missions to Okinawa to propose plans for the development of the island. Brig. Gen. George J. Nold led a team of engineers. His report was positive. "Mr. Voorhees had expressed displeasure at the appearance of the depots and storage yards. By description and appearance, there has been a remarkable change," he wrote.

Voorhees also sent a six-man team to the island led by Raymond E. Vickery, an agricultural economist in his office. Vickery's report on economic and agricultural reconstruction was extremely critical. The first sentence in his seventy-two-page report read: "Four years after the cessation of combat operations, the people of the Ryukyus Islands and especially Okinawa, remain in a state of abject poverty and a continuing burden on the American taxpayer. Little prospect exists for their attaining a significantly greater degree of self sufficiency until an effective program of reconstruction is inaugurated and vigorously pursued."[19]

While the civilian leadership of the army had bridged the differences within the government, the State Department still had to obtain political and legal sanction for American rule of Okinawa. By definition, this task was tightly interwoven with the negotiation of a Japanese peace treaty. A year later, these interrelated assignments fell on the sloping, underrated shoulders of John Foster Dulles.

In 1950 Dulles was the leading foreign policy expert in the Republican Party. A Wall Street lawyer by trade, Dulles was a diplomat by breeding. His grandfather, John Watson Foster, was secretary of state under Pres. Benjamin Harrison and an uncle, Robert Lansing, served Pres. Woodrow Wilson in the same post. His sister, Eleanor, was a Foreign Service officer while his brother, Allen, was drawn to the field of espionage, eventually serving as the director of the CIA under Eisenhower and Kennedy. Dulles's grandfather and uncle gave him an early start in foreign affairs. He enrolled at Princeton when he was sixteen years old, and while still an undergraduate, Dulles served as his grandfather's secretary-clerk at the Second Hague Peace Conference. Lansing later gave him a position on the U.S. delegation to the Versailles peace conference, where Dulles worked primarily on the reparations issue.[20]

The reparations work, Wilson's firing of his uncle, and the Senate's rejection of the peace treaty, along with his own personality, helped mold and shape Dulles's approach to foreign policy. On a strategic level, he operated within the limitations of domestic American politics. He regularly consulted and briefed the members of the foreign affairs committees in both the House of Representatives and the Senate. His public, stern, and austere reputation, combined with his use of rigid language, kept his anticommunist credentials strong. On a tactical level, he avoided "cut-and-dry" proposals. While initially seeming nebulous on an issue, he carefully probed his counterparts, searching for their strengths and weaknesses.

On other occasions, he thought out loud, which often led to misunderstandings.[21] Religion also shaped his analysis. When a friend asked him
how he could forgive the Japanese for the Bataan Death March and other
atrocities, he replied, "Jesus teaches us that nothing is unforgivable."[22]

Dulles knew that personality and personal contacts affected the negotiating process. He traveled to meet and negotiate with his foreign peers.
"He was a man you could absolutely trust," remarked Sir Carl Berendsen,
the ambassador from New Zealand. "You could rely upon him. His word
was his bond." Dulles drew from an incredible constitution to get him
through these lengthy trips. "Mr. Dulles never stopped," John Allison,
his assistant, wrote. "There was always someone else to talk to, something else to see, somewhere else to go, and always it must be done at a
gallop." He would relax from these energetic explosions with a simple
game of catch, throwing a baseball with one of his staff members. "He
handled a glove with a professional touch," C. Stanton Babcock recalled.
He developed close relationships with his small three-man staff. Allison
was the most influential, often disagreeing with Dulles on issues. Babcock,
then an army colonel, was a former Japanese-language officer and advised Dulles on the differing views in the Pentagon. He told him none of
these perspectives were in agreement with the positions MacArthur took.
Dulles required that Babcock and Allison read each other's papers. Foreign Service officer Robert Fearey had no policy input, serving rather as
an administrative assistant and performing secretarial work. His main
duty was taking notes of conversations. Dulles respected these men and
later supported them in their careers when he was secretary of state. In
oral history after oral history, people remarked on the false image of
Dulles's public reputation. "When you got to know him," Allison recalled,
"he was a very human person and a very likable person." William J.
Sebald, a Foreign Service officer working in Japan as MacArthur's political advisor, observed that "he was charming company, socially," and
added that Dulles had a wry sense of humor. Babcock spoke of his "great
warmth and compassion" and believed his formal, austere reputation
covered a painful shyness and awkwardness at public gatherings.[23]

When Dean Acheson gave Dulles the job of negotiating the Japanese
peace treaty, it was an acknowledgment of mutual political need and
weakness. For Acheson the problem was not a treaty with Japan, his
real problem was himself. Senators were calling for his resignation, ques-
tioning his loyalty to the nation, and blaming him for the loss of China

and any other bad things that came to mind. In his memoirs, Acheson called this period "the attack of the primitives." He needed a man who had no previous "contamination" with Asian issues, someone who could deflect partisan attacks. Dulles, on the other hand, had just lost a campaign to defend his appointed seat in the U.S. Senate and was badly bruised and battered. He wanted a position that would help restore some of his stature.[24]

Dulles used two different sets of connections to convince the Truman administration to give him a foreign policy job. Previous writers on this subject have attributed Dulles's appointment to one action or the other, but the documents make it clear that he was using two different approaches to obtain the same goal.[25] Sen. Arthur Vandenberg, the Michigan Republican dying of cancer, wrote Acheson from his hospital bed suggesting he find a position for Dulles. "It is acutely advisable to bring him back into active and important cooperation with the State Department if we are to seriously hope to restore some semblance of unpartisan unity at water's edge." Dulles also had Carl W. McCardie, a close associate and journalist working for the *Philadelphia Bulletin,* call Lucius D. Battle, a special assistant to Acheson, with the message that Dulles would like a position in the State Department. At first Acheson, his undersecretary, and Truman refused, but W. Walton Butterworth and Dean Rusk, the former and current assistant secretaries for Far Eastern affairs, championed the idea, and it began to make more and more sense. Dulles had the necessary political standing to work on a Japanese peace treaty that a Foreign Service officer would never enjoy.[26]

Even after deciding he had to work with Dulles, Acheson was reluctant to give him a meaningful assignment. He despised Dulles, going so far as to resign a day early in 1953 to avoid signing the Republican's commission as the new Secretary of State. With time the malice grew. Following Dulles's death, Acheson shocked a dinner party into silence by saying, "Thank God Foster is underground."[27] He initially offered Dulles a position as a State Department lobbyist with Congress on Asian issues. The job disappointed Dulles. He told Acheson that it "wasn't a very distinguished sounding office." Nevertheless, on April 6 the State Department announced that Dulles would serve as a consultant to the secretary without mission or portfolio. After a few weeks of indecision, Acheson gave the job of exploring the feasibility of a Japanese peace treaty to Dulles.[28]

Was Japan friend or foe? The answer to this question quickly became a major dilemma for Dulles as he began consulting Foreign Service officers with experience and expertise in Japanese matters. The United States had two sure enemies in the Soviet Union and the People's Republic of China. Japan remained an uncertain player. John Allison warned Acheson that the odds were 50-50 that the Japanese would retain the American imposed democratic reforms after the occupation ended. Rebuilding the Japanese military might serve American anticommunist policies, but only at the cost of jeopardizing its own security and that of other nations in the Pacific. "However, the two aspects overlap and it may be possible that a satisfactory security arrangement for one would materially assist in taking care of the other," Dulles suggested.[29]

While Dulles left the solution unstated, Robert Fearey described it bluntly. In an undated memo given to the Australian government, Fearey explained that U.S. troops would act as a brake on any restoration of Japanese militarism: "To the extent that Japan may be considered a potential security threat in its own right, the U.S. forces retained in Japan after the treaty can be counted upon to restrain that threat. The U.S. will not remove those forces until alternative arrangements under United Nations or otherwise have been established to provide effectively both for the security of Japan and security against a resurgence of Japanese aggression."[30] Before beginning his duties, Dulles wanted an assistant experienced in Japanese matters. He found that expert in May of 1950. During a briefing on the peace treaty, John Allison stated that only a "soft peace" held the promise of seeing occupation reforms continued. Dulles agreed, and after the meeting ended, he pulled Allison aside and asked him to serve as his assistant during the negotiations. Following some initial protests, Allison accepted and entered what he called "the most interesting and satisfying" period of his Foreign Service career.[31]

In June, 1950, Allison and Dulles took a trip to Japan to meet with MacArthur and leading Japanese figures, exploring the possibility for a treaty. The Joint Chiefs and Secretary of Defense Louis Johnson also went to Japan to enlist MacArthur's help in blocking the treaty. There were a number of different views in the Pentagon on Far Eastern policy, but Johnson led the opposition to the treaty out of a rivalry with Acheson. Journalists Walter Isaacson and Evan Thomas speculated that Johnson's effort to undercut Acheson was an attempt to gain popularity for a presidential campaign. Both Truman and Acheson, on the other hand, believed that Johnson was mentally unstable. Whatever his motivation, Johnson gave his consent to JCS efforts to scuttle a peace treaty. In their opposition, the chiefs took the military tendency to plan for a worst-case scenario in a legalistic direction. The Joint Chiefs told State Department representatives that a treaty would force the United States out of Japan and give the Communists a pretext to invade that nation, since a legal state of war would still exist between Japan and the Communists countries of Asia.[32]

Sebald greeted two different delegations at Atsugi airfield on June 17, 1950. In the early morning hours he met Dulles and Allison. He then stayed at the field and greeted Johnson, the JCS, and their wives when they arrived later in the day. While making his public comments on the tarmac, Johnson ripped into Dulles, calling him a "do-gooder," and warned that he wanted to replace MacArthur. "The whole thing was smelly and nauseating," Sebald wrote in his diary. Years later, while writing his memoirs, he speculated that the two groups never met while they were in Japan. Evidence on this point remains unclear.[33]

In any case, these meetings went poorly for the Joint Chiefs. MacArthur supported a treaty, saying it was time for an agreement. In a lengthy memorandum, the shogun stated that a treaty would meet all of America's military needs. He also dismissed the JCS stipulation that the Soviet Union and China sign the treaty. "This, of course, is impossible." MacArthur had sided with the State Department. This position stunned the Joint Chiefs, while Dulles asked the general to write another memo that was specific on a few details. The next day MacArthur gave him the desired document. These memos, Dulles wrote, "provided the bridge which subsequently brought together all the branches of our government as to the desirability of a peace treaty."[34]

MacArthur's support ended outright military opposition to a peace treaty. The State and Defense Departments established a joint committee to resolve the many details still in dispute. Maj. Gen. Carter B. Magruder and Allison did most of the negotiating. Allison found the talks long and extremely difficult. "General Magruder had a good, if slow moving, mind," he recalled. In late August the JCS dropped their demand that the United States honor its wartime pledge not to seek a separate peace treaty and have the Soviets and the Chinese invited to a peace conference as signatories. On September 1 Magruder and Allison reached a final agreement and produced a memo establishing the basis for negotiations of a peace treaty with Japan. They agreed that the United States would keep bases in Japan after the occupation ended, no treaty would become operational until the end of the Korean War, and the peace settlement would "secure to the United States exclusive strategic control of the Ryukyu Islands." Acheson and Johnson signed the memo on September 7, and Truman approved the settlement the next day.[35]

John Foster Dulles could begin talks on a peace treaty. On September 14 Truman commissioned him to negotiate two treaties: a peace settlement with Japan and a collective security alliance that would create a Pacific version of NATO. Dulles and Allison, supplemented by a small staff, began negotiating the peace treaty through a series of bilateral talks in what Dean Rusk would later call "one of the finest chapters in American diplomacy." Dulles called it the "eleven months' peace conference." His biographer called it "divide and conquer."[36]

Dulles started negotiations by consulting with wartime allies. He quickly learned that American friends in the region had problems with the type of peace he desired. He had written a short, seven-point memo outlining the peace settlement, among the major elements were: no reparations, no restriction on Japan's postwar military, independence for Korea, United Nations membership for Japan, alliance with the United States and its allies in a security organization, and an American trusteeship for the Ryukyus. Dulles began consultations during the fifth meeting of the U.N. General Assembly. Most of the countries that had fought Japan sent their foreign ministers, giving the Americans an opportunity to obtain authoritative responses. The meeting between Dulles and Soviet deputy foreign minister Yakov Malik went well, even though they agreed on little. His discussion with Sir Percy Spender, the Australian foreign minister, was a different story. Dulles asked for a meeting on short notice, and when they got together Dulles abruptly handed Spender a copy of the memo without any forewarning. The failure to restrict Japanese rearmament offended Spender. "As he read the memorandum his face grew more and more suffused with color, and at one point I thought he would burst a blood vessel," Allison recounted. "Sir Percy did not hesitate to express his opinion in colorful and uninhibited language." Other delegates expressed the same sentiment with a little more tact. In his meeting with Frederick Doidge, the foreign minister for New Zealand, Dulles said American troops in the Ryukyus would provide a buffer should U.S. units leave Japan.[37]

These meetings left Dulles brooding. He confided to MacArthur that he was uncertain of the next step. Bilateral negotiations looked promising and, if he reached an agreement with the Japanese, dealing with other nations would be much easier. Then, he thought, all he might have to concede would be "some placating modifications which will be for form rather than substance."[38] Dulles later found that he would have to concede matters of actual importance.

Dulles began actual negotiations shortly after the new year and made some important concessions on territory and security. In the South Pacific, Dulles compromised on security issues. The Australian goal was simple: protection from Japan. There were, however, splits within the Australian government. Prime Minister Robert Gordon Menzies and Spender were political rivals. Spender, who earned the nickname "Butcher Bird" during his legal career for his treatment of witnesses on the stand, was the subject of idle gossip that often mentioned him as a replacement for Menzies as leader of the Liberal Party. Menzies soon began calling Jean Spender, the foreign minister's wife, "Lady MacBeth" to her face. Spender became minister of external affairs because Menzies figured the post would keep the "Butcher Bird" and his novelist wife from dabbling in domestic politics.[39]

More importantly, Spender and Menzies also differed on foreign policy. Before the war Spender stated that the British were no longer capable of providing protection for Australia. In Spender's view the main threat to Australian security was Japan, a common position in the ministry. When he became the minister for external affairs, Spender began working for an alliance with the United States. Menzies was much more of a traditional Victorian in outlook, expecting England to provide security for Australia and far less worried about the Japanese than Spender. The Australian military also rejected the view of their foreign office on Japanese rearmament, indirectly informing the United States of this. So failing a ban on rearmament, the Australians would accept a formal alliance with the United States that excluded Japan.[40]

New Zealand cautiously followed in Australia's wake with a similar split between an anti-Japanese external affairs ministry and an Anglo-centric prime minister. The diplomats in the external affairs ministry feared that a collective security pact would commit them to defend Japan and the Philippines, preferring instead a presidential statement that the United States would come to New Zealand's defense if it were at-

tacked. Prime Minister Sidney Holland wanted to create a security organization that would include Great Britain and was willing to accept
American stipulations on Japan and the Philippines.[41]

Dulles understood these concerns about Japan and gave up on efforts
to negotiate a collective security pact. Dulles arrived in Australia on February 14 and began negotiations with the Australians and New Zealanders the next day.[42] He spent the first meeting in Australia, making a
factual presentation on conditions in Japan to Australian and New
Zealand diplomats. In a presentation that took most of the day, he implied that pacifism dominated the Japanese, as if the war had taken the
fight out of them. Although the Australians and New Zealanders were
unaware of it, Dulles lied to them when he told them he had not discussed rearmament with the Japanese. "In the main I found Dulles' arguments rather convincing though it would have been unwise for me to
have said so," Spender noted. The Australian and Frederick Doidge, his
New Zealand counterpart, stood their ground. The two foreign ministers played a subtle game of "good cop, bad cop." While Spender insisted
on a formal agreement in treaty format, Doidge said that New Zealand
could accept a presidential declaration that Congress confirmed, which
would have been the same as a treaty. After explaining the American
strategy to build a defensive perimeter that would provide de facto protection against Communist aggression to the island nations of the Pacific,
Dulles asked why the United States should accord special status to Australia and New Zealand with a treaty when it had no plans to do so for
any other country. Spender quickly replied in kind. Australia and New
Zealand were the only two countries with military obligations outside of
the region, referring to their shared commitment to help England defend the Suez Canal and Singapore. The meeting was an impressive gathering of astute and nimble minds on both sides.[43]

When the meeting ended, Dulles still had said nothing about a security treaty. Australian and New Zealand reports of the discussion were
gloomy. Australian diplomat Alan Watt warned Spender that it seemed
unlikely the United States would make a security commitment.[44]

The next day, the "Butcher Bird" dominated events. He forcefully informed Dulles of Australian and New Zealand views even when they di-
verged. He made it clear that Australia would not sign a peace treaty
without a security pact. Dulles reiterated his arguments of the day before and added that the Soviet Union could offer Japan an opportunity to

seize power in the Pacific. By comparison, the United States could offer it little beyond an uncertain existence on the four main islands and had rejected Japanese efforts to regain the Ryukyu Islands. It was critical that Japan be offered peace on lenient terms. Dulles slowly brought up the idea of a mutual security treaty, which might include Japan, although he was willing to consider a trilateral arrangement. He also used Allison and Babcock as his own "bad cops." The two Americans stressed the need to include Japan in any security pact. Since the New Zealanders did not want the Philippines included in the pact and Dulles would not agree to British participation, the alliance came down to the United States, Australia, and New Zealand. Dulles made it clear that he was acting on his own initiative in negotiating a tripartite alliance with Australia and New Zealand; his instructions were for a collective pact. However, the astute negotiator had scored a victory. Dulles had cleverly waited a day, watching his opposites reveal their positions and implicitly tying the two treaties together while giving nothing away. It was one of his more impressive moments.[45]

This compromise actually increased the importance of Okinawa to the United States. Instead of having a solid cohesive anticommunist organization like NATO in the Pacific, the United States was beginning to create a web of anticommunist alliances. The nations of the Pacific were tied together indirectly through the United States but not directly to one another. This pattern would increase as the United States signed treaties with South Korea, the Philippines, Taiwan, and Japan, but none of these countries were obligated to help in the defense of the others. Since American allies had no direct connection to one another, the United States needed a base that it could use without the political hindrance of prior consultation, where it had political flexibility, and could both protect *and* monitor the Japanese. Okinawa became that base.

The Japanese, however, had no intention of surrendering claim to an entire prefecture. The main figure in Japan with whom Dulles had to contend was Prime Minister Yoshida Shigeru. A career diplomat and Anglophile, Yoshida had served as part of the Japanese delegation at the Versailles peace conference and had been the Japanese ambassador to Great Britain before the war; he even had an English nickname, "One Man" *(wan man)*. Removed from his post for his opposition to the Axis alliance and jailed briefly during the war, Yoshida began his political career during the American occupation. Strong, decisive, as well as stubborn and cranky, he helped guide Japan through its most difficult hour. In 1947 he could see that the rift between the Soviet Union and the United States was permanent; in this contest neutrality was not an option. The Soviets had already shown what it thought of Japanese neutrality when it declared war in 1945 despite a nonaggression pact between the two countries. Communists threatened Japan from both within and without. The internal threat came from the Japanese Communist Party, which seemed to be the vanguard of a Marxist revolution. The Soviet Union was the clear external threat. Yoshida initiated planning that would develop an appropriate anticommunist policy for Japan when the occupation ended. This preparation continued even after Yoshida's government fell in April, indicating broad concern about the danger communism might pose to Japan. Five months later, in September, Foreign Minister Ashida Hitoshi handed American representatives a memo that proposed a joint effort to provide for Japanese security. The Japanese would build a strong militarized police force to handle the internal threat while the United States would agree to respond to any external attack. The Japanese wanted to keep U.S. troops out of metropolitan Japan, but they were willing to have American forces stationed in the Ryukyus.[46]

This policy remained the Japanese position after Yoshida regained office. When Dulles showed him the contents of the seven-point memo, he found them "of a far more generous nature than we had been led to expect." Ending Japanese sovereignty over Okinawa was too much to ask, though. Yoshida considered the island an "integral" part of Japan. More importantly, the nationalistic right wing, the same political element that had thrown him into prison, was garnering attention and support with its opposition to the territorial settlement of the treaty. Soon, the left wing too was attacking Yoshida for allowing the Americans to dismember Japan. Yoshida had to find a way to neutralize the opposition before it undercut support for the security arrangement. He approached Sebald at a dinner party and suggested the inhabitants be allowed to keep their Japanese citizenship. MacArthur was opposed to this idea. Undeterred, Yoshida sent Shirasu Jiro, a political confidant, to talk with Fearey when the Dulles mission visited Tokyo in January, 1951. Shirasu asked the Americans to reconsider their position on the Ryukyus. Japan acquired these islands peacefully and should at least be allowed to retain title in some nominal manner. Then, on January 31, Yoshida broached the subject directly, handing a member of the Dulles mission an *aide-*

mémoire on Okinawa. In the document Yoshida stated that Japan would provide whatever land the United States required, under any conditions it desired, if it would only reassess its position on the Ryukyus.[47]

Dulles knew as he read the *aide-mémoire* that the American government had actually just finished doing exactly what Yoshida asked. Sebald, MacArthur's political advisor, had warned the State Department that the fate of the Ryukyus was becoming a partisan issue in Japan, spurring anti-American sentiment. Fearey suggested to Foreign Service officer U. Alexis Johnson, his nominal supervisor, a lease agreement similar to the one for Guantanamo Bay, Cuba. Johnson forwarded this proposal up the bureaucratic chain of command, making his own recommendation. He advised that the United States consider returning the islands after the signing of a treaty, and the conclusion of a security pact would give the military an opportunity to realize all their needs. Acheson politely asked George C. Marshall, the new secretary of defense, if the Department of Defense would consider other ways of meeting American security needs in the Ryukyus. The opposition—the adamant disapproval of the JCS *and* from MacArthur—quickly stopped any move in this direction. That the Japanese had questioned his wisdom was a betrayal and outrage to Douglas MacArthur. He told Dulles the area was an economic drain; the residents were not Japanese; and the Japanese should be glad, no eager, to get rid of these islands. After meeting with the JCS, Acheson accepted their objections on the matter. When Dulles returned to Tokyo in January, 1951, he worried that the Japanese were going to try and play the United States off the Soviet Union. There might be good reasons to reconsider the settlement of the Ryukyus question, but he would do it on his terms and his terms only. In a meeting with Yoshida, Dulles informed the prime minister that the disposition of the islands was not a matter open for reconsideration and told him to move on to the next item of business. Yoshida had little choice but to accept this statement.[48]

The American position was less firm than Dulles let Yoshida think. Dulles never enthusiastically supported the retention of Okinawa. He worried that reactionaries and the ultranationalist right wing would use the territorial issue to "crucify" Yoshida and build up sentiment against the accord, just as had been done in Weimar Germany. He was also concerned that Okinawa might become "another Puerto Rico," creating citizenship, immigration, trade, and civil liberties problems. Still, those working in the Pentagon wanted the island, and Dulles was not going to let the Japanese force him into changing policy. There were, however, people in the United States who could force the change. Senators on the Senate Foreign Relations Committee expressed grave doubts about maintaining Okinawa as a trusteeship. Sen. H. Alexander Smith of New Jersey observed that the treaty gave the United States the right to seek a trusteeship only if it chose to do so, otherwise it could retain the islands indefinitely; was this not imperialism, he asked pointedly. John J. Sparkman of Alabama agreed, saying the treaty asked too much of the Japanese.[49]

On March 22, 1951, Foreign Service officer U. Alexis Johnson had a long conversation with an army lieutenant colonel in a military-government assignment on Okinawa. The colonel stated that if the United States obtained the desired defense agreement with Japan, there would be little need to keep and administer the Ryukyus. This talk helped convince Dulles (he was sent a memo of conversation) that the United States could meet its military needs short of what the Joint Chiefs were demanding. During negotiations in London, Allison told the British that Dulles was beginning to see that the United States faced a number of difficulties in trying to get the consent of the United Nations while maintaining exclusive American control of the island. An argument at a meeting in April between Dulles and General of the Army Omar Bradley, which quickly degenerated into quibbling about the legal nature of "trusteeships" versus "strategic trusteeship," made it clear that the military would accept something else as long as it allowed for exclusive administration. Dulles soon began formulating a response that would handle these legal, political, and military complications. His answer was the legal concept of "residual sovereignty."[50]

According to this theory, Okinawa would become just like the Panama Canal Zone: the United States would administer the territory, but the inhabitants would keep their original citizenship. This solution seemed an ingenious, legalistic compromise that answered all the objections to the disposition of the Ryukyu Islands. Japan would still have legal claim to the islands, and Yoshida would not be open to the charge of selling out Japanese interests. Even though the island would become a territorial issue in later years, the "residual sovereignty" formula ultimately dictated that the matter would be resolved in favor of Japan. This settlement would satisfy the Senate, and the United States would be protected from the charge of imperialism, at least as that term was traditionally and legally understood. The military would have the island without international legal and political complications. And, most of all, Dulles had controlled the decision; the United States would appear generous while keeping the Japanese in line. He discussed the issue with Marshall and the Senate Foreign Relations Committee, obtained the approval of each, but delayed any public announcement.[51]

The peace conference held in San Francisco to sign the treaty with Japan was mainly a ceremonial event, but it drew widespread attention. *Newsweek* magazine ran a front cover article on Dulles, and it even ran a biographical article on Allison, an unknown mid-level civil servant until then. Not to be outdone, *Time* magazine sponsored a television show on ABC and CBS entitled "Your Stake in Japan." The Pennsylvania state senate passed a resolution praising the work of Dulles and Acheson on the treaty. The conference was also the first event broadcast live on national television. Truman's welcoming speech focused even more attention on the gathering. Delegates gave their speeches on the second day after the adoption of the bylaws, which American diplomats had designed to keep the Soviets from disrupting the conference. A shoving match nearly broke out between Acheson and Soviet delegate Andrei Gromyko when Acheson ruled that the Russian was out of order but Gromyko refused to leave the podium. Dulles gave the first speech and announced a new policy for the Ryukyu Islands. "The United States felt that the best formula would be to permit Japan to retain residual sovereignty." Three days later Yoshida gave the last speech. While grateful for residual sovereignty, he made it clear that Japan had not given up interest in the islands. "I cannot but hope that the administration of these islands will be put back into Japanese hands in the not [too] distant future with the reestablishment of world security—especially the security of Asia."[52]

When the San Francisco conference adjourned, the U.S. occupation of Japan quickly came to an end after ratification of the treaty. The United States continued, however, to administer and rule Okinawa. Americans believed they had to protect the Pacific from both the Communists and the Japanese. With Okinawa firmly under U.S. control and Japan restored to sovereignty, Americans set about turning the Ryukyu Islands into an American colony.

CHAPTER 4

The Making of an American Colony, 1950–56

On June 19, 1960, Dwight D. Eisenhower, the president of the United States, landed at Kadena Air Force Base, Okinawa. After some arriving remarks, Eisenhower rode into Naha accompanied by Okinawan chief executive Ota Seisaku, who had taken the initiative to invite the president to the island. An estimated two hundred thousand people, roughly a fourth of the population, lined the fourteen miles between the air base and the city, waving signs and banners welcoming Eisenhower. At the end of this line a crowd of thirty thousand waited to greet the president. A small group of protesters, about two or three thousand in number, positioned themselves in the line at the point it ran into the crowd. Marine guards over-reacted and fixed their bayonets. Media accounts, American and Japanese, gave the protesters a disproportionate amount of attention. Eisenhower passed without noticing, and scheduling kept him busy meeting with Ota and members of the Okinawan legislature.

Eisenhower did observe and remark on the rehabilitation and recovery that had taken place in the fourteen years since his last visit to the island. "I was delighted to see at first hand the many visible signs of progress and prosperity that the people of Okinawa are increasingly able to enjoy," he wrote later.[1] The "prosperity" Eisenhower saw was a direct result of the investment the United States made in turning the island into an American colony and the key to gaining Okinawan acquiescence to American rule, which the military required because of uncertainty about Japanese dependability as an ally in the Cold War.[2]

There was little dispute in the 1950s that Okinawa was an American colony. Americans bandied the term about both in public and private. Vice President Richard M. Nixon warned the National Security Council about Okinawa in 1953. Earlier in the year he had visited the island as part of a tour of Asia. He told the NSC that Communists in Asia were charging that the United States supported colonialism, and American administration of the Ryukyus made this accusation credible.[3] In a positive article about American activity on Okinawa published in 1955, a reporter for *Time* enthusiastically stated, "Without anyone really intending it that way, the U.S. has been thrust into the colonial business." After an article in the London *Times* called the island an American colony, the English-language paper on Okinawa responded, saying there were cases of good and bad colonialism; Okinawa was good. In the Senate, John F. Kennedy, during a famous speech he gave on French rule in Algeria, claimed the United States had a clean record on colonialism. Hubert H. Humphery, the Minnesota Democrat, responded, "The situation on Okinawa at the moment brings these reassuring statements into some doubt."[4] Olcott Deming, the American consul general in Okinawa during the mid-1950s, wrote a lengthy memo about the island when he returned to Washington that circulated for years within the State Department: "It may be denied by some who are skilled political scientists that the United States position in Okinawa is a 'colonial' one; but in the eyes of most of the world our status here is close enough to colonialism so that the label with all its opprobrium will stick and be used. It is, then, an anomaly that the power in the world most against the basic philosophy of colonialism should find itself ruling a foreign area and its inhabitants."[5]

The Okinawans certainly believed they were a subject people. Resentment building up for years exploded on February 1, 1962, when the

Okinawan legislature unanimously passed a resolution accusing the United States of colonialism in defiance of U.N. ordinances. This resolution passed even though a conservative party favorably inclined toward the United States controlled the legislature. Although the Japanese foreign ministry informed the United Nations that the Ryukyus were not a colony, the Diet passed a resolution supporting the Okinawa petition. Lt. Gen. Paul Caraway, the high commissioner of the Ryukyu Islands at the time, stated in an oral history, "They were not an American colony." The charge of colonialism "was just a political gambit." Caraway, however, in his next breath compared the island to French-ruled Algeria. He also wrote the British governor of Bermuda, "you and I are in the same business."[6]

American administration of the Ryukyus had also had its dissenters. The most significant internal challenge to American rule came in 1951 from Gen. Matthew Ridgway, MacArthur's successor in Tokyo. When he took over from MacArthur, the general was no different from others in the U.S. military in his views about Japan possibly becoming a threat again. He warned the secretary of the army that "it would be a dangerously fallacious premise to assume, as seems to have been done already in some quarters, that Japanese thinking has been permanently reoriented into our channels, or that the Japanese people may not revert wholly, or to a large extent, to their previous customs, traditions and way of life." Ridgway had a reputation in the army for independence, and his view of Japan changed during his stay in Tokyo. He came to believe that the retention of the Ryukyus threatened to undermine U.S. policy in the region. When the Government of the Ryukyu Islands was inaugurated, he downplayed the severity of the separation between the archipelago and the rest of Japan. Okinawa would continue to enjoy cultural, economic, and educational ties with metropolitan Japan. He also promised that there would be no restrictions on travel and political limitations would be kept to a minimum.[7]

Ridgway also acted on his concerns, writing a lengthy report that challenged the retention of the Ryukyus. This document initiated a debate within the U.S. government that lasted for over a year and a half. In his memo, he quickly and clearly made his opposition known: "The security of the strategically vital U.S. position along the off-shore island chain in the Western Pacific is in no way dependent upon the perpetuation of U.S. political control, by virtue of a UN trusteeship or other device, over the Ryukyus Islands." In the dense prose that was typical of Ridgway, he explained his reasons. "The effectuation of permanent U.S. political control—or political responsibility, to use a more expressive term—over the Ryukyus Islands will serve not only to burden the U.S. with an economic liability for the indefinite future, but will stand as a denial of the principle of self-determination, to which the U.S. has traditionally subscribed, and might at a later date develop into an irritant to the Japanese of such proportions as to contribute to a breakdown in U.S.-Japanese mutual confidence and friendship." As long as the United States reached an agreement "to retain under our exclusive control such military facilities in the subject islands as are deemed essential by the Joint Chiefs of Staff," he believed reversion would actually improve relations with Japan. "A U.S. sponsored movement for the return of control over the Ryukyus Islands to Japan would constitute an additional step toward the cementing of the already interlocked U.S.-Japanese security objectives in the Far East."[8]

Few on the other side of the Pacific shared that view. A January, 1952, study commissioned by the JCS in response to Ridgway rejected the main thrust of the general's argument that the United States and Japan had interlocked security interests. The report straddled two different views of Japan. One perceived the Japanese as an enemy lying dormant: "The economic cost of administering the area is trivial when balanced against the cost in blood and treasure required to conquer the islands from Japan, their importance to U.S. security, and the expenditure of lives and equipment which might be necessary should the islands be given up and, subsequently, military necessity demand their recapture." The other viewed Japan as an uncertain and unsure ally. The United States needed to keep its bases in Okinawa in case Japan should fail to support the nation in a moment of crisis. "The security interests of the United States require that United States forces, deployed in accordance with war plans, continue to remain in the Ryukyus irrespective of conditions in the sovereign nation of Japan."[9]

News of the Ridgway report's existence leaked to the State Department, causing a split among diplomats. Many lower-echelon Foreign Service officers agreed with Ridgway's thinking and wanted to follow up on the document. Acheson, however, chose not to press the matter, but he did have representatives of the department informally solicit the views of the JCS on the issue.[10]

The Joint Chiefs responded with a memo that indicated a slightly new view of Japan. The JCS opposed reversion because bases on Okinawa "would be relatively useless in war if Japan were hostile, and might involve difficulties even if Japan were neutral." The chiefs were beginning to entertain the idea that Japan, instead of being a foe, might simply be an ally of questionable dependability.[11]

Debate on the Ryukyus stalled shortly thereafter. The civilian leadership in the Department of Defense rejected the opinion of the JCS and asked the State Department to establish an interdepartmental working group. Defense Department representatives, however, were middle-level military officers who repeated the JCS position over and over. Nothing happened other than having the debate leak out onto the pages of *Foreign Affairs.*[12]

The dispute lurched forward immediately after the inauguration of the Eisenhower administration in 1953. John Foster Dulles, the new secretary of state, received a memo from his old friend Assistant Secretary of State John Allison bringing the matter to his attention. Allison recommended that the United States return the Bonin Islands, which included Iwo Jima, and the Amami Islands, which were in the northern Ryukyus. The United States should retain Okinawa as well as the rest of the Ryukyus, and the president should make a clear and plain announcement of this decision. After reading the memo, Dulles penned a note in the margin asking Allison to prepare a paper for discussion at a National Security Council meeting.[13]

The discussion that followed three months later at a NSC meeting in the West Wing of the White House indicated that views of Japan were slowly changing. Dulles made a lengthy presentation and kept the issue away from the merits of retaining the Amami and Bonin Islands, directing the discussion to the larger issue of U.S.-Japanese relations. He made much the same argument Ridgway did; America's future in the Pacific depended on Japan, and the island issue could destroy that relationship. Okinawa was an important exception because of its prime military importance. Secretary of Defense Charles Wilson said the military had profound doubts about Japanese dependability in the Cold War. He would favor reversion of these islands, if the United States could be certain Japan would, in his words, "stay with us." President Eisenhower made some comments at this point. The minutes of the meeting record that he delivered his remarks with power and force. He spoke of the need to keep

American priorities in order. Keeping Japan friendly was the most important goal. If the fate of these small islands put that relationship at risk, then returning them was a "must." With the president's views clear, Wilson backed down and said he had no problem returning the Amami Islands.[14]

During the debate on the Ryukyus, views about Japan underwent a change. The idea of Japan as a dormant enemy awaiting resurrection died. Japan was not an enemy, but that did not necessarily make it a friend. What bothered Americans in particular was the Japanese reluctance, indeed refusal, to rearm and fight the good fight in the anticommunist crusade. "I am terribly disappointed at the way things have been going in Japan," Dulles wrote shortly after the return of the Amami group. "There has not been any rebirth of moral strength, as in the case of Germany." Counting on Japan as an ally should war erupt in the Pacific was considered unwise. In a study of Japanese postwar defense policy, Martin E. Weinstein found that this view was unfair. The Japanese did reject American insistence on a 350,000-man army, but the country made good-faith efforts to develop their self-defense force.[15]

Dulles returned the islands to Japan with a flurry of positive press. In a private meeting during an August trip to Tokyo, he informed Yoshida of the decision. The United States actually returned the islands on Christmas Day, 1953, as a present from one nation to another.[16] Reaction in Japan was positive, but the suddenness of the restoration soon troubled some representatives in the Diet. Members of the opposition wondered if the foreign ministry might have made concessions on the status of Okinawa. Okazaki Katsuo, the foreign minister, clarified the issue and removed any doubt during a debate in the Diet. He said Japanese diplomats had rejected an American suggestion that a note be attached to the instrument returning the islands to Japanese administration that reaffirmed U.S. rights in the rest of the Ryukyus. The American diplomats accepted this rejection. This discarded statement came two weeks later, though, in the State of the Union message when Eisenhower declared, "We shall maintain indefinitely our bases in Okinawa." Journalists on the island and in the United States applauded this statement on their editorial pages. The Okinawans made a distinction that Eisenhower had not intended between the presence of bases and American administration, and many reasoned that the president was leaving the door open for a reversion agreement in the near future in which the bases remained on the island as they had in Japan proper when that occupation had ended.[17]

The main reason—actually, the only reason—the United States made the Ryukyus a colony was its strategic location and function as a forward base. "There was no other purpose—not to free Okinawans, not to right any wrongs. And a military base it remains," a reporter for the *Saturday Evening Post* wrote, summarizing American sentiment about the island. American officials repeated this view time and time again.[18] The United States gained nothing from the island economically, Japanese goods outsold American products in Okinawan markets, and administration was a deficit to the American treasury.[19] The island base gave the United States flexibility in responding to a threat or aiding in the defense of any one of its many allies in the Pacific without having to consult with a sovereign power. "This location is needed to ensure striking power to implement the collective security concept," Dulles wrote in *Foreign Affairs.*[20]

American planners believed the United States had two possible foes in either the Soviet Union or the People's Republic of China. "Okinawa-based medium bombers," the military governor said, "have an effective advantage in that they can reach all important target areas within an arc which includes all of Southeast Asia, the whole of modern China, the Lake Baikal industrial area, Eastern Siberia, and the southern tip of Kamchatka Peninsula." U.S. bombers based on the island could also hit targets in the European territory of the Soviet Union and land at air force bases in Western Europe if they flew one-way.[21]

Okinawa fit into the mission of each military service differently. The navy had no interest in the island. Port facilities were poor and no more than a handful of sailors were ever stationed in the Ryukyus. The air force, on the other hand, had a sizable detachment assigned to the island. MacArthur stated back in 1948 that air power was critical to the American presence in the Ryukyus. After touring military facilities on the island, a reporter for *The New York Times* wrote, "Okinawa is for the Air Force what Pearl Harbor is for the Navy." Maj. Gen. Ralph Stearley, commander of the Twentieth Air Force stationed at Kadena, described the importance of Okinawa to his service: "You can talk all you want about Japan, Formosa, and the Philippines, but to me this is the key to the Pacific."[22]

Okinawa did indeed prove to be an important base during the Korean

War. Three days after the North Korean Army crossed into South Korea, bombers stationed on the island began flying missions over the peninsula. The attack caught the air force off guard. While there were enough pilots, crews, and planes on the island to start operations immediately, support personnel on the ground were in short supply. Officers spent three days rounding up clerks, cooks, and anyone else they could find to act as bomb loaders and ground crews. Poor intelligence and weather hampered the initial flights. The first bombing runs had no defined objectives and planes flew against "targets of opportunity." These missions were blind shots in the dark during the first month of the war—the B-29s either destroyed bridges and roads all over the peninsula or returned home after dropping their loads into the sea.[23]

With each successive bombing run came greater and greater success. Later flights hit railroads, petroleum yards, port facilities, and dock areas on both coasts. Missions also provided close air support for ground troops. The air force bombed enemy tanks, truck convoys, and troop concentrations moving against U.N. combat units. In the first three months of operations, air force units stationed on Okinawa lost only two men and one plane. At the end of the year, the crews based there dropped 24,914.9 tons of bombs in 3,284 sorties. These missions had an effective rate (flights that unloaded their payload over target) of 97.5 percent. "There is never a dull moment on this island called Okinawa," Stearley observed.[24]

There were limits to the effectiveness of the airfields on Okinawa. All bombing missions had to fly out of Kadena Air Force Base, since it was the only airfield in the Ryukyus that had runways capable of supporting heavy bombers. In 1951, when the Joint Chiefs of Staff insisted on the deployment of atomic bombs for use in Korea, combat plans originally called for their storage in the Ryukyus. The proximity of Okinawa to Communist territory was a blade that cut both ways. Having the bombs housed on the island would make them vulnerable to a preemptive Soviet strike. Once planners in Washington realized this they had the location changed to Guam.[25]

The war also caused the air force presence on Okinawa to grow. By the end of the summer, the number of bomb groups on the island tripled (a group is an air force unit commanded by a colonel). A three-year rebuilding program for Kadena Air Base budgeted at just over forty-five million dollars was underway when the war started, and the conflict had the ironic effect of slowing down construction. To friends of his in the army, Stearley gloated in a light-hearted way that his service had bested theirs in getting better contractors and plots of land. After inspecting the structures, he predicted that the Ryukyus would become "the garden spot of the world in another year and a half."[26]

Although the army administered the island, it used Okinawa mainly as a logistical center and supply base. In the early 1950s the 29th Infantry Regiment, a combat unit under the command of a colonel, was on the island, but most soldiers were service and support troops. In mid-decade a military reorganization put the IX Corps on the island, but it was no more than a paper organization. "As a Corps Commander, I didn't have anything there, except the headquarters," Lt. Gen. Paul Caraway, a high commissioner in later years, remarked. "There were about three of us in the IX Corps."[27]

The Marine Corps arrived on Okinawa late. Until 1956, marine units in the Far East were based in Japan. Following an agreement between Pres. Dwight D. Eisenhower and the prime minister of Japan, the 3rd Marine Division began relocating to the island. When they made their late arrival on Okinawa, the air force had taken all the available space for dependent housing, making duty on the island an unaccompanied hardship assignment for the marines; even the generals went without their families. The marines in the Ryukyus had three missions. The first of these was training. The absence of families allowed the division to train at all hours and to stay out in the field for extended periods of time.[28]

The second mission was to serve as a rapid deployment force for the United States in the Pacific. Marine generals argued that the absence of families allowed the unit to deploy without men worrying about their families after their sudden departure. While there might be some truth to that argument, it is also clear that the absence of families hurt morale and reenlistment rates declined.[29]

The final mission for the 3rd Marine Division was to defend Okinawa. Although the army formally had this mission, most of the soldiers on the island were service and support personnel. Nuclear weapons were a key component of marine defensive plans for Okinawa. It was an open secret for years that atomic weapons were on the island, though no proof was ever available before now. According to 3rd Marine Division operational plans, American defenders were prepared to use nuclear weapons in a defensive strategy similar to that devised by Col. Yahara Hiromichi during the battle for Okinawa. The marines would defend the militarily valuable southern end, allowing an invading enemy force to take the northern half of the island. Once the enemy was on the island, the Americans would use tactical nuclear weapons to destroy the enemy force. The operational plan prohibited attacks on civilian population centers, prisoner of war camps, hospitals, orphanages, port facilities, roads, and bridges. The likelihood of such an assault was remote and generally understood. The editors of the *Fort Worth Star-Telegram* noted as much in 1960. The Chinese, the most likely foe, lacked the naval resources to launch an assault on the island.[30]

Since Okinawa fit into the missions of three different military services, the decision to keep the island was an economic boon for the Okinawans. In 1950 Congress appropriated $50 million, which was more than the amount for the previous three years combined. Funding dropped in 1951, but the $36 million for that year was just under the combined total for 1948 and 1949. Base construction was a major economic engine. In order to help foster Japanese and Okinawan economic recovery, Americans intentionally discriminated in favor of Japanese firms, preferably Okinawan ones. Japanese companies accounted for 85 percent of the contracts in the early 1950s, but Okinawan firms obtained some major and prestigious projects. These included the new capital building, worth $1.2 million, and the port terminal building, worth $225,000. Okinawan firms also refurbished 130 Quonset huts and built another 308 new homes in several American housing areas scattered across the island. Throughout the 1950s Okinawan companies progressively won more and more of the construction projects. At the end of the decade, all of the contracts for the building of Camp Hansen, a new marine base, went to local firms. No matter the nationality of the firm, Okinawans provided most of the labor. In this way construction absorbed the agriculture laborers the bases displaced. All told, the United States invested $630,034,800 in base construction during its twenty-seven-year rule of the island, most during the first half of the 1950s.[31]

Military construction altered the landscape. "American military installations on Okinawa have to be seen to be believed," a stunned Foreign Service officer from the Tokyo embassy wrote. "From north of Kadena Air Base to the city of Naha to the south, Okinawa seems to be one continuous American base."[32] A month later the same sites flabbergasted Ambassador John Allison and Deputy Assistant Secretary of

State for Far Eastern Affairs William J. Sebald, MacArthur's former "foreign minister." Sebald recorded in his diary seeing hills leveled and valleys filled. The military was building thousands of homes, numerous clubs, multiple post exchanges, swimming pools, and other "paraphernalia which goes with an American effort when money doesn't mean anything. It is easy to see that the services are convinced that we are on Okinawa for generations." After an aerial tour of the island by helicopter, Sebald began asking difficult questions: How long before weapons technology makes Okinawa obsolete? What if the population turns hostile? What if Japan demands the return of its prefecture? "Those are, of course, nightmare questions which have been swept under the rug. All in all, Okinawa strikes me as a never-never land of the unbelievable."[33]

Despite the massive construction, housing remained a serious problem for the commanding officers on Okinawa. Much had been done about housing in the 1950s. The largest construction project, which consumed most of the money spent in rebuilding Kadena, went to building new housing units that could withstand winds of 120 miles per hour. "The experience on Okinawa has definitely indicated that the Quonset-type buildings are very difficult and costly to maintain and unsatisfactory as family housing," the construction proposal for Kadena stated. Military families lived in low concrete bungalows, which could withstand the typhoons, in neighborhoods that resembled civilian suburbs. Major General Stearley, after inspecting some of these new homes, noted, "They really are a dream set." Quantity rather than quality for dependent housing was the main difficulty now; demand exceeded supply. Geography limited the amount of additional construction, thus complicating matters. While Stearley proudly observed that the wait for assignment for family quarters dropped by half under his command, it still took seven months. One of his successors, Maj. Gen. Dale O. Smith, remarked, "Housing is my number one problem." Some Americans found homes off base, but these domiciles were often expensive and small. Morale and efficiency suffered as servicemen tried to live in cramped off-base quarters, or, more times than not, served on the island without their families.[34]

The marines faced an even more difficult situation. Following the Vietnam War and reversion, the Marine Corps developed a large presence on Okinawa, but during the 1950s the situation was far different. The 3rd Marine Division had only tents and Quonset huts for its men, with no dependent housing at all. A reporter with the *New York World Tele-*

gram and Sun called them "Okinawa's slum dwellers." Supply officers had to scrap and scrounge for basic supplies, like toilets and sinks, to outfit their new camps. Most of this material and the Quonset huts disappeared when the next major typhoon struck the island. An officer later wrote, "We were crammed into barracks with rotting floors and leaking roofs which were infested with termites and mosquitoes; the toilet facilities were unsanitary and continuously breaking down." An official inquiry later found that these charges were essentially correct.[35]

Generals back at USMC Headquarters in Washington worried about these accommodations. An inspection of Okinawa bases in 1957 discovered that the reenlistment rate in the division had dropped 20 percent since its assignment to Okinawa. Housing for the marines, however, never improved; they continued to face an acute housing shortage well into the 1970s.[36]

Providing social and recreational facilities for American service members and their families was an important part in turning Okinawa into a major military base. The presence of these facilities played a significant role in maintaining unit morale and efficiency. "This is a long way from home and you've got to give the people who come here or who are ordered here as pleasant a life as possible, with plenty of recreation," remarked Maj. Gen. Robert S. Beighter, military governor in the early 1950s. The military succeeded in this endeavor. "On Okinawa," the wife of an air force officer said, "the livin' is easy, man. Real easy." There were plenty of extracurricular activities for the children of service personnel, including sports leagues, scuba diving classes, instruction in judo and karate, and summer activity programs. An American family could hire an Okinawan as a full-time maid for between fifteen and twenty dollars a month. Freed from housework, military wives had plenty of time on their hands. Wives' clubs and volunteer work at hospitals and schools were major activities. Learning about Okinawan history and culture was extremely popular; touring the island was a common weekend excursion, and a book on Okinawan culture sold so well on the island that it went through two editions. In this effort Marian Merritt was a pioneer. Although the wife of a mere major—the leadership of the military wives' community usually correspond to the rank and position of their husbands—Merritt took the lead in a number of projects designed to foster good relations between Americans and Okinawans. Society at the time generally considered these activities to be the realm of women. In an effort to eliminate cultural clashes, she established the Okinawan Maid School. The goal of the program was to give Okinawan women a sixty-hour course in how to do ordinary American-style housework. She also mediated disputes between graduates and their employers. More times than not, the Americans were at fault in these matters, failing to appreciate how foreign their ways were to Okinawans, even to those trained to be maids. "Most of your problems will vanish if you will have a heart!" Merritt wrote to American wives. She was a charter member of the International Women's Club, which eventually became quite large. The purpose of this organization of American and Okinawan women was to allow both groups to explore the culture of the other. Merritt even learned Japanese so that she could address Okinawan groups in their own language. She took a course from a Japanese school in flower arrangement, and she had a collection of her letters home published as a book. Although she used language that was at times condescending, Merritt made it clear with explicit statements that there was nothing intrinsically superior about U.S. culture over that of Okinawa despite the greater material prosperity that Americans enjoyed. Her work led *U.S. Lady,* a magazine for military wives, to name her "Lady of the Month" in April, 1956.[37]

The military provided a number of other activities. The air force ran Awase Meadows Country Club, which included an eighteen-hole golf course, driving range, swimming pool, pro shop, and restaurant. Base clubs also did a healthy business. Americans could get steak dinners for under two dollars and mixed drinks for nickels and dimes, while watching live entertainment, including the likes of Sammy Davis, Jr. Veterans organizations, such as the American Legion and the Veterans of Foreign Wars, ran their own clubs on Okinawa. These facilities had slot machines, which were big draws. A total of 150 machines brought in $100,000 a month for the VFW, and the tax-free sale of alcohol produced another $120,000. The managers of base clubs imported slot machines after seeing their popularity in the private establishments. Both types of clubs sponsored dances, bingo nights, and pool tournaments. There was a downside to these businesses, though. Many people, mainly bored housewives with too much free time, whiled away the day with drink and lost large amounts of cash at the slot machines.[38]

Okinawan-run establishments were another entertainment venue for service personnel and were more often than not in prostitution districts.

An air force analysis estimated that 90 percent of all the bars catering to Americans were fronts for organized prostitution. "If it weren't for the easy availability of sex," an officer remarked, "our troops out here would go nuts." The commander of the 29th Infantry Regiment in 1951 made a condescending comment in his diary that "Okinawa is no place to send these kids as they tend to lower their social conduct to the same standards as these under privileged (down trodden) people whose standards of health and cleanliness are very low." A reporter for the English-language Okinawa *Morning Star* wrote, "Gambling, gin, and gals are the three G's that keep lonesome American GI's occupied on Okinawa during their off-duty hours."[39]

The issue of sex, in general, and prostitution, in particular, was in no way unique to Okinawa in either time or space. The presence of camp followers, harlots, and the like has been a matter with which military commanders all over the world have had to deal with since time immemorial.[40] The idea that such commercial perversion reflected inferior social and moral standards of Okinawan society or was the product of the vast economic disparity between Americans and Okinawans was a gross distortion of the truth. One of the best accounts on the sexual interaction between U.S. service personnel and their hosts on the island came from an American sociologist stationed in the Ryukyus in the mid-1950s as an enlisted man. Yehudi Cohen conducted a series of interviews on commercial prostitution in two villages that were adjacent to his base. In one the illicit practice flourished, while in the other it was virtually nonexistent. He found that in Okinawan society the history and moral status of prostitution was roughly the same as that in the United States. Cohen also learned that factors other than simple economic pressure led Okinawans to enter the sex business. The people living in the two towns faced the same sort of financial concerns, but those in the area without prostitution pursued socially acceptable employment opportunities. The greatest difference between the two villages was migration and the presence of family. The prostitutes and brothel owners were new immigrants to their community and had no close kinsmen in the area. The residents in the other town were indigenous and less than receptive to the arrival of newcomers. In his study of the U.S. Army stationed in the United Kingdom during World War II, British historian David Reynolds argued that the service was in many ways a social welfare program for the soldiers. By providing for all the basic social needs of the individual soldiers, the army fostered a climate that essentially eliminated the need for individuals to take personal responsibility for their actions.[41] Taken together, these studies suggest that prostitution on Okinawa prospered because the social forces of shame in one culture and those of sin in the other were absent from daily life.

While there is no denying the heavy amount of prostitution on the island, recreational activities for young, single men were not totally bankrupt of morals. The military built several beach facilities that were open to enlisted personnel of all services, while others existed for officers. With white sandy beaches and emerald blue waters, Ishikawa on the eastern shore of the island was a popular location. "These beaches are *great!*" one marine told the *Triad,* the newspaper of the 3rd Marine Division. "These beaches are the best I have ever seen." Military personnel could go sailing, skin diving, or just have a picnic and barbecue on the beach. Military sports leagues remained another popular pastime. Many competitions were recreational: tennis, swimming, bowling, and horseshoes. Others, such as boxing, football, and baseball were far more competitive. Officers served as coaches, and enlisted men played for unit teams. Service ball teams often had former professional, semipro, and college players on their teams. While competitive, these teams were hardly overwhelming in talent. Every marine in an "Opinion Corner" feature of the *Triad* said interservice competition on Okinawa rated no better than average when compared to other service leagues. Underscoring this fact, the University of Southern California Trojans beat the 9th Marine Regiment baseball team 8-1 in August, 1955.[42]

Self-improvement was another way to spend off-duty time. The University of Maryland extension program offered college credit courses on Okinawa for military personnel. Some foreign-born marines studied for and obtained U.S. citizenship on their own time.[43]

While much of the construction on the island was designed for the benefit of Americans, development also served Okinawan needs. The United States introduced social and cultural programs that were designed solely for the Okinawan people. These efforts went beyond simple increases in pay or gross national product. These initiatives helped improve the living conditions and social standards that Okinawans themselves considered important. This attentive response was a prime reason the residents tolerated the American presence for so many years. The most significant American contributions to the social welfare of the Okinawan people came in the field of education. When reversion came in 1972, there were forty-three high schools, six special institutions (schools for the deaf, blind, disabled, and mentally retarded), five junior colleges, and three universities. Before the war there were no institutes of higher education on Okinawa at all. It is also important to note that instruction took place in the Ryukyuan dialect of Japanese. Had these schools used English, education would have become a form of cultural warfare designed to widen the separation between Okinawa and Japan, making it easier to perpetuate American rule.[44]

In the early 1950s the Okinawans had the responsibility for constructing schools. Allocations for education quickly became the largest item in the budget of the Government of the Ryukyu Islands. Educational funding equaled 29.6 percent of the budget in 1953 and 27.1 percent in fiscal 1954. With less than half of the needed classrooms built, American administrators realized the United States would have to intervene in order to serve Okinawan interests and protect American ones. Maj. Gen. William F. Marquat, chief of civil affairs and military government for the army, explained: "The slow rate at which educational facilities have been restored has been widely used by the Japanese in an effort to develop pressures for the reversion of the Okinawa group to Japan following the recent turnover of the Amami Gunto. Japan is known to have planned substantial measures to provide prewar standard of education in the Amami group as a possible embarrassment to the United States." Most school construction occurred in 1955, but the United States spent a total of fifty million dollars during its administration.[45]

The U.S. Army also established the Ryukyuan Scholarship Program. These scholarships funded college study in the United States for Okinawan students. Between 1949 and 1974, 1,045 students participated in the program: 28 earned doctorates, 263 master's degrees, and 163 their bachelor's degrees. Participants in the program enrolled in diverse schools ranging from Cornell to Whittier, and from the University of Texas to the Massachusetts Institute of Technology. Most, however, chose the University of Hawaii or Michigan State College (as Michigan State University was known at the time). The program started off small, but in 1956 the appropriation jumped from forty thousand dollars to two hundred thousand dollars. Many private American organizations provided scholarships as well for study in either the United States or Okinawa.[46]

The army also played a large role in establishing the University of the

Ryukyus, the first institution of higher learning on the island. The school opened its doors in May, 1950, with a faculty of twenty-eight. Later that year Shikiya Koshin, the former governor of Okinawa, became the institution's first president. An observer for Michigan State, which soon became a sister school to the university, commented on the faculty: "They lack appropriate dress and attire, including shoes of proper size and fit, but are not lacking in native intelligence and drive and sincerity of purpose to develop a valid institution which some day may be worthy of the name 'University.'" At the time, the school did not deserve that title. "The University, by American standards, would not be rated much higher than a senior high school and possibly first year in junior college."[47]

The institution improved quickly. In 1950 the school had an enrollment of 562 students, with an acceptance rate of 60.4 percent. By the late 1960s enrollment had mushroomed six-fold while the acceptance ratio dropped to 19.1 percent. The graduation ratio fluctuated between 80 and 95 percent. The school library, named after Shikiya, gained an average of eight thousand new volumes a year. Books in Japanese and Chinese accounted for 74 percent of the holdings.[48]

Despite heavy American financial support, the administrators and faculty of the school looked to the Japanese educational community for guidance and inspiration. The university modeled itself after the University of Tokyo. In the mid-1950s the school started a program that brought professors from Japanese colleges to teach at the university. The United States had little to do with this endeavor. Because of these connections, University of the Ryukyus graduates began seeking employment in Japan; this migration helped strengthen Okinawan connections to the rest of Japan.[49]

Americans had four distinct reasons for fostering education. The humanitarian impulse was one. Americans have a tradition of trying to live up to their occasionally overblown rhetoric of being a progressive force in international affairs. Okinawa was no different. "The investment is probably one of the most rewarding forms of assistance that the United States could extend to the Ryukyus," Maj. Gen. C. K. Gailey, Marquat's successor, told the House Appropriations Committee.[50]

Second, education programs were American efforts to respond to the interests and desires of the Okinawans as the Okinawans defined them. Marquat's assistant was direct and to the point on this matter. "There are certain things that the Oriental lays great stress upon; that is, we feel we have not helped them enough in the reconstruction of their schools," he remarked. Supporting education, he continued, would "be tangible evidence that the United States is interested in the cultural welfare of the Ryukyu Islands." An editorial in *The San Francisco Chronicle* supported this view. "Okinawa . . . is of immense strategic importance. We must hold it and by that token we must take good care of the progress of the people. Their cry for schools is one to be met without delay."[51]

Self-interest was a third motive. Providing education and training helped alleviate the burden of administration. Documents submitted to the Senate Appropriations Committee during funding hearings make this point distinctly: "An educated citizenry is essential to develop in the Ryukyuans the ability to assume an increasing responsibility of self-government."[52]

Anticommunism was the final reason. Americans assumed that only ignorant people would voluntarily choose communism over the standards of democracy and free enterprise that the United States represented. Marquat made this point clear during congressional testimony. "The friendliness of the native population for the United States, and the consequent loyal contribution to our purposes, best can be developed through educational processes," he asserted in clumsy prose. Stuart T. Baron, the director of economics and finances for the U.S. Civil Administration of the islands, was more direct during this appearance. "The influence is for the sale of American and free world ideals," he remarked. At commencement exercises at the University of the Ryukyus, Maj. Gen. James E. Moore, the high commissioner, put his spin on this view, telling the graduates it was their duty to work at "removing the mask that covers the deceptive promises of communism."[53]

While funding education programs and creating new schools was a key element in garnering the acquiescence of the general population, it did not buy subservience. Military authorities often had to force Okinawan students who wanted to remain in the United States to continue their studies to return or prohibit their departure from the island in the first place, which always damaged American standing.[54] The university soon became a center of reversionist sentiment. During a discussion about Okinawa and the college, President Eisenhower said it troubled him that communists attended schools established with American money. Allen Dulles, the director of the CIA, quickly responded that anti-American demonstrations were more times than not expressions of nationalism rather than communism.[55]

The United States turned Okinawa into an American colony in the early 1950s because of large doubts about Japanese dependability as an ally in the Cold War. Strategic location and military function were the reasons for American interest in this colony. While the U.S. presence was an economic and social boon to the Okinawan standard of living— American rule had indeed brought material benefits to the island—problems developed in the late 1950s that caused leaders in Washington to make a profound reassessment of policy concerning the island. The key figures during this time of difficulty were Dulles, Eisenhower, and a largely unknown ambassador with a well-known name, Douglas MacArthur II.

Figure 1. The Tenth Army comes ashore at Higashi Beach on April 1, 1945. The Japanese Thirty-second Army allowed the Americans to land unopposed, conserving its strength for the defense of the southern half of the island.

Courtesy U.S. Army Military History Institute

Figure 2. The hilly terrain of southern Okinawa aided Japanese troops in defending the island. The U.S. Army relied on artillery to destroy Japanese positions, which were heavily fortified to withstand American shelling.

U.S. Army Photo, National Archives, College Park, Maryland

Figure 3. Lt. Gen. Simon B. Buckner, Jr., and Gen. Joseph Stilwell confer in early June. Buckner commanded the Tenth Army, an amalgamation of U.S. Marine and Army units. Buckner never appreciated the differences in tactics between the two services. Stilwell was a harsh critic of Buckner during an inspection trip. Afterward, General of the Army Douglas MacArthur and Stilwell discussed removing Buckner from command prior to the invasion of Japan. Ironically, Buckner was with marines when he died in a Japanese artillery barrage as the battle neared an end, and Stilwell replaced him in command.

U.S. Army Photo, National Archives, College Park, Maryland

Figure 4. During Stilwell's inspection trip, he visited frontline units. Here he examines the progress of the 7th Infantry Division at a regimental command post. "Seventh has no respect for the Japs," the general observed in his diary. His guide for a good part of this inspection tour was Maj. Gen. Archibald Arnold, commander of the division (left of map). This visit was a homecoming of sorts for Stilwell, who was the division's commander when the war began. In his diary he noted: "Recognized everywhere and got friendly greeting."

U.S. Army Photo, Hoover Institute, Stanford University

Figure 5. On September 7 the Japanese garrison in the Ryukyu Islands surrendered to Stilwell and the Tenth Army. The formal capitulation of Japan had taken place aboard the U.S.S. Missouri *three weeks earlier. The Ryukyu defenders were the last element of the Emperor's military to end their resistance.*

U.S. Army Photo, Hoover Institute, Stanford University

Figure 6. In the early days of the American occupation, there were few recreational activities on Okinawa for either soldiers or their commanding general. Stilwell's diary indicates that letters from home and visiting entertainers were the only breaks from the monotony of life on the island. After a USO show in August, 1945, Stilwell added his signature to the collection on the band's drum.

U.S. Army Photo, Hoover Institute, Stanford University

*Figure 7. General of the Army Douglas MacArthur played a large role
in breaching differences between various elements of the U.S. government on the issue
of Okinawa. In 1948 he met with George F. Kennan of the State Department and
explained that American retention of Okinawa allowed the United States to both
protect and defend against Japan. State Department opposition to the retention of
the island quickly ended after this meeting. Two years later in June, 1950,
the general sided with the State Department against the Joint Chiefs of Staff on
the issue of a Japanese peace treaty. He argued that the occupation had reached its limits
and that American bases acted as both protection for the Japanese and a hedge
against the resurrection of militant Japanese nationalism.*

U.S. Army Photo, National Archives, College Park, Maryland

Figure 8. Undersecretary of the Army Tracy Voorhees visits Okinawa on an inspection. Disturbed about reports of conditions on Okinawa, Voorhees traveled to the island in September, 1949. After his return to Washington, a number of reforms and personnel changes took place. The military governor was replaced before the end of the month, and funding for the island increased dramatically.

U.S. Army Photo, National Archives, College Park, Maryland

Figures 9 and 10. Lt. Gen. Paul W. Caraway served as high commissioner of the Ryukyu Islands from 1961 to 1964. Edwin O. Reischauer represented the United States from 1961 to 1966 as the ambassador in Tokyo. The two had several bitter confrontations over Okinawa. The ambassador wanted the island returned to Japan and favored allowing that nation to provide large sums of economic aid, while Caraway fought efforts to increase Japanese support, seeing it as the first step in stripping the United States of what he considered the most vital base in the Pacific. Although Reischauer enjoyed favorable publicity during his tenure in Japan, his influence within the U.S. government was generally limited to the bureaucracy within the State Department. Caraway had lengthy experience working in high levels of the federal government and successfully blocked the tepid efforts of the Kennedy White House to implement policy initiatives that the ambassador, the Japanese government, and the State Department favored.

Figure 9 courtesy U.S. Army Military History Institute; figure 10 by Yoichi R. Okamoto, courtesy LBJ Library Collection

Figure 11. In 1966 President Lyndon Johnson named U. Alexis Johnson to serve as U.S. ambassador in Japan. The new ambassador started his career in prewar Tokyo as a language specialist and was the senior officer in the Foreign Service at the time of his appointment. In previous years he had earned LBJ's respect and gratitude. As ambassador he negotiated the return of the Bonin Islands. While in Tokyo, he earned Richard Nixon's admiration and trust after providing standard VIP treatment to the former vice-president that Nixon often did not receive. When he became president, Nixon made Johnson the Undersecretary of State for Political Affairs, the fourth-ranking position in the depart- ment. From this position, he conducted the final reversion negotiations.

Photo by Yoichi R. Okamoto, courtesy LBJ Library Collection

Figure 12. *National Security Advisor Walt W. Rostow introduces Wakaizumi Kei to President Lyndon Johnson. Rostow and Wakaizumi were close friends—Rostow was the godfather of Wakaizumi's son—and academic colleagues. Wakaizumi was also affiliated with Prime Minister Sato Eisaku's political faction. In 1967 Sato bypassed his foreign minister, a political rival, sending Wakaizumi to Washington to negotiate secretly with Rostow on the return of Iwo Jima.*

Photo by Yoichi R. Okamoto, courtesy LBJ Library Collection

Figure 13. *Sato and Johnson privately discuss the return of Iwo Jima and the Bonin Islands in the Oval Office. Sato was telegenic, poised, and a master of political timing. He served eight years as prime minister, the longest tenure in Japanese history. Johnson was a larger-than-life wheeler-dealer, best at assessing other people and making deals. While the two enjoyed cordial relations, both attempted to take as much as possible from the other while giving as little as possible in return.*

Photo by Yoichi R. Okamoto, courtesy LBJ Library Collection

Figure 14. President Richard M. Nixon presents a package of Japanese cigarettes to Foreign Minister Aichi Kichi in the Oval Office after reaching an agreement on reversion. Kichi had vowed not to smoke again until Okinawa returned to Japanese control.

Nixon Presidential Project, National Archives, College Park, Maryland

Figure 15. Nixon and Sato at the White House on November 21, 1969, announce the reversion of the Ryukyu Islands. Each is flanked by their foreign ministers: Aichi is on the left, next to Sato, while Secretary of State William Rogers is on the right, next to Nixon. U. Alexis Johnson, in a position symbolic of his career, is above in the back row.

Nixon Presidential Project, National Archives, College Park, Maryland

CHAPTER 5

The Difficult Years, 1956–60

In the late spring and early summer of 1960, a political crisis of the first order rocked Japan. A national debate on a proposed new security treaty with the United States engulfed the country after the accord came before the Diet for ratification on February 5. On April 26 the political Left took the issue to the streets, organizing anti-treaty rallies and demonstrations. Every day for two months the people of Tokyo saw parades, rallies, and demonstrations against the treaty. On May 19 Prime Minister Kishi Nobusuke tried to bring the matter to a close and used parliamentary maneuvers to end debate, including the forced removal from the Diet building of socialist members participating in a sit-down strike. Stunned critics compared the action to the attack on Pearl Harbor. In June, labor unions organized three strikes, each drawing in the neighborhood of six million people. Protesters chanted "Overthrow Kishi, Dissolve the Diet" and "Kill Kishi." Demonstrators fought the police, resulting in much bloodshed and one fatality. In a joint editorial, the seven leading newspapers in Japan openly expressed fears that the protests were either the beginning of a communist revolution or the pretext for a right-wing coup. Even before these protests occurred, the U.S. ambassador warned the secretary of state in a telegram marked "eyes only" that everything, including the future orientation of Japan in the Cold War, was in doubt. The day before the scheduled ratification, the Tokyo police chief warned Kishi that the police department, weakened after having battled demonstrators for two straight months, could no longer protect his official residence. Kishi spent that night expecting a mob to storm the building and kill him. The secretary-general of the Japanese Communist Party had actually rejected plans to take the prime minister's residence, fearing the response from the military and the ultranationalist right wing. Calm returned to Japan when Kishi resigned after ratification.[1]

The treaty crisis was the last in a series of episodes that tested U.S.-Japanese relations during the second half of the 1950s. The incidents involving Okinawa led to a serious reappraisal within the U.S. government of the continuing American occupation of the island. Many, including the secretary of state and the president of the United States, thought that Okinawa risked the more important relationship with Japan. The military saw these events quite differently; these episodes confirmed that Japan was an ally of questionable dependability.[2]

The first crisis that rocked Okinawa was a dispute between the U.S. government and Okinawan landowners on the proper form of rent payment for American military bases. Reimbursement for the land was an issue slowly festering as the island developed into an American boomtown. Until the legal state of war between the United States and Japan ended, the military paid no rent for the land, claiming the soil as a prize of war. When the occupation ended, the United States had to start compensating the landowners for the use of their property. The army appraised the value of the land on Okinawa in April, 1952, and announced that it would make annual rental payments of 6 percent of the property's total value. On average, this figure came to less than twenty dollars. Most Okinawans refused payment on principle.[3]

To resolve the issue, the army proposed that a payment equal to the value of the land be made that would grant full use, but not title. The military would also fund a public works program to develop uninhabited areas of the island. Okinawans received this idea poorly. Higa Shuhei, chief executive of the Ryukyu Islands, explained why: "The landowners consider lump-sum payment of rental unfavorably because there is no distinct difference, it seems to them, between such payment and the sale of their land. It is also believed that lump-sum payment will not assist the landowners in any considerable way in relocating themselves in undeveloped or unused areas in the Ryukyu Islands."[4]

On July 26, 1955, House Armed Services Committee chairman Carl "The Swamp Fox" Vinson appointed a special subcommittee, under the leadership of Melvin Price of Illinois, to investigate the land situation on Okinawa. The subcommittee traveled to Okinawa and held two days of hearings in Naha. Higa, other members of the Okinawan government, legislators, an American missionary, and two displaced farmers testified during those proceedings. Most of the Okinawans spoke through an interpreter, which lengthened the sessions. A speaker on the second day explained the cultural significance of the land to the subcommittee and why there was so much resistance: "In Okinawa, land truly represents family inheritance—the benefit of which should be equally enjoyed by the descendants. Its loss in one generation in return for cash is considered to be practically a gross betrayal of trust to the family line. In Okinawa, there is no precedent for such lump-sum payment, and it is considered to be similar to the purchase of land."[5]

The Okinawans made a counterproposal. The United States should make annual payments to landowners equal to the amount of income the plot would produce. Philip W. Kelleher, counsel for the Armed Services Committee, responded to this proposal with an interrogation of Higa. He suggested Okinawan farmers wanted a guaranteed source of income without having to work.[6]

When the subcommittee released its final report a year later, on June 13, 1956, it came much closer to the army's position than the Okinawan one. The undervalued land should be reappraised, but payment should be made in one lump sum. The military would have free use of the land, but Okinawans would keep their title. The subcommittee wanted to find a solution that would end agitation on the land issue and believed annual rental payments would only allow the matter to fester and explode sometime later. It appears that the members never seriously considered anything other than a lump sum payment.[7]

Okinawa exploded in protest. On June 20, a week after the release of the report, one hundred thousand Okinawans, roughly one-sixth of the population, assembled in fifty-five different locations on the island to protest the recommendations of the report. The entire legislature and the chief executive threatened to resign if the Americans implemented the plan.[8] Significant opposition also appeared in Japan. The American consul in Nagoya reported: "The recommendations of the Price Report find strong opposition among virtually all classes of Japanese people." The timing of the report was also bad. The document became public during the middle of elections for the upper house of the Diet, handing the opposition an issue that it used to considerable advantage.[9]

In Washington there was little immediate understanding of how extensive and deep the opposition was to this report. Dulles initially recommended the release of a few clarifying statements.[10] John Allison, by then the U.S. ambassador in Tokyo, sent telegrams explaining that the opposition to the Price report was strong and deep. "By acting as if we were in Okinawa permanently, we do not get rid of Japanese pressure for return of administrative control but in fact increase it," he warned. He recommended that the United States obtain twenty- or twenty-five-year leases.[11] Dulles trusted Allison implicitly in Japanese matters and immediately changed his position. He proposed to the secretary of defense that their two departments establish an interdepartmental committee to review policies for the Ryukyus. The Defense Department rejected this proposal, insisting that the Price plan be implemented. The military did agree, however, with Dulles's suggestion that the acquisition of more land be canceled.[12]

Continued Okinawan opposition eventually forced the army to retreat. The United States postponed the implementation of lump sum payments and agreed to reconsider the entire land issue.[13] The army opposed this gesture. Gen. Lyman Lemnitzer, army vice chief of staff, noted in a meeting with Undersecretary of State Christian Herter and Secretary of the Army Wilber M. Brucker that it would be tough to get any other policy from Congress since the Price committee had helped establish the current policy, which had never been given a fair chance. This argument lost much of its force when Rep. Walter Judd informed the administration that lump sum payments had little support in Congress, including among members of the Price commission.[14]

Resolution of the issue came on American terms, except for the lump sum format. The military finally conceded the point on June 30 in a meeting between Secretary of Defense Neil McElroy and Dulles in the latter's office. Lemnitzer said the army would make annual payments to landowners and periodically review the amount. On July 30 Lt. Gen. James E.

Moore announced the new rental payment program. The land issue soon lost its importance as a diplomatic concern between the United States and Japan after 1958, when other matters moved to the forefront. Landowners, however, remained deeply interested in the fate of their property for years to come.[15]

As the land issue developed, negotiations between the Soviet Union and Japan made Americans uneasy. In 1954 conservative Japanese politicians, fearing the strength of the recently reunified socialists, decided to unify their separate political parties. Prime Minister Yoshida Shigeru opposed a merger and was forced out of office by a coalition that included a number of his own supporters. Hatoyama Ichiro replaced him and, a year later, the conservative parties formed the Liberal Democratic Party (LDP). To differentiate himself from his predecessor, Hatoyama wanted to pursue a foreign policy independent of the United States and to negotiate a treaty with the Soviet Union that would outdo Yoshida's work with the West. In 1951 Soviet diplomats had walked out of the San Francisco Peace Conference. A state of war technically still existed with the Soviet Union, and Hatoyama decided to pursue rapprochement with Russia. Rumors floated that Japan might even go as far as to sign another nonaggression pact.[16]

Territorial issues proved to be a major difficulty in the negotiations. Japan's one-legged foreign minister, Shigemitsu Mamoru, was nothing if not an anticommunist. He insisted that the Soviets return the four Kurile Islands they had seized during the waning days of World War II. The Soviet counterproposal was two. Talks broke down and restarted only to founder on this one issue. Talks resumed again in Moscow in August, 1956. When negotiations stumbled yet again on the Kuriles, Shigemitsu publicly suggested that Japan concede the issue to the Soviets.[17]

These talks unnerved Dulles. Shigemitsu only added to these concerns in April, 1955, when Japan distanced itself from U.S. policies in Southeast Asia at the conference of nonaligned nations held at Bandung, Indonesia. Maybe Japan was about to "go neutral" after all. Worse still, a resolution of Japan's territorial disputes with the Soviet Union would direct nationalist sentiment south toward Okinawa against the United States. A week later Dulles arranged a meeting with Shigemitsu in London, where both were attending the conference on the Suez Canal dispute. Dulles reported finding his Japanese counterpart in a "worried and distraught condition." He quickly added to Shigemitsu's concerns. Dulles told him that the peace treaty accorded the same status to both the Kurile and Ryukyu Islands. In other words, "if Japan recognized that the Soviet Union was entitled to full sovereignty we [the United States] would assume that we were equally entitled to full sovereignty over the Ryukyus." He also made this threat public in a press conference ten days later.[18]

This pressure apparently was unnecessary. Allison reported from Tokyo that the cabinet was unanimous in its opposition to Shigemitsu's proposal. Hatoyama never got the treaty he wanted. At the end of the year he made a summit visit to Moscow and formally ended the state of war, agreeing to exchange ambassadors. This accord was enough for the Soviets; they ended their practice of vetoing Japanese admission into the United Nations. Japan joined that body on December 21, and the next day, the Hatoyama cabinet resigned. Shigemitsu died a month later. Nevertheless, a secret NSC study of the U.S.-Japanese bilateral relationship warned, "The major U.S. objective—a firm alliance in the Pacific—is not being achieved."[19]

As this crisis resolved itself, another one developed to take its place. On Christmas Day, 1956, the voters of Naha elected Senaga Kamejiro mayor. Senaga won with a plurality of only 40 percent, but what made his electoral victory an issue was that Senaga was president of the Okinawan People's Party, the communist party on the island. His election drew much embarrassing attention to the fact that the Okinawans chose a Communist in a supposed showcase of American democracy. Novelist Vern Sneider, author of *The Teahouse of the August Moon,* wrote another novel lampooning American authorities. In *The King from Ashtabula* the people of a fictional island reject American rule in a plebiscite, choosing instead to reinstitute the traditional monarchy.[20]

Observers offered a number of explanations for his victory. An analysis in the *Okinawa Taimusu* argued that four factors were responsible for the outcome: the superior organization of the Okinawan People's Party; the split of the majority of votes between two conservative candidates; voting residents in some newly incorporated neighborhoods expressing their resentment toward the civic administration through the election; and a protest vote by others against what they considered the arrogant attitude of many wealthy businessmen toward the electorate. The political advisor to the commander in chief of the Pacific fleet argued that American goals and Okinawan interests were in conflict with one another. "In any colonial situation of the past, if you had subjected the policies of the colonial power to the will of the people, it would not have received their support."[21]

Efforts to remove Senaga began almost immediately, which only served to exaggerate his importance. A majority of the city council—twenty-seven out of thirty—pledged to vote "no confidence" in Senaga, but ordinances required he serve at least three months. The United States cut off all funds to the city, and Okinawan businesses and businessmen refused to pay their taxes. Lt. Gen. James E. Moore, the military governor, established a committee to take actions to ensure that nothing like this ever happened again. Roderick Gillies, deputy civil administrator, chaired the committee. Donald Vorhis of the Central Intelligence Agency began funneling money to the conservative politicians of the Okinawan Liberal Democratic Party. Such an effort was a standard, stock response of the agency in countries where the political left enjoyed electoral success. (The best-known case was the support the CIA provided to the Christian Democrats in Italy; a 1994 *New York Times* story revealed that the agency also gave money to the LDP in Japan proper from the late 1950s into the 1970s.)[22]

Initial efforts to remove Senaga backfired, making him even stronger. On June 17, 1957, the city council voted "no confidence" in the mayor. Senaga responded by dissolving the council, initiating another election. On August 4, despite heavy rain, 72 percent of the electorate voted. Senaga supporters won twelve seats, making it impossible to convene the quorum of two-thirds needed to remove his honor from office.[23]

The stalemate continued on into the fall. The mayor's supporters walked out of every council meeting that tried to vote on his removal. On one occasion, when their opponents had guards block the exits, the Senaga faction went out the windows. One Senaga backer left his pants behind when another councilman tackled him. The council failed to approve a budget, which allowed the mayor to implement an emergency spending plan. His power was actual increasing during the stalemate.[24]

Developments in Washington soon allowed American intervention to break the impasse. On June 5, 1957, Pres. Dwight D. Eisenhower signed Executive Order 10713. The State and Defense Departments had worked on this document since the early days of the administration. The order acted as a de facto constitution, or basic law, for Okinawa and replaced the military governor with the high commissioner of the Ryukyu Islands, who would answer directly to the Department of the Army. The executive order charged the military with developing democratic government and improving the welfare and economic conditions of the Okinawans. The two departments reached an agreement, but after Senaga's election, the Defense Department withdrew its clearance and insisted that the document be rewritten. The revised order gave the high commissioner the power to veto any act of the Okinawan legislature, remove any official of the Okinawan government, and appoint the chief executive. These powers led a State Department official to call the order a "facade of democracy and self-government." The problem with the document was simple: "If the Ryukyuans are to develop a democratic form of Government, they must be allowed sufficient leeway in which to experiment, develop and, as is unavoidable, make mistakes."[25]

The high commissioner saw otherwise and used the powers the executive order invested in him to resolve the deadlock. Council members met with Lieutenant General Moore and petitioned for his assistance. A number of mayors from other cities and towns on the island made similar requests. Moore decided to change several city ordinances, making it easier for the council to remove Senaga. He informed Olcott Deming, the American consul general in Naha, of his plans and asked Deming not to report the matter to Washington. Deming reluctantly agreed, and the general promised to protect him if there were repercussions. Despite this precaution, the State and Defense Departments learned of Moore's intentions but acquiesced, aware that he had to act before the council adjourned for the year. On November 24 Moore revised a number of regulations that made it easier to remove Senaga. Now, the council needed only a simply majority for quorum. The general also gave the council the power to select a temporary mayor and prohibited a convicted felon from serving in that office. (Senaga had been convicted of perjury earlier in the decade.) The next day, the council removed Senaga on a 16-10 vote.[26]

There was no military rationale for Moore's actions. A study conducted by the Air Force Inspector General's Office of Special Investigation found that the Okinawan People's Party lacked the capacity to conduct sabotage operations. Infiltration by Chinese Communist spies was a far greater threat.[27]

The ouster of Senaga unleashed a firestorm of criticism in the United States, Japan, and Okinawa. A businessman on the island commented to a marine officer, "You say you are giving us the vote and if you don't like who we elect you change the laws—this is your wonderful democracy?"[28] Japanese commentators agreed, called the action undemocratic, and questioned America's commitment to its own principles and ideals. These critics had a legitimate point. Senaga might have been objectionable, but he had won an honest and fair democratic election. "This is an A-1 example of Defense's ineptitude in civil affairs," a Foreign Service officer wrote in an analysis of Senaga's rise and fall. He also predicted another American setback in the coming mayoral election since the parties left of the political center were better organized.[29]

On January 18, 1958, this forecast came to pass as Kaneshi Saichi, the socialist candidate, won the election, delivering another blow to U.S. prestige. In his study of Okinawan politics, Higa Mikio attributed Kaneshi's victory to better political organization. Americans choose to see it as a referendum on their administration. "The election brought basic and widespread dissatisfactions of the Ryukyuans out into the open," Walter Robertson, assistant secretary of state for Far Eastern affairs, stated in a letter to his counterpart in the Defense Department.[30] Press accounts treated the outcome as an example of Americans reaping what they had sowed.[31] "The Government of the United States ought to take over the administration of Okinawa from top to bottom and tell the Japanese on the island that we shall have no more nonsense, that we shall tolerate no communists and that spies will be hanged on lampposts as has been customary in that part of the world ever since they got lampposts," an editorial in the New York *Daily Mirror* declared.[32]

Self-interest and calm heads avoided a solution as extreme as the one the editors of the *Daily Mirror* advanced. The Americans had few options. A reporter for *The Christian Science Monitor* observed that the removal of Kaneshi would totally repudiate universal adult suffrage. The mayor, on the other hand, had just seen his predecessor removed and needed to reach an understanding with American authorities to avoid the same fate. George Roderick, assistant secretary of the army, had reason for the optimism he expressed in his response to Robertson. "While I recognize the unfortunate political aspects of the recent election, I do not believe that because we continue to have problems there, our situation there is deteriorating." Shortly after his inauguration, Kaneshi announced he would run municipal matters in a nonpartisan fashion. The socialists expelled him from the party, but he was the first mayor of Naha to serve a full term in office since the end of the war.[33]

The crisis faded in March with island-wide elections for the legislature and in September with a number of municipal votes. With covert CIA funding, the Okinawan Liberal Democratic Party, an organization to the right of the political center, won these contests, which were better gauges of Okinawan sentiment. Although these conservative politicians favored reversion, as did socialists and communists, they favored a gradual approach and were far more willing to work with the Americans in the meantime.[34]

As the electoral issue began to fade away, a currency crisis developed to take its place. One of the major figures in this episode was the new ambassador in Tokyo—Douglas MacArthur II. A 1932 graduate of Yale, MacArthur's receding hairline, dark brows, and somber eyes gave the misleading impression of a timid, retiring man. Nothing could be further from the truth. A football letterman in college, the ambassador shared a similarly lofty demeanor and sense for the dramatic with his uncle and namesake. He also had a temper with a bite, and it showed at an exchange of interned diplomats at Lisbon, Portugal—the Vichy France puppet regime had handed over MacArthur and the rest of the U.S. embassy staff to the Nazis for internment after the American invasion of North Africa. During the exchange, MacArthur snapped at the French ambassador to the United States after a remark that he had lost weight, "You would probably have lost weight yourself, sir, if we had handed you over to the Japanese." Although not particularly close to the MacArthur family following the premature death of his father, a naval officer with a promising career, he followed family tradition and joined the army after graduation. After two years he resigned his commission and entered the Foreign Service.[35]

MacArthur brought a combination of power, prestige, and influence with him when he arrived in Tokyo in 1957. At first glance, he seemed a poor selection for the assignment. Tokyo was his first ambassadorial posting. He had spent his entire career in European diplomacy, spoke no Japanese, and knew little about the history and politics of Japan. His strengths, however, outweighed these shortcomings. First and foremost was his name. He discovered that being the shogun's nephew added stature. More importantly, he had personal relationships with both Dulles and Eisenhower. He had just finished serving as the counselor of the department and, before that, had been the political advisor to the first commander of NATO forces, General of the Army Dwight D. Eisenhower.[36] Japanese foreign minister Fujiyama Aiichiro recognized and appreciated the personal connections that the new ambassador brought to his job.[37]

MacArthur was concerned about Japanese politics and wanted his staff to stay abreast of current events in Tokyo. He diligently read *The Japan Times*, the major English-language daily in Tokyo, and had his language officers report on issues covered in the paper. If an article was wrong, he wanted to know the correct facts. The ambassador had critics, though. Edwin O. Reischauer, the Harvard University historian, made the most important contemporary assessment of MacArthur's administration. In an article in *Foreign Affairs,* Reischauer argued that the embassy had limited itself to a small circle of officials and had little knowledge of the larger mood of the country. MacArthur called Reischauer into his office, told him he was wrong, and showed him the cables and reports his officers had written to prove his point. Reischauer admitted some of his criticism was too harsh and tempered his comments in a Japanese translation.[38]

The currency crisis that MacArthur faced centered on the replacement of B-yen script used on Okinawa since the occupation of Japan. The Judge Advocate General of the U.S. Army held in an informal opinion that the army had no authority to issue the script after the legal state of war with Japan ended.[39] The Constitution clearly and distinctly charges Congress with responsibility for issuing currency. Both the civilian and uniformed leadership of the Department of the Army wanted to keep legislative involvement in Okinawa to a minimum. Army leaders worried that a congressional debate on the basic premise for American occupation might start if they sought the proper legal authorization for occupation script. Replacing B-yens with dollars was the easiest and safest response.[40]

The only problem with the army plan was that no one bothered to inform the president. When, in the course of a phone conversation, Dulles told him of the pending replacement, Eisenhower ordered the move stopped. There was no reason for the action, he said. The United States had never used a dollar-based economy in occupied territory before.[41]

Many people at the time mistakenly believed that MacArthur was responsible for this postponement. The day before the Dulles-Eisenhower conversation, MacArthur met with Prime Minister Kishi Nobusuke and Foreign Minister Fujiyama and informed them of the pending move. "I gather they feel they have been had," MacArthur reported. Kishi said he understood the economic reasons for replacing the occupation script but added that the people would see the move as the first stage of an American annexation. He asked that the announcement be delayed, which MacArthur recommended in his report. Lt. Gen. Donald P. Booth, the high commissioner of the Ryukyu Islands, delayed the introduction of dollars but explained that Okinawans enthusiastically endorsed the plan. He also warned that if the Okinawans learned of a successful Japanese intervention, it would reduce U.S. influence.[42]

Dulles broached the subject with Eisenhower again, only to have the president reject the idea a second time. He was angry and even took the time to write down his objections. "This proposal seems to be one of doubtful wisdom, particularly because of its possible effect within Japan." His fears were similar to those of Kishi. "I am sure that the use of American currency in the Islands would be interpreted in Japan as an unexpressed but nevertheless latent ambition of this country to annex those Islands. The mutual friendship and trust that have been built up between our country and Japan are extremely valuable and I do not see why we should chance damaging them in the effort to achieve a greater administrative efficiency." The only way he would reconsider was if MacArthur talked to Kishi and got his approval.[43]

Dulles made no case for substitution. As secretary of state, he addressed a number of issues every day. Dulles remembered nothing of the reasons for substitution and said little in response to the president. Only afterward did he learn of the constitutional issues involved. The president, however, had made his decision, and Dulles had a telegram sent to MacArthur instructing the ambassador to meet again with Kishi. Dulles informed MacArthur that the issue was "urgent" since currency and coin had already arrived in Naha.[44]

MacArthur reacted quickly after receiving the message and arranged a meeting with Kishi within a day. The prime minister mistakenly believed that Eisenhower postponed conversion at his request. Kishi appreciated this action as a reflection of a real partnership between Japan and the United States. After hearing MacArthur explain the economic, political, and constitutional reasons for replacing the script, Kishi said he understood the American reasoning and no longer had any objections. He would offer no support, but neither would he do anything to oppose the action. Timing, however, was critical. He asked that the United States make the public announcement during the Diet recess. He also insisted that the land issue be resolved. Walter Robertson, the assistant secretary for Far Eastern affairs, told Dulles that Kishi had gone as far as he could on the matter. In another meeting, Dulles explained these qualifications to the president and Eisenhower agreed to them.[45]

General Booth announced the conversion on September 15 at the ratio of B-¥270 to the dollar, better than the official exchange rate of 360 Japanese yen to the dollar. The exchange of currency and script took place between September 16 and 30. Then, the Americans weighed down the B-yen notes with concrete and dumped them into thirty fathoms of indigo-colored water off the Okinawan coast. Roderick Gillies, the deputy civil administrator, told an Okinawan audience afterward, "The introduction here of the most sought-after currency in the world has placed the Ryukyu Islands on the threshold of economic possibilities which were beyond reasonable expectation[s] a year ago." Okinawans initially shared these optimistic, positive views, but second thoughts began to develop. Conversion caused inflation to jump as many local businessmen used the transfer as an excuse to raise prices and gouge consumers. Just as Kishi and Eisenhower had dreaded, some saw the introduction of dollars as an American move toward annexation. Gillies later called these concerns "groundless."[46]

Another crisis developed shortly after the resolution of the currency issue. Barton M. Biggs, a former marine officer who had served on Okinawa, wrote a devastating attack on the U.S. administration of the island that appeared in the December, 1958, issue of *Harper's Magazine.* "When I saw the election returns this spring," he explained later, "I knew what had happened. That's when I decided to tell the story." He wrote his article in an effort to alert Americans to the precarious conditions that jeopardized a key U.S. base.[47]

In "The Outraged Okinawans," Biggs made, according to a later military analysis of the article, twenty-five different statements of fact. If reduced to one point, the article declared that U.S. actions were alienating the Okinawans. This behavior was a military problem, Biggs argued. American exploitation was creating an external environment that was hostile and an internal one that was detrimental to the military presence. "We must realize that merely raising the standard of living will not create good will in an underdeveloped people if we insult their sense of personal dignity at the same time," he wrote of the external environment. The election of Senaga was only one expression of this sentiment. Officers in the Pentagon might have simply dismissed his argument were it not for his evidence and the serious social problems for which he claimed the U.S. administration was responsible: the American administration openly tolerated white slavery when Okinawan fathers sold their daughters into prostitution; venereal disease was so rampant it was affecting unit performance; combat readiness was low; marines lived in hovels; and troops rebelled in race riots.[48] These accusations grabbed the attention of the military brass.

The military response and handling of these charges contained the crisis. On November 28, Adm. Harry D. Felt, commander in chief, Pacific—the man headquartered in Hawaii and in command of all U.S. forces in the region—directed the high commissioner to establish an investigative committee to examine conditions on the island and to send him periodic reports. On December 3 Booth complied, appointing an interservice commission of eight officers. The chairman and all the members came from the very commands under examination, which automatically limited the vigor and critical extent of the inquiry.[49]

The board spent a month collecting information from various unit commanders and taking testimony from twenty-seven witnesses. Much of what they uncovered supported Biggs's charges about the American military community's interaction with the Okinawan population and the care of its own troops. In the official response of the IX Corps based on Okinawa, a captain wrote: "White slavery does exist. This is an age-old practice of the Orient." The housing situation of the 3rd Marine Division was poor but endurable. Marines still lived in Quonset huts, some of which were rotting. In its final report, the board concluded some of the huts "do not meet acceptable standards of habitability." They discovered no marines housed in tents, as Biggs had suggested.[50]

This American exploitation—particularly the sexual exploitation of Okinawan women—backfired, creating many internal problems, including a military health crisis. In the article, Biggs reported that venereal disease kept 10 to 15 percent of his marine company from reporting for duty. If so, his unit was one of the luckier ones. The earliest available public health figures for the division, September, 1957, revealed that a fourth of the 3rd Marine Division reported to sick bay with some form of venereal disease. The percentage of infected marines continued to increase steadily. In September, 1958, these diseases incapacitated 37 percent of the division.[51]

Another internal problem that the board avoided altogether was the declining efficiency of the 3rd Marine Division. Poor maintenance, a sure sign of lax discipline and low morale, was rampant. From 24 to 45 percent of major equipment, depending on the type of machinery considered, was inoperable. Outside investigators discovered 97 percent of division tanks in need of some type of repair with 38 percent out of service. This trend continued well into the early 1960s. A General Accounting Office report found that many of the division's unit reports to higher commands were vague, deceptive, and misleading. These shortcomings were extreme examples of systematic problems that plagued the entire Marine Corps in the 1950s. The service faced a crisis in morale as it downsized in the wake of the austerity measures that Eisenhower demanded to keep the federal budget balanced. Poor internal marine leadership made the situation worse. The difficulties that the servicemen faced on Okinawa began to improve only after Gen. David M. Shoup became the new commandant and initiated reforms that led to a marked improvement in unit effectiveness throughout the Corps. A recipient of the Medal of Honor, Shoup had briefly served on Okinawa as the division commander and stressed improvements in personnel issues such as physical fitness, leadership, training, and military bearing. Despite the renewed emphasis on issues that marines had always viewed with high regard, improvements on Okinawa began only after Shoup returned to the island on an inspection trip. Even then, it took another two years before the commandant could tell the Senate that the division was combat ready.[52]

The commission included none of this material in its final report, which stated: "Mr. Biggs' article, 'The Outraged Okinawans,' presents a grossly exaggerated picture of the military/civil environment on Okinawa." There were no race riots, discipline was high, and combat readiness was acceptable. The board agreed with Biggs that American-Okinawan relations were important: "If we assume that the entire Ryukyuan labor force is in a position to bring about a major strike or slowdown, we do have a problem. However, all evidence indicates that such a possibility is extremely remote."[53]

Little came of this investigation, which was the intent of the military administration all along. The board made a few tepid recommendations at the end of its twenty-one-page report, and Booth concurred with the conclusions. Unit commanders took no action on this matter, and venereal disease remained the largest public health problem among Okinawans for another decade.[54]

The Biggs article was also unique in that it was one of the few critical accounts of American rule in the Ryukyus that made it past the various mechanisms the army used to control and limit press coverage. The concern in the military was that attention from the press might challenge an assumption that most Americans held dear: the United States was different and unique from other nations in its practice of world affairs and was a progressive force in the international community. If this assumption were challenged, it would no doubt initiate the dreaded congressional debate. As a result, the military made it difficult for reporters to travel to the island. Controlling physical access limited the number of stories written about Okinawa. In addition the army insisted on briefing every journalist that visited Okinawa. This briefing stressed the strategic location of the island and the utility of American air bases in the Ryukyus. The public relations office of the U.S. Civil Administration also routinely controlled reporters, arranging safe interviews, which were often meaningless, and denying them support resources, such as access to the post exchanges. As a result of these efforts, Bob Trumbell, chief of *The New York Times* Tokyo Bureau and one of the few American journalists to write about Okinawa on a frequent basis, never produced any quality work about the island. His articles often had only one unidentified source.[55]

The American press resident on the island was even easier to control. The Okinawa *Morning Star* was the main English-language publication on the island and was the voice of the American expatriate community. Founded in 1954, the paper enjoyed a symbiotic relationship with the Civil Administration. Retired and reserve army public relations officers found civilian employment with the paper. Stringers for the Associated Press, United Press International, and *The New York Times* normally held full-time jobs with the paper and were threatened with unemployment should they write stories critical of American rule. When *Washington Post* columnist Drew Pearson wrote an editorial blasting the Civil Administration for its control of the press, *Morning Star* editor Robert M. Prosser fired back in its defense. The editorial positions of this paper displayed an ethnocentric belief that Americans on the island knew what was best for Okinawa, more so than the Okinawans themselves. The paper favored the introduction of dollars on the island, hoping the use of the currency would cement the separation from Japan. On another occasion the paper admitted that American rule was colonial but defended the practice, arguing it was necessary for national security and the revitalization of the island. Through these various factors and efforts, the army successfully limited popular interest in, and media access to, the Ryukyus until the late 1960s, when reversion talks began. Neither the public nor its representatives in Congress ever challenged the basic premise of the military colony. This vacuum of public involvement was a major reason that the uniformed and civilian leadership of the military was able to maintain a real consistency in policy concerning Okinawa.[56]

Even without public pressure, though, the collective weight of the difficulties with Okinawa that had wracked the U.S. government and its relations with Japan led Dulles, MacArthur, and Eisenhower to a serious reappraisal in 1958 of U.S. policy toward the Asian nation. MacArthur initiated this review with a series of telegrams and letters to Dulles and Walter Robertson, assistant secretary of state for Far Eastern affairs, stemming from the ambassador's outrage at what he considered arrogant behavior by the military on Okinawa during his visits. The discussion focused on two issues: revision of the U.S.-Japan security treaty and American administration of Okinawa.[57]

In an eight-page letter to Dulles, the ambassador warned that continued occupation of the Ryukyus jeopardized the U.S. relationship with Japan. "Return of administrative rights in Okinawa is bound to be a basic long-range national policy objective of all Japanese including the Conservatives, and the issue will also continue to be exploited by the Left as long as it is unresolved. We should recognize, therefore, that the time may well come in the next few years when, for one reason or another, we conclude that the national interest is best served by the return of administration of the Ryukyus to Japan." Until that time came, he recommended that the United States institute a number of reforms, including a new form of rental payment and a civilian, rather than a military, administration. *"Okinawa is not a military problem but a political one."* In his closing paragraph, MacArthur wrote that it was time for action. "In my judgment the situation is deteriorating, and, while I believe it may still be manageable for a certain limited time, a trend has set in which if not reversed will do incalculable damage to our own interests."[58]

The letter found a receptive audience in Dulles. A few weeks before, he had written, "If we try merely to sit on our treaty rights, we shall end by being blown out by popular sentiment, spearheaded by a Japanese

government of hostile and neutralist, if not pro-communist, sentiments."
He believed the United States should make concessions to bolster Kishi,
since he was a strong and certain friend and the best prime minister
America would have in Japan for years.[59]

Two months after MacArthur sent his letter, Dulles raised the issue
with Eisenhower. He told the president that he thought Okinawa put
the relationship with Japan at risk. He suggested establishing a military
enclave and returning the rest of the island. Eisenhower endorsed the
idea enthusiastically. He had suggested a similar concept during his tenure as army chief of staff. The issue of Okinawa had been troubling him
as well. "The situation could become unpleasant," he wrote in one of
his diary-like memos. "While I do not expect the matter to assume the
importance of the Cyprus difficulty with Britain, nor of the Algerian with
France, still there could easily develop a situation that would create much
embarrassment for us. The lesson is that we should be forehanded with
offers that the Okinawans will clearly recognize as generous and understanding and which will have the effect at least for some years of fore-
stalling trouble." Eisenhower saw enclaves as the best way to achieve
these two exclusive goals. This settlement would satisfy Japanese nationalist sentiment, and the United States would have the required
bases.[60]

The president became an ardent advocate for making an initiative on
the Ryukyus. Dulles could have asked for nothing better. While he was
making a foreign junket to Turkey in February, he had the Office of Far
Eastern Affairs review the American position in the islands and consider
MacArthur's suggestions for reforms. The Defense Department refused to
cooperate and even objected to having an NSC meeting on the topic.[61] On
April 9 Eisenhower called Dulles and asked about the progress on the
Okinawa question. The secretary explained the bureaucratic gridlock and
said some presidential intervention might be necessary. Six and a half
hours later, the two shared another phone call on Okinawa. Dulles suggested that the United States return everything except the bases and challenge the Russians to do the same with the Kuriles to the north. Eisenhower
warily agreed, but said he wanted the matter studied and wanted the Defense Department to explain its position at an NSC meeting.[62]

The position of the Joint Chiefs was simple: reversion was bad. "A major requirement for the ultimate security of the United States is the ability of the United States to maintain strategic control of the Pacific Ocean.

The entire United States strategic position in the Pacific would be seriously jeopardized if the Ryukyus were to come under the control of Japan, whose political instability might lead to a denial of the use of these bases by U.S. operating forces at a critical time." The military still saw Japan as an ally of uncertain reliability.[63]

Two days after Eisenhower inquired about progress on Okinawa, Robertson, described once as a "thoroughly affable Southern gentleman capable of uncompromising obstinacy," proposed to Dulles that he commission MacArthur to open talks with Japan on returning the Ryukyus on an enclave basis. MacArthur actually rejected this idea, mainly because the Japanese were in the midst of a Diet election.[64]

As a result of the reassessment that had taken place in interdepartmental meetings that spring, the United States was prepared when the Japanese initiated discussions on revising the security treaty. Eisenhower took the view that a treaty was no good if one party objected and agreed to revise the security pact. Dulles and Foreign Minister Fujiyama met in Washington and on September 11, 1958, announced that negotiations for a new treaty would begin immediately.[65]

The military was equally well prepared to oppose reversion during treaty negotiations. "I believe that Japan's growing sympathy for neutralist views is an overriding reason why we should oppose any change in our present position in the Ryukyu Islands," Gen. Lyman Lemnitzer, commander of U.S. Army forces in the Far East, asserted. "Our military position in Japan can be so impaired by Japanese harassment or by Treaty revision or renunciation that Okinawa could well become the only base on which we could fully rely between Korea and Taiwan, or between these countries and Guam." The service chiefs were of a similar opinion. In a letter sent to the secretary of defense over the signature of Chairman Nathan Twining, the Joint Chiefs argued, "The entire United States strategic position in the Pacific would be seriously jeopardized if the Ryukyus were to come under the control of Japan, whose political instability might lead to a critical denial of the use of these bases by U.S. operating forces at a critical time."[66] The Joint Chiefs also feared that the Japanese might use an agreement to respond to an attack on the Ryukyu or Bonin Islands as a lever to bolster claims for reversion, and they insisted that the operational area the new treaty covered not include these archipelagos.[67] Military concerns on this latter point were well founded. Kishi had told the Diet two months earlier that the inclusion of Okinawa in the Japa-

nese defensive zone would be a partial extension of Japanese administration.[68]

Eisenhower accepted the JCS recommendation—temporarily. On January 19, 1959, he ordered a feasibility study on enclaves. The issue was
still alive as far as the president was concerned as long as MacArthur
was negotiating. Several months passed without action, and Eisenhower
began to suspect that the army was preparing a massive study that would
defend the status quo. Nevertheless, he did nothing, waiting to see the
conclusions of the report that he had commissioned.[69]

The president had good reason to be suspicious. Documents indicate
that the Joint Chiefs opposed consolidation and intended to slant the report against enclaves before it reached the NSC. As it turned out, the
analysis that General Booth sent to the Pentagon needed no modification.
In the first sentence of his report, Booth stated, "The existing military
installations and the various neighboring civil communities interspersed
throughout the U.S. Forces base complex are so interwoven with dual
purpose and mutually complementing civil-military roads, power lines,
water lines, and communication cables that it is impossible to classify
the military complex on Okinawa as an 'enclave' capable of separation
from the Okinawan community."[70]

The Joint Chiefs readily endorsed this view. "The southern half of
Okinawa does not really contain a series of bases but should be classified
as a single military base complex," the JCS declared.[71]

The report finally reached the White House ten and a half months
after the president requested a feasibility study. Gordon Gray, the national
security advisor, read key portions of the report to Eisenhower. Gray then,
according to his notes, told the president he doubted "there was any profit
in pursuing this matter further as he would never succeed in getting acceptance in Defense of the notion of concentration." Dejected, Eisenhower agreed.[72]

The president gave way to the Joint Chiefs on this issue due, in large
part, to the lack of Japanese pressure for reversion. Eisenhower was actually more concerned on the issue of Okinawa than Kishi. When the
prime minister first met with MacArthur to announce his interest in a
new treaty, he wanted to include these islands in the defensive zone of a
new agreement if reversion was impossible. This statement surprised
Togo Fumihiko of the American Affairs Bureau in the Japanese Foreign
Ministry and the other diplomats attending the meeting. Kishi said he

wanted to pursue a treaty even though there might be difficulties with ratification in the Diet. There was opposition almost immediately. The day Fujiyama left for the United States to meet with Dulles, a number of Diet members, many associated with, and protégés of, former Prime Minister Yoshida Shigeru, formed a group to oppose any revision of the treaty. Some Diet members wanted to exclude the Ryukyu and Bonin Islands from Japan's defensive zone to keep from being drawn into an American war. The leadership of the defense agency also stated that Japan lacked the resources to protect the two island groups. When Fujiyama took the initiative and proposed that the islands be excluded, other Diet members attacked him, saying the treaty had to include the two chains. The public statements of both Fujiyama and Kishi became muddled and vague on Okinawa and the other islands. An industrialist and businessman before entering the cabinet, Fujiyama had little political or diplomatic experience and resented the attacks on his policies, thinking they were attempts to use him to get at Kishi. MacArthur finally maneuvered the negotiations so that it was the Japanese who proposed excluding the Ryukyus from the defensive zone.[73]

One important development that took place with the treaty was the establishment of a ten-year limit to the accord. After 1970 either country could cancel the alliance with one year's notice. If neither nation gave notice, the treaty would remain in force indefinitely. This provision would require the United States either to heed the political demands of the Japanese in 1970 or to let Japan go its own way.

The second half of the 1950s were difficult years for the American-Japanese relationship. A number of key figures in the U.S. government believed that the difficulties America faced in Okinawa put this relationship in jeopardy. The Joint Chiefs of Staff and the civilian leadership of the Department of Defense thought otherwise. The problems the United States had with Japan only increased the need to retain administration of the Ryukyus. The military won this debate and would best another administration that attempted to tackle the issue.

CHAPTER 6

Reischauer vs. Caraway, 1961–64

Pres. John F. Kennedy received two important visitors in March, 1961. One he had known for a long time—Douglas MacArthur II—the other he had never met before—Edwin O. Reischauer, his appointment to replace MacArthur.[1] In his meeting with the new president, MacArthur warned that Okinawa was an issue in the making and would be a continuing problem until the United States returned the island to Japan.[2] Nothing of consequence transpired in the meeting with Reischauer, which would become symbolic not only of Reischauer's five years in Tokyo, but of Kennedy's foreign policy toward Japan. In the brief age of Camelot, Japan did not rate highly in American foreign policy because nothing went drastically wrong. Okinawa was the main issue in U.S.-Japanese relations at this time, but with Reischauer's tactical, and bureaucratic defeat at the hands of Lt. Gen. Paul W. Caraway, the high commissioner of the Ryukyu Islands, ensured that little change occurred.

The rivalry between Reischauer and Caraway is well documented. "So bitter is the feud between [the] State Department and the military over the question of Okinawa," a reporter for *The Washington Post* noted, "that the High Commissioner . . . frequently withholds important information from the U.S. Embassy in Tokyo, and embassy officials have been known to exaggerate grossly reports of the military's autocratic rule."[3] Of the two principals, only Reischauer penned memoirs. Although he down-played the intensity of their feud, "our personal relations always remained very cordial," he described Caraway as "a rigid, bull-headed man."[4] Caraway used even sharper language. "The Ambassador was useless in almost every case," he stated bluntly. "He's useless. He's a menace, because he thinks he knows everything. He had a lot of information, and he knows nothing."[5] Reischauer's interpretation of events is better known. A talented publicist, he enjoyed good relations with the press, granted many interviews, testified often before Congress, and produced several books on U.S.-Japanese relations that presented his ideas as more "sophisticated" and "cosmopolitan" than the military point of view.[6] This activity conceals the fact that while in a high-placed government post, he failed in his efforts to revise the American position on Okinawa. Like Kennedy, his success was stylistic, not substantive.

When Edwin Reischauer became the U.S. ambassador to Japan, he was *the* American academic expert on that nation. Born and raised in Tokyo by missionary parents, Reischauer earned a Ph.D. from Harvard University in East Asian studies. Tall and gaunt with large ears and fore-head, his owlish looks were the type that actually improved as age lined his face and grayed his hair. During the war he served in the military intelligence branch of the U.S. Army, analyzing intercepted Japanese messages. At war's end he was awarded the Legion of Merit, a presti-gious decoration awarded for distinguished achievement in high office, even though he held the relatively junior rank of lieutenant colonel.[7]

After the war he was largely responsible for the establishment of Japa-nese studies in the United States as an academic discipline. In 1948 he chaired the founding meeting of the Far Eastern Association and, then as its president, in 1955 supervised its transition into the Association for Asian Studies, its publication becoming *The Journal of Asian Studies*.[8] He edited and translated some works of Japanese literature but focused the majority of his efforts on foreign policy.[9] The books he produced were broad surveys, easily adaptable for classroom use and accessible to the reading public.[10]

After the death of his first wife, he met and married, in a whirlwind romance, Matsukata Haru, granddaughter of Prince Matsukata Masa-yoshi. Haru Reischauer's grandfather was a founder of the modern Japa-nese state, serving fifteen years as finance minister and two terms as prime minister. Her mother had grown up in New York and Connecticut, and her maternal grandfather established a silk trade between the United States and Japan. Her family was still prominent in Japanese banking, business, and government circles in the 1950s. She had gone to college in the United States at Principia College, a small Christian Science school in Illinois. Afterward she worked as a correspondent for *The Christian Science Monitor* and *The Saturday Evening Post* in Tokyo.[11]

Contrary to popular opinion in both Tokyo and Washington then and since, Reischauer's appointment had little to do with any Harvard or Boston ties with Kennedy. In January, 1961, he arranged a meeting with Undersecretary of State Chester Bowles through James C. Thomson, a former student then serving as Bowles's assistant. The second-ranking officer in the State Department, Bowles was responsible for the appoint-ment of ambassadors. Thomson kept suggesting Reischauer for the To-kyo assignment. When Reischauer arrived at the undersecretary's office for a meeting to pass on a message from the Korean prime minister, Bowles quickly dismissed talk on Korea and offered him the post in Ja-pan. Stunned, Reischauer asked for some time to consider the offer. His wife opposed the move. She feared that the American military and diplo-matic community would not accept her, and the Japanese might con-sider her a traitor. "Despite Haru's violent opposition, I realized from the start that I had no choice but to accept," Reischauer wrote in his mem-oirs. Haru Reischauer had good reason for concern. The Washington society columnist for the *New York Journal-American* reported that there was much grumbling in the State Department that a Foreign Service officer with a Japanese wife never would have received the assignment.[12]

The long delay in getting clearance from the Federal Bureau of Inves-tigation, typical following the many appointments of a new administra-tion, made Reischauer regret his decision a bit. Rumors, mostly in Japan, abounded about opposition to his appointment and his policy views. In the end, his confirmation was painless. When he arrived in Tokyo on April 19, a mob six hundred strong, mainly journalists, greeted him at the airport terminal. He read a statement in both English and Japanese while television news carried the event live.[13]

The new ambassador had strong views on Okinawa when he arrived. He gave a lecture at the National War College before leaving for Tokyo. His notes for this lecture read: "Okinawa issue: potential dynamite; if choice between Japan and Okinawa bases must have a quick escape possibility." These views were nothing new for Reischauer. In his book *The United States and Japan,* he wrote, "there was no moral or legal justification for the removal from Japan of the Bonin, Ryukyu, or Kurile Islands." He called the island an American colony and recommended that the United States "begin to face the problem of removing this stumbling block in our relations with Japan before we come to grief over it."[14] These comments obscured the fact that he had supported, or at least acquiesced to, American retention of the islands in 1950. Shortly after John Foster Dulles started negotiating the Japanese peace treaty, the Council on Foreign Relations held a dinner meeting to discuss security issues related to the treaty with Dulles. Reischauer was one of those attending. According to the summary of the discussion, the talk focused on questions of how, rather than if, to protect Japan and to station American troops on the islands. The participants briefly mentioned the Ryukyus and Bonins with no dissent or major discussion. At the time, he accepted the basic premise of double containment. "The primary role of our bases in Japan, I feel is to help insure that this country [Japan] does not fall or gravitate into Communist hands or into a neutralist position." Unfortunately, the Pentagon seemed "to be judging them solely on their secondary value as bases for the defense of other areas in the Far East," which caused the military to emphasize the freedom of action that Okinawa offered.[15]

Reischauer's rival in Okinawan matters had arrived in the Ryukyus two months earlier to a similarly hospitable reception. A newspaper reporter noted that a crowd of several hundred at Kadena Air Force Base greeted Maj. Gen. Paul Caraway, the new high commissioner for the Ryukyu Islands, with a "warm cheer" as he deplaned. Short and stocky with a receding hairline and military haircut that accentuated his round face and weak chin, he was wearing the three stars of a lieutenant general. The high commissioner assignment and the accompanying command of the IX Corps automatically brought with it a third star. Though Caraway's name was still on the promotion list awaiting Senate confirmation, he thought it was important to him to establish as much standing with the Okinawan public as quickly as possible, and believed wearing three stars would be more impressive. The danger was that the Senate could have learned of his action and rejected his promotion, offended that he assumed he had an automatic confirmation. Nothing came of this episode, but it was indicative of Caraway's actions in the Ryukyus: he never considered the ramifications of his decisions beyond Okinawa.[16]

The general was no stranger to politics, and the Caraway name was well known in Washington. His father had represented Arkansas in the U.S. Senate. When Caraway's father died in office, his mother finished her husband's term and then served another two of her own, eventually losing reelection in 1944.[17] Paul Caraway, like his brother, chose a military career, graduating from West Point in 1929. After the academy, he attended law school at Georgetown University, earning his degree in 1933. During World War II Caraway served in a number of staff positions, never getting any combat experience, and spent a good chunk of the war in the China-Burma-India Theater. Despite his lack of combat experience, he became a general, again, like his brother.[18]

After the war, his assignments sent Caraway back to Washington and Asia. As a brigadier general he served as military aide to Vice President Richard M. Nixon and accompanied him on his famous 1953 tour of Asia, which included a stop on Okinawa. In this function, Caraway attended meetings of the NSC. Apparently he did not enjoy service with Nixon— he had all mention of it removed from his official biography. Later, as a major general, he commanded a division in Korea.[19]

Caraway was a workaholic. "General Caraway thrives on work," one of his aides reported. His official biography stated, "General Caraway has few active hobbies apart from a continuing off duty interest in military and international problems." He did have an interest in collecting and shooting guns, but even these related to work. The general and his wife had no children, which might have been the cause or a consequence of his intense work habits, but he avoided making excessive demands on staff, allowing them to spend time with their families.[20]

The general, however, was a bit peculiar when it came to uniforms. He wore his rimmed visor with gold braid too tight; it always left a mark on his forehead and a crease in his hair. He wanted his staff to wear the same class of uniform he did, but he never decided the uniform of the day until that morning. His aide made it a habit of never dressing, waiting in his living room in his underwear, until he got a phone call from the general's orderly telling him what uniform Caraway had chosen.[21]

The general liked his position in Okinawa. In a letter to his mother-in-law he explained: "The duties of my new assignment are the most interesting I have ever been given. Each day's problem is different, each one has just enough danger inherent in it to make me consider it very carefully." He also enjoyed the people he met and worked with. "The Ryukyuans are nice, cheerful, pleasant and very able persons. Their politicians remind me of the ones I used to know in Arkansas."[22]

He had no intention of dealing with Okinawan officials as equals, though. "I'm the guy who is responsible here," he said once, "and I am the high commissioner. I am the locus of power, and I'm going to exercise the power."[23]

Caraway held views that were almost exactly opposite to those of Reischauer on American administration of Okinawa. He believed the American occupation of the Ryukyus was in the best interest of both the Okinawans and the Japanese. He proudly noted the economic gains the prefecture had made under U.S. rule. He believed that if the island reverted to Japanese administration, the Okinawans would once again suffer authoritarian rule and discrimination. The status quo was in the best interest of the Japanese people as well. Caraway assumed the Japanese were happy to have nothing to do with a people they considered inferior. Given these beliefs and assumptions, Caraway never could fathom the nationalistic sentiment in either the Ryukyus or Japan for reunion. The general also believed American rule was a stabilizing influence in the Pacific. In an op-ed piece he wrote after he retired, Caraway warned that reversion would make Japan's southern flank vulnerable to attack. In private, he worried about a resurgent, remilitarized Japan and believed that Okinawa was America's best check against such a development. The United States would lose its leverage keeping Japan in the alliance if it returned the islands.[24]

The immediate issue over which Reischauer and Caraway clashed was economic aid. Both agreed that the island needed more funding, but they had strong differences about the sources for an increase in appropriations. This issue was a front for their differences on the larger issue of American administration. Reischauer wanted to let the Japanese provide more money as a first step toward ultimate reversion, while Caraway opposed any action, large or small, that would lessen American control over what he considered the most important U.S. base in the Pacific.

The issue came to the forefront early during their tenures, when

STRATEGIC IMPORTANCE OF RYUKYU ISLANDS

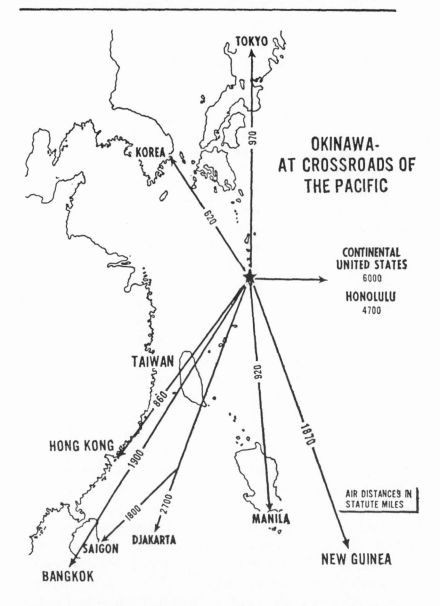

Map 2. Representatives of the U.S. Army used this map in congressional hearings to show the strategic location of Okinawa in East Asia. From air bases on this island the United States could strike almost every major city in the region.

Kennedy hosted Japanese prime minister Ikeda Hayato aboard the *Honey Fitz*, the president's yacht, on June 21, 1961. In an interesting study in contrasts, Ikeda complained to Kennedy about living conditions in the Ryukyus while they cruised along the waters around Washington. He told his host that the tax burden in Okinawa was higher than that of the poorer Japanese prefectures. In front of a group that included the senior leadership of the Foreign Ministry, Ikeda told Kennedy he had no interest in seeking restoration of Japanese administrative authority. As long as American security interests required the deployment of nuclear weapons, he believed it was in the best of all concerned that the United States govern the island. The financial inequities between the Ryukyus and other comparable Japanese prefectures, however, helped to foster pressure for reversion. Such a development was not in the strategic interests of Japan. Ikeda wanted to seek financial resolution of Okinawan needs through the framework of the U.S.-Japanese alliance. Kennedy responded defensively, saying that the American presence on the island was strategic rather than colonial. Ikeda engaged the president further, making his position clear. Kennedy responded once he fully understood the limited thrust of the prime minister's position and agreed to initiate action in the U.S. government to rectify discrepancies between the Ryukyus and other Japanese prefectures.[25]

Reischauer was in Washington for this conference and witnessed the Kennedy-Ikeda conference but played no major role. The only interesting entry in his memoirs for this episode occurred when he replaced an absent Douglas Dillon, the secretary of the treasury, at the head table of a White House luncheon. He was sitting next to Mamie Eisenhower. "She proved a much more interesting conversationalist than I had imagined," he observed. She made several mean and snide remarks about the Kennedy-run White House: There was never an embarrassing vacancy at a head table when she and her husband lived in the executive mansion.[26]

Back in Okinawa, Caraway saw little of consequence resulting from Ikeda's visit. In another letter to his mother-in-law he wrote: "The meeting between Mr. Kennedy and Mr. Ikeda had a rather unsettling effect on the people here in Okinawa. However, things are settling down again since nothing really earth shaking from their points of view came out of the meeting."[27]

Caraway was wrong. Kennedy's promise to Ikeda led to the creation of a task force that would investigate the administration of the Ryukyus.

Caraway showed no enthusiasm for this idea. He scored an important bureaucratic triumph before the president signed the memo creating the commission. In meetings with Reischauer, Caraway agreed to support the task force's creation if it would investigate social and economic issues only. Reischauer agreed to these terms even though Secretary of State Dean Rusk wanted a broader license for the board. Kennedy signed a memo that created a presidential task force but limited the thrust of investigation. The group was to study social and economic conditions in the Ryukyus only, avoiding political issues such as reversion. The ambassador, however, scored an important victory in his own right when Kennedy appointed Carl Kaysen, a Harvard University economist then a member of the White House staff, to lead the commission on the strength of Reischauer's recommendation.[28]

The creation of the task force and the Kaysen appointment was the high-water point of Reischauer's authority and power on Okinawa policy. His influence at the decision-making level of the Kennedy administration, never strong, withered and vanished as his patron, Chester Bowles, foundered in Washington and was forced later to accept assignment as the U.S. ambassador to India. Reischauer's academic credentials and expertise carried weight at lower levels of the bureaucracy, but his ideas rarely seemed to get past the subcabinet level.[29]

Concern about economic development in the Ryukyus predated Reischauer and the Kennedy administration. Economic assistance to the Ryukyu Islands rapidly dropped in the mid-1950s from its high level of $50 million in 1950. In 1957 American funding amounted to $1,058,000. This decline began to get press attention and worried Ambassador Douglas MacArthur II, still unsettled from his trip to the island. "We should exercise our administrative rights in Ryukyus so that inhabitants are reasonably contented," he told Assistant Secretary Walter Robertson in telegram language. "Japanese attitudes about Okinawa strongly reflect Okinawan attitudes," he wrote Dulles. "If the situation is quiet in Naha, it is not likely to be too successfully agitated here in Tokyo."[30]

The problem was not so much economic in nature, but political. The Okinawan per capita gross national product (GNP) had skyrocketed compared to its prewar size. In 1960 the per capita GNP in the Ryukyus was $202 compared to an average of $25 between 1934 and 1936. Compared on a per capita basis, the Okinawan GNP humbled other economies in East Asia: it was twice the size of the Taiwanese and Filipino GNPs, three times that of Korea, and four times the Indonesian economy. Okinawa, however, lagged behind the Japanese national average by about a third and had a cost of living slightly higher than that of Tokyo. Okinawa was not the poorest prefecture in Japan, but it fell in ranking as the Japanese economy took off in the early 1960s. The gap between the Japanese national average and Okinawa grew to almost 50 percent. A polarization in the Ryukyus further complicated matters. Many Okinawans were on social welfare, while a small minority had made a fortune.[31]

MacArthur began lobbying visiting members of Congress to increase aid levels. Melvin Price, the same House member who chaired the land rental committee, sponsored the measure. The long legislative process ironically culminated just after the security treaty crisis, when Eisenhower signed the bill on July 12, 1960. Economic assistance jumped to $3,349,000 for that year compared to the $1.3 million for 1959.[32]

The task force held its first organizational meeting on August 25, two weeks after Kennedy authorized its creation. The commission had members from the Departments of Defense, State, and Labor. Kaysen decided the group would collect information and determine which issues were the most important. He assigned areas of study to individual members on various topics and asked them to prepare papers for the rest of the board. Topics included wage differences between Okinawans and Japanese, long- and short-term economic issues, land, and legal issues of citizenship. Kaysen planned to have the task force make a trip to Okinawa of several weeks' duration in order to solve these problems.[33]

The commission worked in relative obscurity until A. M. Rosenthal of *The New York Times* broke a story with a Naha dateline revealing the existence of the group and its pending visit to the Ryukyus. When the group arrived, Okinawan expectations for change in favor of reversion were rather high. Speculation appeared in the press that the commission would bring significant changes to the administration of Okinawa. These hopes remained vague, however, and led Okinawans to expect results far beyond the scope and mission of the task force. To a certain degree, these exaggerated hopes were understandable. The Kaysen commission was the highest-ranking group to study Okinawa since the Price committee held hearings in 1955, and it was the first ever with a presidential warrant. An editorial in the *Okinawa Taimusu* was close to the mark, noting that little would change as long as the task force ignored the fundamental problem of American administration.[34]

Caraway feared that the task force would adopt Reischauer's recommendation of allowing increased levels of Japanese economic assistance. He saw Japanese funding as the beginning of a slow erosion of U.S. power on the island. "We said that Reischauer was not the ambassador of the United States to Japan, that he was the Japanese ambassador sitting in the United States embassy," the general recalled. "He never protected a single American interest while he was there." Caraway wanted economic assistance increased, but he wanted it to come from American sources. He tried to get the Peace Corps to send volunteers, but Sergeant Shriver, the program administrator, refused.[35]

Caraway decided to contain and limit Japanese aid even before the task force wrote its final report. In one of his regular biweekly meetings with Ota Seisaku, the Okinawan chief executive, Caraway explained that he would consider aid in two phases. Funding current projects was the first priority. Japanese aid would go to specific programs. The U.S. Civil Administration would then plan new projects based on the current ones. American decisions and funding would determine the new programs. Ota immediately realized that Caraway's plan would result in no increase in Japanese funding. Yes, the general said, but it was important to keep the United States and Japan from getting into a bidding war for the favor of the Okinawans. Ota might very well have wanted such a contest but said nothing. There was little he could do, because Ota served at the high commissioner's pleasure, and Caraway had evidence that would have convicted him on felony charges of price gouging and speculation. Caraway's initiative was a brilliant bureaucratic move: it contained Okinawan requests for larger sums of Japanese money and forced Reischauer into a position of rejecting offers from Tokyo to increase appropriations as unnecessary, since the Okinawans had not asked for more funding.[36] Japanese economic aid sowed the seed of reversion, but Caraway had devised a system that would prevent anyone on either side of the Pacific from harvesting the crop.

From Caraway's point of view, the Kaysen task force report was a disaster; from Reischauer's, it was a beginning. In a preliminary summary, Kaysen argued that American "control is in fact conditioned both by the domestic political situation in Okinawa and by the reflection of that situation in Japan." (The commission established after publication of "The Outraged Okinawans" in *Harper's Magazine* reached similar conclusions.) The United States had to meet Japanese and Okinawan needs. He recommended action in three areas. First, the United States should work to reduce the differences between Okinawa and Japan in areas such as education, health and welfare, per capita income, and pensions. Second, Kaysen also argued that the United States should develop programs in tandem with the Japanese government designed to close these gaps. Finally, he recommended that lessening of the American political hold on the island, even though the commission of the task force limited it to an investigation of social and economic matters. Kaysen remained vague in his assertions and avoided specifics in the preliminary report.[37]

After a few weeks of interdepartmental meetings, the task force finalized its findings in a sixty-two-page report. The recommendations generally conformed to those Kaysen made. In order to develop closer ties with Japan, the commission advocated making the Japanese a party to all assistance programs and the creation of an intergovernmental committee to handle issues involving Okinawa. "We can only continue to use the Okinawan base freely if the Government of Japan gives us at least tacit cooperation," the report declared. In economic matters, the final report called for a retirement and pension plan for government employees retroactive to 1952, larger appropriations for economic aid, an increase in the ceiling for U.S. assistance in the Price Act from six million dollars to twenty-five million dollars, and a relaxation of rules prohibiting foreign—primarily Japanese—investment in the Ryukyus. In the political arena, the commission endorsed the appointment of a civilian as civil administrator, nomination of the chief executive by the Okinawa legislature, criminal jurisdiction of Okinawan courts when an Okinawan was the defendant, abolishing prior approval of publications, and ending restrictions on travel from and entry into Okinawa.[38]

The report went before the NSC on March 5, 1962, even though a number of key people in both the military and the State Department had reservations about the document. In the Pentagon, the secretary of the army "strongly endorsed" the first two sets of recommendations in the final report, but he objected to the political ones, calling them restrictive and urging the secretary of defense to give the high commissioner "flexibility for the exercise of first-hand knowledge and judgment." Across the Potomac in the State Department, U. Alexis Johnson made a telling observation. The senior officer in the Foreign Service and a deputy undersecretary of state who had started his career in Tokyo, Johnson spoke with authority on Japanese matters. He told Dean Rusk that the "recommendations of the Task Force fail to come directly to grips with the heart of the political problem, namely, the fact that the Ryukyuans are neither 'fish nor fowl.' They are neither American nor Japanese." Johnson, nevertheless, advised Rusk to support the task force conclusions because they did offer some temporary relief to the problems in the Ryukyus.[39]

Army sentiments and reservations carried the day on March 5, when President Kennedy signed a new National Security Action Memorandum. Kennedy ordered some specific modifications of Executive Order 10713, including the appointment of a civilian as civil administrator, and specified that the Okinawan legislature could determine its own districts and would serve for three years. In all other political matters, the president instructed the high commissioner to make reforms, but the extent and range of change was up to him. The high commissioner had discretionary authority over appointing more civilians to his staff, extending civil rights to the Okinawans, and limiting his veto authority. In another field, the president committed his administration to seeking an increase in the Price Act ceiling.[40] However, the presidential directive did little to change conditions on Okinawa. The highly qualified and vague language made implementation optional, and Caraway had already made his position clear. He had successfully blocked any change in a direction he thought detrimental to U.S. interests.

Two weeks later, the president made a statement that White House speechwriters had apparently drafted. The language was ringing and evocative. "I recognize the Ryukyus to be a part of the Japanese homeland," he declared, "and look forward to the day when the security interests of the free world will permit their restoration to full Japanese sovereignty." Modifications in the executive order also accompanied this statement. His remarks said much without saying anything.[41] The Joint Chiefs, however, were suspicious. A year later Gen. Earle Wheeler, chief of staff of the U.S. Army, made a presentation on the strategic importance of Okinawa. Gen. Maxwell Taylor, JCS chairman, noted in his memorandum of conversation that Kennedy "expressed no disagreement, indicating that he had no intention of giving up the island."[42]

Reaction to the Kennedy statement was quite positive in the United States and Japan. *Newsweek, The New York Times,* and the Washington *Evening Star* printed positive editorials and accounts of the decision. The American Civil Liberties Union also praised the move.[43] In Japan the announcement was banner headline news, and the next day it was the subject of the lead editorial in every major paper. During a session of the Diet, Ikeda called the Kennedy statement "a great step forward." While taking different tones, most Japanese commentators agreed that the policy was a major change.[44]

In Okinawa reaction was much more reserved. Caraway's staff solicited the view of leading Okinawans and found little enthusiasm. "In general terms the change is nothing much," the director of Okinawan television remarked. In a secret study done a year later, a student at the U.S. National War College accurately summarized Okinawa reaction to the executive order: "It was recognized as a bone."[45]

If there was any doubt, the optimists on Okinawa had their illusions shattered in early May after Deputy Assistant Secretary of Defense for International Security Affairs William Bundy testified to Congress. Bundy's testimony and that of Johnson, Caraway, and Undersecretary of the Army Stephen Ailes were part of the Kennedy administration's effort to build congressional support for raising the ceiling of the Price Act and getting more economic assistance. "The recommendations of the President's Task Force on the Ryukyus represent the best hope of achieving a political and economic environment under which our security interests can be sustained for the indefinite future," Bundy said; the other witnesses reiterated this view.[46] The hearing stunned those who thought the Kennedy policy represented a major change.[47]

As the Kennedy administration began its efforts to achieve the new policy, Caraway received even more power to block implementation. When the president signed National Security Action Memorandum 133, he also directed Secretary of State Dean Rusk to begin negotiations with the Japanese. Rusk was to get continued Japanese contributions to economic assistance programs that tacitly recognized American long-term intentions to administer the Ryukyus. "In the conduct of these negotiations, Ambassador Reischauer should maintain close contact with Lieutenant General Caraway, the High Commissioner of the Ryukyus so that he can play his appropriate part," Kennedy instructed. Kaysen later defended this passage, saying the directive clearly authorized the State Department to carry on negotiations while only giving Caraway an advisory role. Whatever the intended purpose of this language, it clearly gave the general even greater authority to thwart initiatives he opposed.[48]

The execution of the proposed reforms depended on Caraway's judgment, and his opposition to any change was well known within the bureaucracy in Washington. The prevailing sentiment was that he would have to live with the coming changes. He proved far more obstinate than expected. In most cases, Caraway simply took no action, claiming he was still reviewing what powers he could transfer to the Okinawan government or what civil liberties Okinawans could enjoy. A transaction he had little power to prevent was the appointment of Shannon McCune as the new civil administrator. A former provost and vice president of the University of Massachusetts and current chairman of the geography department at Colgate University, McCune was born in Korea to missionary parents—together Reischauer and his brother had developed a standard form for romanizing Korean characters. McCune's experience in Okinawa was unpleasant. Caraway ignored him and consolidated power in the office of the high commissioner, which circumvented the former academic. As one of McCune's subordinates noted, he "floundered."[49]

While Caraway thwarted reform, negotiations started between representatives of the State and Defense Departments in Washington to create working guidelines that defined the exact meaning of the president's language. Like Caraway, Defense Department officials wanted to avoid a bidding war between the United States and Japan on economic assistance for Okinawa. The military wanted to limit Japanese aid to existing programs, and the Japanese had to provide their figures before the United States determined its budget. In return for allowing the Japanese to provide economic assistance to Okinawa, the Defense Department wanted at least implicit Japanese acquiesce to American rule of the prefecture. Caraway, for his part, was willing to accept an increase in Japanese aid now, realizing it was best to contain and limit Japanese inroads. He set conditions and refused to allow a Japanese economic mission to visit the island until Reischauer agreed to a set of restrictive rules on Japanese contributions that ratified the general's earlier stand.[50]

A motivating factor for the Defense Department's position was a concern about congressional willingness to fund larger outlays for Okinawa. Diplomats admitted, at least among themselves, that the military had a point. If there was any doubt on this matter, it ended in June when the issue of raising the ceiling of the Price Act went before the Senate Armed Services Committee. After listening to Undersecretary of the Army Stephen Ailes make his presentation, committee chairman Richard Russell of Georgia said, "I think you are asking for too much money." A few minutes later Mississippi Democrat John Stennis said the presentation was lacking in facts and organization. In September the committee authorized only twelve million dollars instead of the twenty-five million dollars the Kennedy administration requested.[51]

From Tokyo Reischauer reported adverse public reaction to the Senate committee action. Japanese government officials put the best spin on the decision, pointing out that the Senate had authorized an increase over current amounts. In private they warned the American embassy that it would be difficult to live within the Caraway-imposed parameters since the United States had failed to fulfill its commitments.[52]

If there were any doubt about Caraway's triumph, it came to an end during May of 1964. A five-part series titled "America's Unhappy Bastion" appeared in *The Washington Post.* The first article appeared in the paper's Sunday "Outlook" section, and each day thereafter, new articles appeared on the front page. Although the series had a critical tone, Rafael Steinberg, author of the series and former Tokyo bureau chief for *Newsweek,* was a good journalist and presented both sides of the issues. He interviewed Caraway for the series and quoted the general when his policies were discussed. A major criticism Steinberg made of American rule was the failure of the military to live up to the spirit of Kennedy's executive order; Steinberg noted, "Caraway admits this readily." In a later series about the island, Steinberg called Caraway an "unapproachable proconsul."[53]

The double defeat Reischauer and the Kennedy administration received at the hands of Caraway and Congress brought matters to an end on Okinawa in the early 1960s. Reischauer was successful in his efforts to get the U.S. government to allow the Japanese to provide Okinawa with economic aid. Caraway devised an appropriation system that gutted the impact of this achievement. Reischauer won a hollow victory, failing to make any significant progress on an issue that he thought put the entire U.S.-Japanese relationship at risk. Caraway's bureaucratic victory was so complete it even outlasted his tenure on the island. Reischauer failed to make any progress on Okinawa even after Caraway retired from the army. Caraway's success in preventing any erosion of U.S. authority—namely that of the U.S. Army—in the Ryukyus was the high-water point of military influence on Okinawa policy. Soon, the United States and Japan started down the road to reversion. Leading the two countries down this path was Ikeda's successor, Sato Eisaku.

CHAPTER 7

The Road to Reversion, 1964–67

On November 9, 1964, Ikeda Hayato, prime minister of Japan, lay in his hospital bed dying of cancer. Although he did not know the extent of his condition, he realized he no longer had the strength to perform his duties and had designated that day as his last in office. Leaders of the Liberal Democratic Party (LDP) gathered in his hospital room, and Ikeda announced his decision to appoint Sato Eisaku as his successor. He then brushed in the characters of Sato's name on a prepared statement. The party assembled later in the day and ratified Ikeda's selection.[1] This day was the first on the road to reversion. In Japan this path was a political one, while in the United States it was bureaucratic. Sato led the way for the Japanese while U. Alexis Johnson, soon to be the U.S. ambassador in Tokyo, did so for the Americans. Both men knew that they had to have some kind of resolution to the issue before 1970.

Two fundamental considerations shaped Japanese policy toward

Okinawa. The first factor was the Japanese political structure. The political spectrum of officeholders in Japan stretched from the Communists on the Left to extreme nationalists on the Right. Given this broad range, agreement on foreign policy was rare. Yet, there was consensus on Okinawa. All political parties and politicians agreed on reversion. Japanese politicians, however, differed profoundly on how to bring this about. The Communists believed Japan was on the wrong side in the Cold War. Party dogma called for the return of the Ryukyus and an end to the American security alliance. Since the Communists held only a few seats in the Diet, they never had a chance to put their ideology to a test.[2]

The Socialists held similar views on Okinawa and the alliance with the United States, but a split developed within their party. One bloc took the view that the party should strive for its maximum goals: the return of Okinawa and the end to the American alliance. A more moderate section believed the return of Okinawa was the priority, even if this translated into accepting a continuation of the U.S. alliance. These differing views on Okinawa had helped split the Socialists into two factions, the Socialist Party of Japan and the Democratic Socialist Party.[3]

The Liberal Democratic Party, the ruling alliance, had complicated views on Okinawa. The LDP was actually an umbrella organization for a number of small political cliques of conservative politicians. Each faction was a political machine dedicated to the advancement of its members. These factions were often the product of mergers between competing political groups, and personality was far more important than ideology in the formation of these organizations. Faction members often had their own suborganizations of supporters in their electoral districts. The key element in unifying these factions was a unique form of two-way loyalty. Younger, junior members had a duty to support their leaders in political and policy debates while the senior members had a duty to promote and develop the careers of their supporters. Funding normally came from specific business corporations.

The LDP was to the right of the political center, although the competition between the factions muddled the party's ideological stand and foreign policy. Party leaders agreed that they wanted unification with Okinawa and supported the American alliance, but the nature of their support differed. Some LDP Diet members favored the status quo: an unarmed Japan closely allied with the United States. Others in the Diet wanted to rebuild the military and pursue an independent, Asian-oriented foreign policy. A third body of opinion in the party wanted to keep Japan unarmed and pursue an independent Asian-oriented policy. A final group of LDP members wanted Japan to rearm and provide vigorous support for U.S. anticommunist efforts. The factions had no partisan orientation on foreign policy. An organization simply supported whatever happened to be the view of its leader.

Since Japan utilized a parliamentary system, LDP control of the Diet gave it the authority to form the government and fill the cabinet, with the president of the party also serving as prime minister. The key to becoming prime minister was not popularity, but rather leadership of a faction and an ability to create a coalition with other faction leaders. Cabinets were a collection of the prime minister's supporters, rival faction leaders, and members of rival factions who found temporary unity in supporting the prime minister. Although the post had more power than it did before the war, the office of prime minister was still weaker than the American president, or even prime ministers in other parliamentary democracies.

The bureaucracy was extremely important in Japan. The vice-minister and other bureaucrats provided stability in policy. The senior position for bureaucrats in any particular ministry was the post of vice-minister. The *Gaimusho* (foreign ministry) had a strong pro-American orientation. The key to career advancement was expertise on the United States. American specialists in the ministry were called the *shin-bei-ha* (pro-American clique). Serving as the ambassador in Washington was a position equal in status and seniority to that of vice-minister. The American-dominated occupation, the postwar purges of career civil servants, and the security alliance with the United States were the main reasons for the heavy American orientation in the *Gaimusho.* Japanese diplomats looked at calls for reversion cautiously, afraid of jeopardizing or weakening the alliance.

The person most responsible for initiating action on Okinawa was Sato Eisaku, prime minister of Japan from 1964 to 1972. Sato was the son of Sato Hidesuke, a sake brewer. Originally born into the Kishi family, the elder Sato took his wife's name when her father adopted him. Eisaku was the youngest of the Sato brothers, all of whom went on to accomplishment and fame. Sato Ichiro became a vice admiral in the Imperial Navy, while Kishi Nobusuke enjoyed a successful career in the civil service before entering politics and becoming prime minister. (Kishi was adopted back into his father's family when he married his first cousin.)[4]

Sato Eisaku's tenure as prime minister was the pinnacle of two highly successful careers in public service. His first career was in what is now the Ministry of Transportation. Through diligent studies in high school, Sato managed to enter Tokyo Imperial University. After an average academic career, he entered the civil service. While his brothers' careers soared—Kishi was a cabinet minister before the war started—Sato's languished. At the end of the war he was in Osaka, running the railway section, while his wife and children stayed with his brother Nobusuke in the false belief that Tokyo would be safer.[5]

It was only during the occupation that Sato's bureaucratic career took off. In 1946 General of the Army Douglas MacArthur purged all civil servants who were advocates of "militant nationalism and aggression." This action removed most of the senior leadership in the Ministry of Transportation. Two years later Sato was the vice-minister.[6]

In this position he came to the attention of Prime Minister Yoshida Shigeru. A former bureaucrat in the Foreign Ministry, Yoshida was recruiting accomplished civil servants to join his Liberal Party. In July, 1948, the party announced that twenty-five high-ranking bureaucrats were joining, including Sato and his high school classmate Ikeda Hayato, then vice-minister of finance. Ikeda and Sato quickly became the star pupils of the *Yoshida gakko* (Yoshida school). Yoshida also began preparing his protégés to replace him as prime minister. Sato had a good sense of timing and an ability to meet the career needs of others, earning the nickname "Eisaku, the quick eared."[7]

A major blow to Sato's political career came in 1954. The Japanese government had, for several years, subsidized shipbuilding to help the merchant marine fleet recover from the destruction it suffered during the war. The shipbuilding industry considered the current subsidies insufficient, and a number of firms gave bribes to politicians and government officials, including Sato, to get a new law. The police arrested the presidents of five major shipbuilding firms, and the chief public prosecutor of Tokyo issued a warrant for Sato. Yoshida had the minister of justice order the prosecutor to drop these charges, but Sato continued to have legal problems and was indicted again later in the year. Ultimately, the charges were dropped in 1956 as part of a general amnesty program. Although Sato avoided conviction, the case hurt him politically, staining his reputation for years to come.[8]

Sato became a faction leader after his mentor lost his hold on power. Politicians in the Liberal Party and conservatives in the Democratic Party wanted to merge their organizations to keep the Socialists from taking control of the cabinet. Yoshida, for a variety of reasons, refused to reach an agreement with his main rival, Hatoyama Ichiro. A number of Yoshida's supporters, fearing the Socialists more than Yoshida, forced him out of office, voted in Hatoyama, and merged the two parties, forming the Liberal Democratic Party. Sato, along with Yoshida, refused to join the new organization. Hatoyama lost his hold on power two years later, due in part to Yoshida's efforts. The Yoshida faction split as Ikeda and Sato disagreed on whom to support as Hatoyama's successor. Ikeda favored Ishibashi Tanzan, while Sato supported his brother Kishi.[9]

The split with Ikeda actually put Sato in a pivotal role in the new party. Ishibashi won the election, but poor health forced him to resign two months later. Kishi and Ikeda led the two largest factions in the LDP, and Sato served as a fulcrum between them. Sato was a member of the dominant coalition and a cabinet member for all but two years from the time Kishi succeeded Ishibashi in February, 1957, until his own retirement in mid-1972. He had, however, little foreign policy experience. His cabinet and political posts were limited to positions dealing mainly with domestic issues.[10]

Sato's triumph and inauguration as prime minister came only after one of the greatest setbacks in his political career. In 1962 Ikeda ran for a second term as president of the party and, given LDP control of the Diet, prime minister. Sato seriously considered challenging him for the post before declaring his support. Ikeda won an unopposed race. In forming his second cabinet, Ikeda demoted Sato, giving him a subcabinet post. This action effectively forced Sato into the intraparty opposition. Two years later, when Ikeda broke with tradition and decided to run for a third two-year term as president of the LDP, Sato challenged him. Sato made this decision after a shouting match with a drunken Ikeda on the phone. Ikeda won an absolute majority on the first ballot, but his vote total was much lower than expected. Realizing he was losing his hold on the party, Ikeda decided to resolve his differences with Sato. He installed several of Sato's faction in the cabinet, healing the breach.[11]

Shortly after this political peace making, Ikeda went to the hospital with a sore throat, which his doctors diagnosed as cancer of the larynx and told him nothing about his condition, choosing instead to inform his subordinates Ohira Masayoshi and Maeo Shigesaburo. Ohira and Maeo, fearing the political ramifications of this news, asked the doctors to keep the facts secret from everyone, including the prime minister. Ohira, Maeo, and the doctors convinced Ikeda to have radiation treatments for his "pre-cancerous" condition. After a month and half in the hospital, Ikeda realized he was too weak to continue in office and announced his decision to resign. This news set off a mad scramble to replace him. The party vice president and secretary-general met with Ikeda and agreed that he should announce his successor since Ikeda was only a few months into his term as party president. Sato was in the best position of the faction leaders for the post, having finished second in the balloting three months before. He faced strong challenges from rival faction leaders Kono Ichiro and Fujiyama Aiichiro. Sato and Kono led strong factions, but many members of the LDP disliked them. Fujiyama, on the other hand, headed up a small faction and hoped to win as a compromise candidate. Each camp began lobbying Ikeda's close political associates, but Ikeda sent a message to Sato early in the process alerting him that he would be the new prime minister.[12]

Sato's hold on power appeared weak early in his tenure. A U.S. intelligence estimate sent to the White House predicted a short Sato administration. According to this analysis, the new prime minister was not good at making compromises and had powerful enemies among the other faction leaders.[13] Unforeseen events, however, diluted the opposition and reduced the pressure on Sato. The Ikeda faction split apart following his death. Kono also died in 1965. These two deaths removed the greatest political threats to Sato; there was no one else with the stature and support to challenge him.[14]

There were four main elements to the foreign policy that Sato pursued while in office: a close partnership with the United States, a strong economic aid program, a role for Japan as a link between the East and West, and multilateralism. The most important of these factors was the relationship with the United States. Sato firmly believed in supporting U.S. foreign policy without an independent military. This view was close to that of his mentor, Yoshida, but different from that of his brother. Kishi wanted to rebuild the military and pursue a foreign policy independent of the United States, although he generally supported the anticommunist elements of U.S. diplomacy. Yoshida advocated an American alliance as a measure that would allow Japan to rebuild its economic strength and gain its rightful place in the international community as a world power.[15] Sato supported U.S. efforts to such a degree that he visited Saigon, making him the only foreign leader other than Lyndon Johnson to make that trip.[16] (Contrary to popular thinking at the time, this action carried little weight with Johnson.) The president believed the United States had treated Japan well and was disappointed with Japanese armament efforts. He had no interest in surrendering territory just to keep Sato happy. Secretary of State Dean Rusk and Secretary of Defense Robert McNamara, however, were grateful for the prime minister's support in Japan of U.S. efforts.[17]

Okinawa was a paradox for Sato, and 1970 was the deadline for a resolution of the dilemma. The security alliance treaty had a set term of ten years, after which time either party could terminate the agreement with one year's notice. The Ryukyu Islands were a key element in U.S. strategic planning for the Pacific, which Sato supported, but continued American occupation threatened to focus nationalist sentiment against the United States and the security treaty. Reversion might require the removal of American bases and nuclear weapons, weakening the U.S. military presence in the Far East and the alliance. Sato personally had no problem with the bases remaining in a postreversion Okinawa. As early as his run against Ikeda in 1964, Sato made it clear that reversion would take place "within the context of the Japan-U.S. partnership." He was even willing to consider allowing the United States the right to store nuclear weapons on the island after its return. The real question was, would the Japanese public tolerate such agreements?[18]

A second area Sato emphasized was economic aid. Since Japan had no military, it had to use its economic resources to full advantage. In a speech given in New York, Sato said it was a national priority for Japan to help eliminate disease, poverty, and hunger in Asia. "Until we do so, long-lasting stability and peace in Asia will elude us," he declared.[19] Efforts to secure markets for Japanese goods and other economic motivations, however, were the primary motivation for this aid.[20]

Sato also wanted Japan to serve as a link between East and West. In his first speech to the Diet as prime minister, he stated Japan's main mission was to "contribute positively to the preservation of world peace." Sato emphasized this theme a few months later in Washington during his first state visit. "We would feel most fortunate if the Japan of today could be held up as an example to the other countries of Asia." Although

Sato did offer to mediate peace negotiations in Vietnam, his ideas on serving as a bridge between the East and West remained vague and undefined. The main purpose of this effort was to rationalize Japanese trade with China.[21]

The final element in Sato's foreign policy was multilateralism. "I see no shame in Japan's dependence on collective security with the U.S.," he told the American magazine *U.S. News and World Report.* Sato wanted to work in tandem with other countries and international organizations on issues such as economic aid. After interviewing the former prime minister, political scientist John Welfield speculated that Sato's emphasis on alliances and partnerships was the "lesson" Sato learned from Japan's defeat in World War II.[22]

Talks that would mark the beginning of the reversion process started on January 12, 1965, as Ambassador Edwin Reischauer and Secretary of State Dean Rusk, their breath hanging in the cold air, waited for the arrival of Sato's plane at National Airport. In July, 1964, when Sato challenged Ikeda for leadership of the LDP, he produced a campaign pamphlet titled "The Fight for Tomorrow." In this booklet, Sato put himself in front of the issue and on his own terms. "Within the context of the Japan-U.S. partnership, Japan will demand from the United States the reversion of Okinawa," the document stated. Political scientist Masumi Junnosuke has dismissed this stand as campaign posturing but, after only two months in office, Sato was in Washington talking about Okinawa.[23]

The new prime minister knew he faced a 1970 deadline and initiated these talks. On his second day in office, Sato pulled Reischauer away from a garden party at the Imperial Palace and told him that he wanted to visit Washington and meet Lyndon Johnson.[24]

The meeting between the two leaders was a study in contrasting political styles. In public appearances, the telegenic Sato appeared comfortable and dignified compared to a clumsy and stilted Johnson. In private, though, the American dominated. In an Oval Office meeting that lasted forty-five minutes, Johnson sat in his chair with his feet propped up on the end of a coffee table while Sato sat on the sofa running alongside the table and perpendicular to the president. Johnson's dramatic gestures and forceful personality made Sato visibly uncomfortable.[25]

Sato came to Washington to talk about Okinawa, and no amount of physical intimidation was going to stop him. During both their private meeting and a large conference with their ambassadors and foreign min-

RYUKYUS - U. S. INSTALLATIONS & FACILITIES

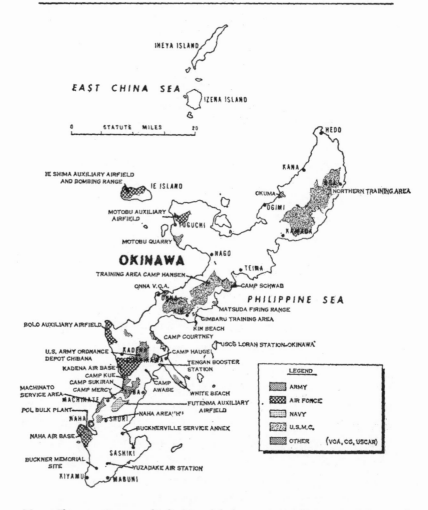

Map 3. This map gives a good indication of the heavy mass and interconnected maze of U.S. bases on Okinawa during the mid-1960s.

isters, Sato raised the issue with Johnson. He complained that there was no movement toward self-rule that had been promised in Kennedy's 1962 statement. Sato pursued another facet of the issue the next day in a private luncheon meeting with Rusk at the State Department. With an interpreter as the only witness, Sato proposed that the United States return all the Ryukyu Islands except Okinawa. This suggestion was the first Japanese action for actual reversion. Rusk answered with diplomatic silence.[26]

Thwarted in Washington in his efforts to initiate movement toward reversion, but still determined to begin the process, Sato decided to travel to Okinawa itself. In doing so he became the first Japanese prime minister since the war, and only the second ever, to visit the island. (Gen. Tojo Hideki, wartime prime minister, was the first.) The trip was a clever political gesture. The prime minister, in one act, put himself at the head of the reversion movement, denied the opposition a potential damaging issue, and used the symbolism of his visit to focus nationalist sentiment in the directions he wanted. Sato flew to Okinawa in August, the twentieth anniversary of the end of the war, which only added to the heavy emotion of his visit. At the airport he announced: "The postwar era will not end until the return of Okinawa to the homeland is realized." Newspaper editors in Tokyo made this statement banner headline news.[27]

The prime minister's tour of the island was an unqualified success. A crowd estimated at thirty thousand lined streets and highways to see him. Sato, politician that he was, worked the crowd several times, shaking hands and greeting onlookers. He put flowers on a monument dedicated to Generals Ushijima and Cho, and the prime minister broke down at the Cave of the Virgins, where a number of young nurses died during the battle. These tears moved a number of Japanese reporters and editors, convincing them that Sato had a real interest in Okinawa. Less publicized trips to smaller islands in the Ryukyus also drew big crowds and again reduced Sato to tears.[28]

Sato held many meetings during his stay that had important, unintended consequences. He talked with a number of civil leaders and held a roundtable discussion with Okinawan legislators. In a question-and-answer session, he promised to increase economic-aid levels and improve education. These public comments were more important than either Sato or his Okinawan audience realized, effectively scuttling the appropriation system Caraway had devised for controlling Japanese economic aid.

The U.S. Civil Administration could no longer claim that Okinawans had no interest in seeing an increase in Japanese funding. Sato was a witness to a public request that the Americans could not deny had been made of him. Sato, however, did not realize the importance of this exchange. In a moment of candor, he admitted he had no definite plan on how to achieve reversion. "I am wracking my brains," he said.[29]

Not everyone on Okinawa was happy to see Sato. The political Left opposed the foreign policy of the LDP, including the alliance with the United States. The Reversion Council, Okinawan Teachers' Association, Okinawan People's Party, and many labor unions hoped to use reversion to force U.S. bases out of Okinawa and terminate the U.S.-Japan security treaty. Sato was their enemy. He had already publicly committed to reversion in a context that would preserve the American alliance.[30]

These groups held a protest rally at a Naha high school that attracted ten thousand people. A torch-lit parade snake-danced its way to Sato's hotel. Senaga Kamejiro, the former mayor of Naha, urged the crowd to "grab Sato at the hotel and throw him out." While a mob of between five thousand and eight thousand people gathered in front of the hotel, Sato dined at a reception held for him at the Ft. Buckner Officers' Club. Warned as he returned that there was no way his motorcade could get through the crowd, Sato ordered the convoy to the Japanese government liaison office, arriving there roughly at midnight.[31]

Yasui Ken, director general of the prime minister's office, met with representatives of groups that had organized the rally. He accepted from them a six-part petition that requested Okinawan representation in the Diet and the direct election of the chief executive but also blasted American and Japanese foreign policy in the Pacific. As Yasui negotiated with the representatives, the rioting mob began to melt away. Americans eager to teach the Okinawans a lesson bitterly noted that Sato restrained the police from taking "forceful action" against the crowd while Yasui negotiated. An attack that was nominally on the behalf of his personal safety that resulted in physical injuries to Okinawans would be devastating politically to Sato back in Tokyo. At 2:00 A.M. an exhausted Sato decided to spend the evening in American VIP housing rather than at another Naha hotel. Editorials in Tokyo the next day attacked him for seeking refuge on an American base.[32]

Around 2:30 A.M. eight hundred Okinawan police officers charged into a crowd that had dwindled to about one thousand. The police battled protesters for an hour before the area was secure. The next day broken glass, fallen store signs, banners, and other debris littered the area.[33]

For the most part, the riots were secondary news, although the *Mainichi Shimbun* did give the episode front-page coverage. Reports of the overall trip overwhelmed the attention paid to the riots. Sato dismissed the disturbance as an "accident," saying it was not an accurate reflection of public sentiment on the island. Some commentators argued that the government should heed the frustration of the Okinawans and begin working on reversion. These comments ignored the political context and motivation of the rioters. Many others praised Sato for his efforts and noted that his controlled reaction was an indication of his sincerity on the Okinawa issue. Many reporters, editors, and columnists declared that the visit was a turning point.[34]

These journalists were correct. The trip was extremely important and supercharged Japanese reversion efforts. The Japanese government soon realized the importance of the public request, and Sato pledged to provide more economic aid. In his memoirs, Reischauer claims it was the retirement of Caraway that led to increased levels of economic aid. The numbers did improve a bit when Lt. Gen. Albert Watson II became the new high commissioner. Watson later said methods rather than objectives were the major differences between himself and Caraway on questions of improving the lot of the Okinawan people. He saw himself as less rigid and more willing to accept additional Japanese aid. Tokyo-funded aid did increase after Watson arrived but began rocketing only after the Sato trip. Japanese levels jumped 40 percent in 1966. In 1967 aid from Tokyo doubled the previous year's totals, surpassing American numbers in the process. Japanese aid grew another 50 percent the following year and another 50 percent the year after. American expenditures grew but lagged far behind those of Japan. Still, this increase was more than enough to anger some Americans. When Otto Passman, the chairman of the congressional committee responsible for appropriating funds for Okinawa, saw these increases, he lost his temper. "You too, have acquired the habits of the Great Society. That is, to spend money you do not have, for things you do not need, having to borrow most of it, no doubt, from unborn generations," he told General Watson and a deputy secretary of the army when they appeared before his committee. A year later, a secret Central Intelligence Agency report sent to the White House warned that the Japanese were using increased levels of aid to increase their influence on the island and "integrate Ryukyuan institutions into the social, legal, and economic framework of Japan." Lt. Gen. Ferdinand Unger, in his first press conference as high commissioner, said sustaining the high economic growth on the island and preserving the U.S. bases were his two major and mutually supporting goals. Sato took other steps to direct the debate on reversion. Before his visit to the island, he declared that Japan would respond to any attack on Okinawa. He also created a special cabinet committee on reversion.[35]

Sato had totally neutralized the political Left on Okinawa. The CIA, in an analysis of Japanese politics, reported that Sato was in firm control of the Okinawa issue. The *Beheiren,* the Japanese anti–Vietnam War organization, inadvertently helped him in this matter. Fearing reversion would kill the antiwar movement, the *Beheiren* avoided the issue altogether for years. The first major reversion rally in Japan proper did not take place until April 28, 1969. The protest was a "fiasco" in the words of one scholar. Student organizations were denied rally permits and went on a rampage. Riots broke out in central Tokyo, the Ginza district, and several subway stations, all of which the police managed to contain.[36]

A far more dangerous political challenge for Sato came from within the LDP. After a brief trip to Okinawa, Mori Kiyoshi, administrative affairs director of the prime minister's office, proposed that Japan negotiate for resumption of individual government services one step at a time. Mori proposed education as the first function Japan should regain. The idea became extremely popular; it seemed to offer an actual concrete step forward. This popularity also helped Mori in his struggle with Nakasone Yasuhiro for control of the Kono faction, now that Kono was dead.[37]

Official reaction to functional reversion was cautious and guarded in public. Cabinet Secretary Aichi Kiichi, a dependable Sato subordinate, said blandly the idea would receive thorough study. A story in the *Mainichi Shimbun* quoted an anonymous foreign ministry source who said the separate reversion of government services was difficult legally but withheld any final judgment.[38]

In private, reactions were strong and negative. High Commissioner Watson and Chief Executive Matsuoka Seiho both rejected the idea as unworkable. "If this isn't a political football, then I haven't seen a football game," Watson remarked scornfully. His successor had similar opinions. The *Mainichi Shimbun* also reported that the Johnson administration was not interested in the idea, although no American official would say so on record.[39]

Mori's proposal put Sato in a difficult political position. The idea seemed unworkable but enjoyed enormous popularity. Opposing this popular idea was unwise; supporting it, however, would be equally imprudent. His initial reaction was to do nothing, and Sato waited five months before commenting on Mori's idea. In January, 1967, at a campaign stop in the city of Otsu, Sato said he favored full reversion over any partial measure and effectively dismissed functional reversion by coming out in favor of full reversion.[40]

The statement caught observers off-guard. Mori claimed he suggested functional reversion only after getting Sato's approval. With this in mind, editorial writers and columnists wondered if Sato had a plan to regain the Ryukyus. Many commentators failed to note that Sato's remarks were a clever way of eliminating the pressure on him to take action on functional reversion without being seen as an obstacle among Okinawans. Sato had adroitly removed himself from a no-win situation.[41]

While Okinawa was a political issue in Japan, it was a bureaucratic concern in the United States. Little action took place in 1963 and 1964. Lyndon Johnson had a caretaker government with an uncertain future and had greater domestic and political concerns to worry about than Japan or Okinawa. Reischauer was the most ardent reversion advocate in the government, but he lacked influence.

When Caraway retired in 1964, Reischauer's position should have improved. The new high commissioner was Lt. Gen. Albert Watson II, a veteran of the battle of Okinawa. Watson wanted a close relationship with the ambassador. "I asked him to not hesitate to call me anytime and if necessary I will come up here to Tokyo or if you want to come down and see me you'd be welcomed," Watson recalled. He went out of his way to meet with Reischauer, traveling to Tokyo even before he arrived in Okinawa. The two agreed to exchange cables and discuss their differences so they could present a united viewpoint to Washington. Reischauer proved unable to live up to the agreement. Watson complained that the ambassador's speeches were too strident and partisan on the subject of reversion. A month before he resigned, Reischauer ignored his agreement with Watson and sent a cable to Washington complaining about the military administration's failure to keep him informed on Okinawan matters. Watson was in Washington at the time, and the State Department desk officer for Japan asked to meet with him. When he saw the cable, Watson said he would take care of the problem. When he returned to Japan, the general had in his own words a "heart to heart talk" with the ambassador. Reischauer refused to admit fault, but the next day an embassy officer showed the general a message the ambassador had just sent telling the State Department to ignore the cable in question. In his memoirs Reischauer blames the misunderstanding on Watson's staff.[42]

The only major Okinawa-related initiative during Reischauer's time in Tokyo came as a direct result of Sato's trips to the United States and Okinawa. In a series of cables written during the summer of 1965, Reischauer predicted a major crisis would develop before 1970 between the United States and Japan over Okinawa.[43] Reischauer spoke with powerful credentials and expertise on Japan that Washington bureaucrats could not ignore, even if they disagreed with his views. As a result, these cables initiated debate and action.

Events on the island and the buildup of the Vietnam War supported Reischauer's arguments. Although the army administered the island, it used Okinawa mainly as a logistical center and supply base. The largest number of soldiers on the island were service and support troops. During the Vietnam War, the 2nd Logistical Command relocated to Okinawa. "I remember visiting them at night," Watson recalled. "They were on a 24 hour basis." According to the commander of U.S. Army forces in the Pacific, the maintenance facilities on the island allowed the army "to overhaul and rebuild well forward—with resultant rapid response to maintenance requirements and substantial savings in work unit costs, pipeline inventories and shipping expenses."[44] After the 3rd Marine Division left for duty in Vietnam, the main combat unit on the island was the Fifth Air Force. This disposition of units was appropriate in a way. General of the Army Douglas MacArthur originally pushed for American retention of Okinawa because its strategic location would allow U.S. bombers to strike a number of locations on the Asian mainland. Watson also explained the strategic significance of U.S. administration of Okinawa: "It was a base from which we could operate without having to ask authority of any other power." While this might have been true in a legal sense, as a practical matter it was quite incorrect. The air force made almost no use of these airfields during the Vietnam War because of local opposition. In 1965 it sent Okinawa-based B-52 bombers on combat missions over North Vietnam. Protesting Okinawans mobbed the gates of Kadena Air Force Base, and Japanese observers made a number of sharp, critical comments against this flight. The air force waited three and a half years before using Okinawa-based planes a second time, and even then only for a few weeks. Watson learned something from this episode. "My whole administration was conducted with one eye on the people of the Ryukyu Islands because as long as they were content to support us, we were able to perform our mission," he stated. "They had the power to shut down U.S. Military operations in the Ryukyu Islands by failing to work."[45]

Shortly after this episode and Reischauer's cables, the Department of Defense proposed allowing the legislature to elect the chief executive of the Ryukyu Islands. At that time the high commissioner appointed the chief executive. Watson hoped the announcement would reduce some of the pressure on the island for the direct election of the chief executive. The duty of responding to this proposal for the State Department fell to the highest-ranking Japan expert in Washington at the time, Douglas MacArthur II. Then an assistant secretary of state, MacArthur said the State Department had no strong view on the proposal, but he thought it could not hurt matters. With no strong opposition, the proposal went through the bureaucracy quickly and arrived at the West Wing of the White House for the president's signature in a short amount of time. At Watson's request, the announcement of indirect elections occurred just before the start of the new legislative session.[46]

The revision of the executive order did little to change the administration of the island, but Okinawans looked on it favorably. The English-language edition of the *Okinawa Taimusu* called indirect elections "a step forward." The selection of the chief executive fell to the Okinawan LDP, since it had a majority in the legislature. Watson, however, proved extremely clever in manipulating the factions of the Okinawan LDP into electing the candidate he favored.[47]

In the debate on reversion that followed Reischauer's cables, the military made it clear that it still thought of Japan as an ally of uncertain character. Three days after the president signed the executive order, the Joint Chiefs of Staff sent the secretary of defense a memo on Okinawa. The chiefs argued that American bases on the island were worthless without American rule. "Unilateral U.S. control of Ryukyuan administrative procedures is essential for as long as we maintain major bases there to prevent the direct imposition of political limitations by another country upon the utilization of our Okinawan-based forces, equipment, material, and other resources." The war in Vietnam, the dangerous, threatening, militant rhetoric of China, and the uncertain dependability of the Japanese prohibited any thought of, or movement toward, reversion. "Less than full U.S. administrative control of Okinawan would inhibit the operational flexibility of US military forces based there and might directly affect our nuclear capabilities in the Far East. Therefore, any transfer of administrative rights over the Ryukyus to Japan would severely dilute the military value of our Okinawan bases, particularly if there should be a change adverse to US interests in the Government or policies of Japan."[48]

Secretary of Defense Robert S. McNamara rejected this stand. When Morton Halperin, one of McNamara's civilian staff, sent a memo to him arguing that the United States should return Okinawa, the secretary responded with a note scratched on the first page: "No need for meeting. Give it back. R McN." McNamara considered Japan an ally, perhaps a reluctant one, but an ally nonetheless. He wanted to use Okinawa as a lever to force Japan into a more active role. He told his Australian counterpart he was willing to return the Ryukyus to Japanese administration under certain conditions. Japan had to start spending more on defense and to help the United States with its balance of payment problems. The Japanese would also have to start sending troops overseas and providing active political support for U.S. military actions in Asia. He knew the United States needed Japanese acquiescence to operate the bases on Okinawa. The incident with the B-52s indicated that the leadership of the uniformed services had overestimated the utility of American administration. McNamara hoped to use reversion to get more support for the American presence. During Sato's second visit to Washington in 1967, he told the prime minister that reversion was a political issue that was bound to happen sooner or latter. The real question was the role of the bases. Reversion and base use, he said, were tied together. He would support reversion only if it would not weaken U.S. commitments to other nations.[49]

The State Department was more unified on the Okinawa issue than the Defense Department. Bureaucratically speaking, the agency simply adopted Reischauer's view that Japan was an ally and Okinawa put that partnership at risk. In interdepartmental meetings, State Department representatives based their views on Reischauer's cables and a paper he wrote, even though many believed he had overstated his case. "Present

U.S. policy in the Ryukyus has not succeeded in creating a stable environment for our bases or a relationship with Japan and the Ryukyuan people that will remain viable for long," declared one paper. Since "the basic source of dissatisfaction is the U.S. Civil Administration of the Ryukyuan people rather than the presence of our military bases," the United States could return control of the island to Japan. Reischauer suggested an enclave settlement similar to the one Eisenhower had favored eight years before.[50]

In Washington, Defense Department bureaucrats were writing studies and preparing for interdepartmental meetings in "an atmosphere of urgency" until Reischauer sent another series of cables in mid-February. The Japanese were now more sympathetic toward U.S. policies than they had been in the previous summer, he wrote. These telegrams eliminated the motivation bureaucrats in the Defense Department needed if they were to take action. Unwittingly, Reischauer had scuttled his own policy initiative.[51]

Interdepartmental meetings continued but with results of little consequence. McGeorge Bundy, the president's former national security adviser, visited Japan during these debates and believed that Japan was a crisis waiting to happen. Bundy sent a memo to the president, warning him that "We have about six months in which to frame a careful and forward-looking policy which will allow us to trade with the Japanese effectively." Bundy—his brother was the chairman of the interdepartmental group discussing Okinawa—suggested presidential intervention on the issue. "Okinawa by its very nature needs to have a White House push." His successor, Walt W. Rostow, endorsed this view. "I've looked into the situation and it is this: Defense has thrown a block across interdepartment work looking to the future of the Ryukyus," Rostow reported.[52] Lyndon Johnson, however, did nothing.

Then, six weeks later, an unforeseen development gave the president an opportunity to take major action. In July Edwin Reischauer resigned. There was only one man on LBJ's list to replace him, U. Alexis Johnson. The ultimate bureaucrat, Alex Johnson had risen to influence through a combination of competence, a preference for work in the shadows, a willingness to let others take credit for decisions, and a detached respect for authority and power. He started his career in Tokyo as a language officer under the supervision of Ambassador Joseph C. Grew. One of the first Americans to make a professional career in the Foreign Service, Grew had a record of mentoring young diplomats, and Johnson was one of his greatest students. Interned by the Japanese at the start of World War II, Johnson's career rocketed after the conflict ended. He helped negotiate an end to the Korean War and then represented the United States in a series of negotiations with the People's Republic of China that took place in the 1950s after the end of the Korean War. In 1966 he was the senior officer in the Foreign Service and, as deputy undersecretary of state for political affairs, held the fourth-ranking job in the State Department. He was highly regarded in Washington. "You are one of the great professionals," McGeorge Bundy wrote while he was still national security advisor, "and I hope you know that all the amateurs know it." Seeing Johnson arrive to testify at a congressional hearing, Sen. Richard Russell said, "You have brought up the heavy reserves and now we are overpowered." Norman Mailer made him a character in *Harlot's Ghost,* his novel about the CIA. In retirement, Johnson summed up his career with the title of his memoirs, *The Right Hand of Power.*[53]

Alex Johnson had two relationships that Reischauer never enjoyed. The first and most important was an association with the president that was both long standing and personal. He had gained Lyndon Johnson's respect when he stood up to the then vice president, protecting another Foreign Service officer in a staffing assignment dispute. He then gained the president's gratitude when he accepted a demotion, agreeing to serve as the second man in the Saigon embassy with only three days notice. His wife, Pat, was upset, but the president promised her that she would get the assignment she desired. "Anyone who knew Pat knew that her heart's desire was to return to Tokyo as the wife of the Ambassador," Johnson remarked. The president lived up to his word despite rampant speculation in the press about the appointment, which Lyndon Johnson hated. Returning to Japan gave the ambassador "a lot of emotional satisfaction."[54]

Observers on both sides of the Pacific approved of the appointment. Reischauer had always enjoyed good press coverage, and his resignation drew a flurry of stories and editorials. Much of this publicity praised Alex Johnson as well. An editorial in the Baltimore *Sun* declared that his appointment was "a clear indication of the importance the Administration continues to give to the Tokyo assignment." His confirmation was painless. Japanese observers also noted the importance of the Johnson appointment. Although it no longer had the bright atmosphere that had existed under Reischauer, the U.S. embassy appeared more professional and efficient under Johnson. These commentators also expected he would carry more weight in the State Department than Reischauer, since the new ambassador had previously worked for Dean Rusk in the Truman administration.[55]

The other relationship that was critical for Ambassador Johnson was a friendly partnership with the new high commissioner, Lt. Gen. Ferdinand Unger. A graduate of West Point, Unger saw combat in Europe during World War II as an artilleryman. Like Johnson, he was also an avid golfer. On October 3, while the two new appointees were still in Washington, Johnson and Unger met to establish operational procedures between themselves. Johnson described Unger as "quick" and "sensitive." Unger said of Johnson: "Alex knew more about the broad military-political issues than some of the military people knew. He just had a feel for it. In addition, his interests, his heart and his motivation were not exclusively State, for he understood the important role that the military played in the conduct of our country's international relations around the world. He understood our on-coming missile systems. He understood power and the feelings of foreign peoples towards power. He understood what we could do and what we couldn't do." In his memoirs Johnson recalled starting the meeting by saying that "I expected him to be my problem and me to be his problem." Unger agreed to a Johnson proposal that they exchange reports with one another and work out their disagreements before sending the messages to Washington. Johnson proudly noted that they never had to refer a split to Washington for resolution.[56] The disputes of the Reischauer years were a thing of the past.

When Unger agreed to this arrangement, he knew his job was primarily political in nature. "It was clear," he recalled, "that my major function was to develop and maintain a stable and political climate in the Ryukyus—an umbrella, as it were, under which the missions of all military services could be successfully performed without local interference."[57] Even though his position had little to do with military matters, Unger liked his assignment. "I couldn't wait to get up in the morning to find out what in the hell was going to go wrong that day," he remarked. "It was this challenge that made the task of the High Commissioner the most unique and the most exciting position in either the military or diplomatic service of the United States at that time."[58]

When Johnson and Unger arrived in their posts, relations between Okinawans and their American rulers were in a nebulous state of flux that was neither good nor bad. In a series of articles for *The Washington Post*, Rafel Steinberg, a Japanese-speaking American journalist, found that the citizens of the island had strongly mixed feelings about their rulers. Okinawans generally appreciated that the Americans were largely responsible for the material and economic prosperity of the island, but they also realized that their guests had done so out of self-interest. "Our hearts are afflicted," Ota told Steinberg. "Although there are a few points that have the look of progress, there has been no real advance commiserate with our hopes." A political rival in the legislature agreed, saying, "What we cannot endure, is that we have given up, have lost, all these things which we would have as part of Japan—development of industry, a sense of nationality, freedom of travel, welfare benefits—just in order for the bases to be here, to safeguard the peace and so forth." A college student said, "We know America is trying in some ways to help us, but most of us feel that we are poor, because the U.S. is here, we are not free, because the U.S. is here, we cannot travel, or govern ourselves because the U.S. is here." A year earlier, the *Yomuri Shimbun* ran a series of its own called the "Americans of Okinawa" and came up with a slightly more negative assessment. The Japanese paper reported finding widespread and mutual mistrust built on cultural misunderstandings. Many Americans told the *Yomuri* that the Government of the Ryukyu Islands was corrupt—an assessment that the paper agreed with—but one which the Americans refused to recognize that they had helped create and perpetuate.[59]

The ambiguous sentiment also found expression in Okinawan literature of this period. In *Kakuteru paatii* (The cocktail party), Oshiro Tatsuhiro used irony and sharp contrasts to make this point. In the first two pages of this short story, Oshiro makes it clear that relations were uneasy between the Americans and Okinawans. When the narrator of this story attempts to have charges filed against a soldier who raped his daughter, he learns that despite their amicable and generous nature, Americans were hardly the friends of the Okinawan people. The unnamed narrator goes to an American he has known socially for assistance in his effort to seek justice for his daughter in the U.S.-operated judicial system. The American, a military intelligence officer, refuses because it might be divisive and jeopardize American-Okinawan friendship. After the meeting, the narrator passes a street banner displaying, in English, a toast Commodore Matthew Perry made in the 1850s at a state dinner after the first contact between Okinawans and Americans:

> *Prosperity to Ryukyuans*
> *and may Ryukyuans and Americans*
> *always be friends.*

This quote rings hollow after the narrator's talk with his American "friend." Oshiro's use of irony is apparent when the narrator visits the site where his daughter was raped, describing it as beautiful and scenic. He also uses this literary device in his general depiction of Americans. Despite the unjust nature of their legal system, they are a friendly lot, responsible for postwar recovery and the improvement in the Okinawan standard of living. This friendship is superficial, however, and the rape shatters that thin veneer. This story is more than a subtle anti-American diatribe. Oshiro also shows the ambiguity Okinawans felt toward Japan. The narrator dismisses George Kerr's *Okinawa: The History of an Island People* as a justification for U.S. policy since it emphasizes the differences between Japan and Okinawa. He argues that Okinawa is part of Japan but finds himself using language that often refers to Japan and Okinawa as distinct and separate entities. A reviewer in the *Okinawa Taimusu* called this account an "astute observation and, in a way, acute criticisms of present-day Okinawa."[60]

Another literary work depicting this ambiguity was Higashi Mineo's *Okinawa no shonen* (Child of Okinawa), in which the author utilized sexual issues to explore the influence of the occupation on Okinawan life. The protagonist of this story, set in early 1950s, is Tsuneyoshi, an idealistic boy in his early teens. Tsuneyoshi's parents run a bar/brothel catering to American servicemen. The boy is appalled that his parents are so concerned about making money that they never consider the moral implications of their business. Higashi's portrayal of Americans was less than positive, but his central character gains empathy for the foreigners as he discovers his own sex drive. Tsuneyoshi's real resentment and disappointment is with his parents—Okinawans who prostitute themselves physically and morally. Higashi was upset not so much at the Americans or the occupation, but at what Okinawans let foreign rule do to themselves.[61]

This ambiguity also found expression in contemporary Okinawan journalism. The editorial positions of the two Japanese-language newspapers, the *Ryukyu Shimpo* and the *Okinawa Taimusu*, favored the eventual, gradual reversion of the island to Japan. According to this view, there was a difference between the presence U.S. bases and American administration. The newspapers supported U.S. foreign policy in East Asia and tolerated the military bases on the island. This position contrasted to the view of left wing political activists who wanted an immediate end to U.S. rule and the removal of all American bases. The editors of the papers declared that reversion required a step-by-step process that would take time. As a result, the papers favored liberalization of travel restrictions, the use of Japanese passports, the flying of the Japanese national flag on fishing boats, the direct election of the chief executive of the Ryukyu Islands, and the repeal of foreign investment laws that prohibited the introduction of Japanese capital as preliminary steps proceeding reversion.[62]

American officials looked at these newspapers the same way the journalists looked at them—with conflicting views. Although military administrators appreciated the editorial support of these publications, they saw the papers advancing positions that would weaken U.S. control of the island. Caraway's contradictory views of Okinawan journalism was a good expression of this ambiguity: "They [Okinawan and Japanese reporters] were really quite friendly to me, personally, and to the American administration in general." He also observed that "the Okinawan Press was . . . at that time, very unfriendly to the military. That's what sold their tickets, they liked that part of it." His successor showed less ambivalence. "The local newspapers were controlled by individuals who were, I thought, generally friendly towards our administration," Watson said. "I would say that the press was . . . really quite helpful and useful. I found that none of their coverage was adverse."[63]

A series of issues related to nationality and citizenship came to the forefront and cut through the uncertain sentiment on the island just as Johnson and Unger arrived in their new positions. It was these issues and the 1970 deadline that forced major steps that would lead to reversion rather than changes in international affairs, such as the U.S. withdrawal from Vietnam. John Foster Dulles originally created the "residual sovereignty" concept to avoid just these problems. The ruling in *U.S. v. Shiroma*, a 1954 court case, appeared to confirm the ingenuity of Dulles's solution. In 1897 Ushi Shiroma was born in Okinawa but had lived in Hawaii since he was sixteen. In 1954 the forty-seven-year-old Shiroma refused to register as a resident alien, claiming that the peace treaty had made him a U.S. national even though he was not a citizen. The U.S. attorney in Hawaii and the Ninth Circuit Court disagreed. The court credited Shiroma with a "novel defense" but held that Japan retained sovereignty over the Ryukyu Islands. Okinawans were neither U.S. citizens nor nationals.[64]

The Shiroma case actually complicated legal issues on the island. Who would issue passports for Okinawans? What was the registry of Okinawan fishing boats? Which flag would these vessels fly? Since these instruments were tools of sovereignty, the court decision ruled out the use of U.S. documents and the American flag. So the real issue was, could the Okinawans use instruments of Japanese sovereignty? Americans believed not. These items were representations of administration, and the United States was the governing power for the Ryukyus. The United States now faced just the situation Dulles had hoped to avoid. Moreover, these legal issues quickly became supercharged with nationalist sentiment. In 1959 Lieutenant General Booth, the high commissioner, had warned visiting Congressman Walter Judd that nationalism was a threat to the bases on the island.[65] Although these issues involved complex legal questions between the United States and Japan, they also provoked strong nationalist sentiment among Okinawans.

When he arrived in Tokyo, Johnson decided to use these issues to reduce the pressure for reversion. The first subject for resolution was the flag issue. This dispute had stimulated the most emotion and public sentiment, since it touched the lives of almost all Okinawans. The United States had always allowed Okinawans to fly the Japanese flag above private residences but, in the late 1950s, displaying the flag above schools and public buildings during holidays became a point of contention. Prime Minister Kishi discussed the matter with Eisenhower when they had met in 1957. The president refused the request because of strenuous objections from the Pentagon. Nevertheless, public sentiment in Japan and Okinawa refused to accept this judgment, forcing reconsideration in 1960 after Ambassador MacArthur recommended that the United States take another look at the problem. President Kennedy finally gave permission in 1961.[66]

In 1966 the flag issue moved on to the ensign that Okinawan fishing boats flew. Before either Johnson or Unger arrived in their posts, Yasui Ken of the prime minister's office asked Watson to allow Okinawan boats to fly the Japanese flag. Progress on the issue predated Johnson's arrival, but it was a perfect opening exercise for the new ambassador and high commissioner. Johnson believed in "quiet diplomacy," which he defined as "discussing and working out between the two governments solutions to problems while they are still small and not permitting them to get large and doing so in as quiet a manner as possible." Unger also wanted to settle the flag issue. "My tenure could be capsulized as a continuing race between the ever-increasing political momentum of the Okinawans for reversion and the efforts of the United States to provide meaningful palliatives which might delay or slow down the timetable for reversion." The flag issue channeled energy away from reversion. The solution that the Americans settled on was clever. Okinawan boats would fly a flag divided into two parts. The lower half of the design was the Japanese flag and above that was a pennant with the word "Ryukyus" printed in red English and kanji characters. At a press conference during a visit to Okinawa, Johnson carefully explained the policy: "this is simply a change in the design of the flag which Ryukyuan-registered vessels will fly. It does not in any other way affect the status of the vessels with respect to the Government of the Ryukyus or the Government of Japan."[67]

Nationality problems were only preparatory exercises for Johnson and Unger. Johnson decided to initiate action on the election of the Okinawan chief executive. Indirect election had not reduced the public's interest in electing its leader. A reporter for the *New York Herald Tribune* had observed back in 1962 that greater self-government would help "still rising clamor for reversion to Japan." Steinberg, in his second series for *The Washington Post,* disagreed. He reported that American and Okinawan leaders agreed that reversion would be the issue in a direct election of the chief executive. Both groups agreed that the political Left could win such a contest with a strong campaign for immediate reversion if it could put its divisions aside. As a result, the Okinawan Teachers' Association, a vanguard of both the political Left and the reversion movement, insisted that Okinawans should have the privilege of choosing their own political officials with the ballot. "We insist on direct elections," Yara Chobyo, the president of the association said. "It's not unreasonable. The Americans taught us to want elections as the ABC of democracy." Americans found it hard to challenge this position in public. In private, though, they had a different reaction. "Direct election is a dream," Watson, the high commissioner, said. He feared the leftists would win an election, creating a situation similar to the rise and fall of Mayor Senaga. Unger, though, thought differently. After a meeting with the ambassador, he decided to support the idea. The general suspected that the legislature would not choose a new executive in 1968 because of the public's interest in direct elections. Having to appoint a chief executive or deal with a leaderless government were options he found untenable. Unger also agreed to make the proposal to Washington. It would be harder for bureaucrats to oppose the idea if it came from the high commissioner rather than the ambassador.[68]

Opinions in the military had slowly coalesced around the views of McNamara about reversion, but the bureaucracy in the Pentagon still opposed direct elections. Undersecretary of the Army David E. McGiffet sent a long message to Unger explaining current thinking in Washington in an effort to get the general to drop his support for direct elections. "There is a strong feeling here on all sides that Japan must share a greater part of the burden and responsibility for Asian security and development than it has to date and that is the quid pro quo which we should exact from the Japanese before we alter our present position on Okinawa," McGiffet wrote. The election of the chief executive was "one of the few important palliatives remaining to us and should therefore be used with great caution; second, the granting of direct elections might be taken as a significant step towards reversion, thereby aggravating pressures in both Okinawa and Japan." This argument had little impact on Unger. "When I was there, Okinawa was nothing more than an Oriental form of irredentism that had existed in other places in the world. People just don't like to have a foreign power administering them, no matter how benevolent it is," he told Army War College students after his retirement. "It was hard for people in Washington, some of the most senior military people to understand this. They weren't there. They didn't understand it." The senior interdepartmental group studying the proposal supported the idea and sent the suggestion to the White House. On February 1, 1968, Lyndon Johnson put his name to Executive Order 11395, and with that act the Okinawans had the right to conduct a direct election.[69]

In the mid-1960s, the United States and Japan slowly began the process of reunifying Okinawa with Japan. Reversion started to move forward only because of Sato's initiative and the able work of a new American ambassador. In order to preserve the U.S.-Japanese alliance, both men knew that they had to have a resolution of the issue before 1970. The two set out to reach that objective, even though one of them soon had to give up his job.

CHAPTER 8

Reversion, 1967–69

In an off-the-record White House press briefing, U. Alexis Johnson stated, "Without being rhetorical or oratorical, I think it is fair to say that this is an historic occasion."[1] The occasion he was referring to was the release of a joint communiqué between Pres. Richard M. Nixon and Prime Minister Sato announcing the return of Okinawa to Japanese administration. Johnson had good reason to be proud of the events transpiring on the White House lawn. As the U.S. ambassador in Tokyo and then as the undersecretary of state for political affairs in the Nixon administration, he was the key player in the events leading up to this statement and a settlement of the Okinawa issue. This agreement met the needs of both countries. Japan recovered a conquered province while the United States preserved an alliance critical to the international system that made it the dominant power in the Pacific. The return of these islands ensured peace and stability in the region. In one sense, reversion was part of the American effort under the Nixon Doctrine to disperse defense responsibilities to other Asian nations as the United States began reducing its presence in Asia. Just as important to American interests, reversion also guaranteed that the United States would remain in the Pacific, assuring other nations in the region still concerned about a resurgent Japan.[2]

When diplomatic negotiations began on reversion, it was the Japanese government that initiated the talks. On July 15, 1967, Foreign Minister Miki Takeo raised the subject of the Bonins while discussing Okinawa. He said it was "common sense to recognize a difference" between the two island chains. Johnson agreed but did not concede the point, knowing that Washington was unprepared to make a decision regarding the Bonins. He also believed that any action on these islands could increase demands for the return of Okinawa.[3]

When he relayed Japan's request to Secretary of State Rusk, Johnson advised returning the island chain for the sake of U.S.-Japanese relations. "If the Bonins are returned, I am inclined to believe it will strengthen the hands of those in both Japan and Okinawa advocating faith and confidence in [the] U.S." Privately, he thought the Japanese were using the Bonins to stall for time. As long as war raged in Vietnam, the Americans would need the bases on Okinawa. If the United States returned the island, administration would formally involve Japan in the war. This was an entanglement Johnson believed the Japanese government wanted to avoid. Miki later confirmed Ambassador Johnson's suspicion when he told the American diplomat that he hoped the return of the Bonins would satisfy public sentiment.[4]

Discussions soon began within the U.S. government on the Bonins and U.S.-Japanese relations. Members of the Johnson administration wrote memos on this topic in the late summer and early fall. They discussed Japan and the island issue at a formal NSC meeting at the White House on August 30 and at a smaller gathering of foreign policy advisors at the president's Texas ranch on November 4. The most important views in the administration belonged to Lyndon Baines Johnson. There were two major elements to his thinking: First, he believed the security alliance was one-sided; American military forces provided Japan with national security for free, and Japan gave nothing in return. Second, Johnson wanted the Japanese to take a more active role in world affairs, which might include providing troops for peacekeeping activities.[5]

Rostow, the national security advisor, recommended immediate action. He suggested returning the Bonins within a year and beginning

talks on Okinawa immediately. In return for the restoration of the islands, Rostow wanted the Japanese to increase their purchases of U.S.
goods, give more to the Asian Development Bank, and increase
significantly their economic aid to the United Nations. "In all of this, I
see the makings of a mutually advantageous package deal," he informed
the president.[6]

The issue had the Pentagon bureaucracy divided. The civilian leadership of the Defense Department had adopted the view of Robert
McNamara—the United States should use the reversion of Okinawa to
get the Japanese to increase their defense spending. McNamara, however, recognized and appreciated the support Sato had given the U.S. effort
in Vietnam, including a visit to Saigon, and believed the United States
should repay him by returning Iwo Jima. He told President Johnson: "You
should push the Japanese, but this [Iwo Jima] is not the issue. This will
only weaken Sato. That guy put his political future in his hands when he
went to Vietnam."[7]

The leaders of the uniformed services opposed the policy that
McNamara, their constitutional superior, advocated. On July 20 Gen. Earl
Wheeler, chairman of the Joint Chiefs, gave McNamara a memo that
opposed the return of either island chain. "Reversion of the Ryukyus to
the Japanese Government would weaken the U.S. strategic posture and
our military position in the Far East." The chiefs also went on record
against any action that would surrender Iwo Jima. "Also important is
the requirement to retain U.S. control over and freedom of action the
Bonin–Volcano Islands." Relations between McNamara and the military
services, to put it mildly, were poor at this time. The defense secretary
had shown contempt for military traditions and officers since he arrived
at the Pentagon, while Wheeler referred to his boss as Robert "Very
Strange" McNamara. "We think the proposal before the President goes
too far too fast, especially with regard to Chichi Jima and Iwo Jima,"
Wheeler told Johnson at the latter's ranch. The military saw a decision
about Iwo Jima as a precedent for Okinawa. Although the Bonin Islands
were the topic of discussion at the NSC meeting in August, Gen. Harold
Johnson, army chief of staff and a survivor of the Bataan Death March,
argued that the United States needed unrestricted use of Okinawa.
McNamara disagreed. The B-52 incident in 1965 (mentioned earlier) indicated that American use of the island was less than the letter of the
law stated. The navy, however, was the biggest obstacle to the islands'

return. Wheeler represented naval opinion at the Johnson ranch meeting, arguing that the submarine fleet needed the island as a forward storage facility for nuclear weapons. The navy also claimed that the islands might become important as a base if American forces were pushed out of Japan, Okinawa, Taiwan, and the Philippines. "I thought this was nonsense," Alexis Johnson bluntly recalled. "If we were driven from the rest of the Pacific, we certainly could not hold the Bonins or mount a worthwhile counteroffensive from this insignificant cluster of rocks."[8]

There was less division in the State Department about the islands. Ambassador Johnson critically assessed affairs between the United States and Japan when he arrived in Tokyo. "Relations between our two countries were still at an immature and unequal stage, not befitting the great nation Japan had become." He also believed that "many aspects of the relations between our countries needed bringing up to date."[9] He warned the president and the National Security Council that the Japanese found it "unnatural" to have Japanese territory controlled by an American general. The islands, he said, were the last unresolved matter between the two countries and were quickly becoming a major issue in Japanese politics. "We had to devise a solution to Okinawa that would allow us to maintain real and enduring military effectiveness," he recalled in his memoirs. He also believed the United States should force Japan to make some hard decisions about its national security strategy. "The Japanese were trying to have their cake and eat it too, taking the benefits of American military protection without acknowledging they really wanted it or assuming any concomitant responsibilities." Johnson wanted the Japanese government to affirm the value of the security treaty to Japan. "Our bases would be useless unless Japan fully supported our having and using them." He often got the impression that the Japanese thought they were doing the United States a favor by allowing American bases in the archipelago. "If we were going to maintain any effective American military presence in Japan the Japanese had to want it, freely, openly, and out of a conviction that it served Japan's interest."[10]

Rusk shared many of these views but rejected doing anything about Okinawa. In 1951 he had urged Dulles to return Okinawa to Japan, but Rusk had reservations about doing so in 1967. He was reluctant to restrict the military's use of the island while war raged in Vietnam. More importantly, he wanted the Japanese to decide how they would fulfill their security obligations before the United States agreed to return the Ryukyus.

During a September meeting with Miki, the secretary took a hard line. Miki proposed that a rough deadline be established for returning the islands. Rusk rejected this suggestion out of hand. Iwo Jima, however, was a different matter. The island did not figure into American strategy, and he was willing to return the Bonins, hoping it would take some of the pressure off the Okinawa question. He appreciated Sato's support for U.S. foreign policy. "He's the most pro-American Prime Minister Japan has had since World War II," he informed the president. "Besides, we are only a squatter on the Bonins."[11]

All of Lyndon Johnson's key foreign policy advisors agreed that the United States needed to return the Bonin and Ryukyu Islands. They also agreed that Japan should give something for the islands and take on more international obligations. "It was important that they go out in the world, instead of being in a tight bilateral relationship with us," Rostow explained.[12] There was no agreement on what exactly the United States should demand, though. The American failure to settle on a price ensured that the United States would get little beyond a continuation of the status quo. Continuity, however, was what the Americans wanted most of all.

After the administration reached consensus, Ambassador Johnson began negotiating with Miki on the return of the Bonins. He concluded that Miki was positioning himself to challenge Sato for the LDP presidency and was hoping to use reversion to that end. According to Ambassador Johnson, the foreign minister constantly delayed negotiations, challenged wording, and twisted public information to make it appear as if he, not the prime minister, was the sole defender of Japan's interests against the American colossus.[13]

One issue that nagged at Ambassador Johnson was the potentially negative domestic American reaction to returning the sites of two bloody battles. Just before his departure for Washington to attend the Johnson-Sato summit meeting, he had an opportunity to alleviate this concern. Senators John Sparkman of Alabama and John Tower of Texas, both of whom served on the Senate Armed Services Committee, as well as Gen. Matthew B. Ridgway, the former commander of Allied occupation forces in Japan, were in Tokyo as official U.S. representatives for the funeral of Yoshida Shigeru. Johnson met with them and explained developments from the Japanese point of view, and the senators assured the ambassador that they foresaw no domestic problems. Aware of Tower's service in the Pacific during World War II, Johnson pointedly asked the Texan if returning Okinawa or Iwo Jima might cause any problems in the United States. The senator reassured him once again.[14]

Despite all his caution, Johnson made a promise that nearly brought negotiations to an end. The Marine Corps had built a small memorial atop Iwo Jima's Mt. Suribachi. Concerned about American public opinion, he told Ridgway, Sparkman, and Tower that the landmark would remain after reversion. In making this pledge, Johnson assumed that this memorial was similar to the one near Arlington National Cemetery. Only when he visited the island did he realize the mistake he had made. Instead of finding an Arlington-type statue, he discovered only a small bronze plaque. The official marine monument was down at an unattended U.S. cemetery. Yet Johnson felt bound to deliver on his promise to the senators. He went as far as to suggest to Miki that the entire island be designated as a war memorial and retained by the United States. Miki said this idea was an unacceptable solution. He understood American sentiment about the island and was willing to do something about the situation, but Miki warned Johnson that American retention of Iwo Jima would "blunt" reversion. He also suggested that Johnson find an alternative to the flag. Johnson refused to back down and the issue festered. In December, Rusk told Johnson that Iwo Jima was not a designated battlefield monument and the Marine Corps would maintain the cemetery in accordance with the arrangements in the Japanese peace treaty. In essence, the flag was a nonissue. Still, Johnson wanted some type of banner but was also trying to find a way to retreat while honoring his pledge. He soon contacted Lt. Gen. Victor "Brute" Krulak, Marine Corps commander for the Pacific, and asked him if a bronze flag might be added to the existing plaque at the top of the mountain. Krulak told him that it would actually be much easier to maintain than a cloth one. Thus, with the ranking marine in the Pacific supporting Johnson's compromise to a nonissue, the matter came to an end.[15]

Prime Minister Sato watched the Johnson-Miki negotiations and worried, knowing that Miki wanted to replace him. Wary of his foreign minister, Sato circumvented formal diplomatic channels. To ensure that his meeting with Lyndon Johnson produced an acceptable communiqué, he sent one of his advisors, Wakaizumi Kei, a professor of international relations at Kyoto University, to negotiate with Rostow a few days before he arrived in the American capital. Wakaizumi was a smart choice, because he had talked with the president before and enjoyed a close friendship with Rostow, who was the godfather of Wakaizumi's son. Sato was well aware of the Rostow-Wakaizumi relationship, as he mentioned in Wakaizumi's letter of introduction. Rostow proudly noted that negotiations through this channel never became public or leaked to the news media.[16]

Wakaizumi and Rostow met three times in late October and early November of 1967. They agreed that the United States would return the Bonins as quickly as technical issues allowed. Wakaizumi then made a proposal that, in Ambassador Johnson's words, threw Washington "into something of an uproar." He wanted the communiqué to commit the United States to Okinawa's return "within a few years." Rostow said timing was difficult because it was impossible to predict the length of the Vietnam War, Chinese actions, or "Japan's progress towards its responsibility in the field of security." Wakaizumi agreed with these points. He told Rostow he had argued with Sato against offering the proposed language, but the prime minister believed public interest and political pressure in Japan now demanded reversion. The return of the Bonins would not been seen as much of an achievement. Wakaizumi suggested to Rostow that the United States could use the vague language to delay reversion until as late as 1980. In a written statement that Wakaizumi left with Rostow, he declared: "We don't mind as long as we have some prospects of the reversion so that we could say to one million Ryukyu people as Japanese 'Wait until 1975, 78, 80, and in the meanwhile we have a lot to do to smooth the way for the actual reversion.' Then, I am sure they will [be] patient to wait, and cooperate with Americans to maintain the effective bases there." When Sato's plane landed in Seattle, Ambassador Johnson was waiting for him. He informed the prime minister that the "within a few years" wording stood little chance of gaining presidential approval. The next day this supposedly secret meeting was front-page news in Japan.[17]

Johnson's prediction was wrong. At Sato's request, the prime minister and the president had a private meeting in the Oval Office on November 14 with only an interpreter present—Sato wanted Miki excluded when he made his proposal. When Sato suggested the "within a few years" phrase, President Johnson was cautiously receptive. Immediately after the meeting, he grabbed his ambassador to Japan and dragged him into the Oval Office. The two Johnsons had a long meeting in which the president told his ambassador about Sato's proposal.[18]

The president's primary concern was congressional reaction to the proposed language. Administration officials had already addressed this issue, talking to a number of key senators and representatives about reversion. In addition, Senate Majority Leader Mike Mansfield had delivered a speech on the Bonins only two months before in Japan, during which he said: "There are no major U.S. military installations there and strategic considerations do not appear to be involved in any significant way. In sum, there would appear to be no major blocks—at least I know of none—to the restoration of the Bonins."[19]

Despite this sentiment and the initiative of his staff, President Johnson still remained concerned; in particular, the reaction of Sen. Richard Russell of Georgia, the chairman of the Armed Services Committee, particularly worried him. The senator recorded that administration officials visited him five times on November 14. His notes indicate he was reluctant to see reversion take place but was hardly an active opponent: "I did not stop but gave them pause and caused revision of plans for reversion." Assistant Secretary of State for Far Eastern Affairs William P. Bundy reported to the president that Russell "did not think well" of including a time element in the communiqué. Since Johnson wanted Russell's support, he had the administration arrange a dinner meeting between the senator and Sato, with McNamara, Rusk, and Ambassador Johnson in attendance. However, nothing that was said that evening changed Russell's mind, and the president gave up on making any further efforts to return Okinawa in the immediate future. (It is important to note, though, that the senator never had overt approval authority over Okinawa as John Welfield suggested in *An Empire in Eclipse*.) The next day, the Americans and Japanese reached a compromise: Japan would express a desire for Okinawa's return "within a few years" while the United States would agree to Okinawa's reversion without committing to any date. Bundy reported that Senators Mansfield, Russell, and J. William Fulbright of Arkansas, chairman of the Senate Foreign Relations Committee, found this language acceptable.[20]

Johnson and Sato met one last time. During this meeting the president hit his guest with the price for the return of the Bonins: an increase in economic aid to Indonesia and a Japanese-built educational television system for South Vietnam. Sato gave his host an evasive response, which he did not intend as a promise. Johnson detected this ambivalence and immediately announced this "deal" after their private meeting. Outmaneuvered, Sato sat silently and listened.[21]

But Lyndon Johnson had a little joke at Alexis Johnson's expense first. When the prime minister and president joined the assembled delegations in the Cabinet Room, Johnson announced that he could not accept the language in the proposed statement. According to the ambassador, "absolute silence gripped the room for thirty seconds." The president's words crushed him; his mind raced trying to figure a way to salvage the meeting and avoid a public confrontation. The president then directed his next comment to the prime minister: "I think my Ambassador to Japan just had a heart attack, and I think we had better relieve his mind." The two had actually reached complete agreement and the room burst out into relieved laughter.[22]

After leaving the White House, Sato went to the National Press Club to deliver a speech on the importance of the islands to U.S.-Japanese relations. In Japanese, he spoke of the work still waiting: "The early return of the Ryukyus to Japan, I am certain, would vindicate itself in establishing the relationship between our two countries, Japan and America, on an even firmer foundation and would contribute towards the achievement of the security and peace throughout the whole of Asia." According to a reporter for the *St. Louis Post Dispatch*, he delivered this passage emphatically. The journalist also noticed that Sato omitted the section expressing support for the American war, allowing his interpreter to read that part in English. The prime minister then tended to ceremonial duties; he went to Arlington National Cemetery and laid wreaths on the graves of the Unknown Soldier, John F. Kennedy, and John Foster Dulles.[23]

Reaction to the summit was reserved. Editorials in several American newspapers expressed disappointment that the United States had not returned Okinawa. "The longer such a negotiation is put off, the more our country will be playing into the hands of the extremists and their relentless drive to poison Japanese-American relations and undermine free Asia's security," declared an editorial in the Washington *Evening Star.* Japanese editorials called the agreement a mediocre success or an out-and-out failure. Okinawans, however, were quite happy; reversion was next.[24]

On November 11, 1968, the Okinawans forced reunification to the front of the political agenda between the United States and Japan. The Ryukyus held the first popular election for the office of chief executive. Much as American leaders had feared, the political Left had unified behind the candidacy of Yara Chobyo of the Okinawa Teachers' Association. Since Yara and the association were two major centers of power on the left side of the Okinawan politcal spectrum, officers in the military intelligence branch of the U.S. Civil Administration had long been trying to find ways to break them. An ad hoc committee in the Civil Administration studied the situation. The committee recommended that the best way to control the Teachers' Association would be to have the Okinawan legislature pass a bill prohibiting political activity on the part of teachers, as was done in Japan, and support the creation of rival organizations. The committee recommended against revoking the organization's charter or arresting its members. The Teachers' Association, like any large organization, had a small group of members that played a large role in determining the activities of the group than the bulk of its membership. Intelligence officers believed that the leaders of the association were advancing political issues and views that lacked the support of the majority of the organization's membership. As a result, the Civil Administration covertly supported the formation of splinter organizations. Money was funneled to these organizations from local businessmen and the Okinawa Liberal Democratic Party (OLDP). Sensing the threat to its existence and power, the Teachers' Association used picketers and peer pressure to break up organizational meetings of the splinter groups. As a result, Yara went into the election with his power base intact.[25]

The contest gave the Okinawan voters two clear and distinctly different choices. The candidate of the governing OLDP was Nishime Junji. A former mayor of Naha and member of the legislature, he had extensive administrative experience and support among the majority parties in Okinawa and Japan. He was a former student of Yara. Nishime favored a gradual approach to reversion, but Yara called for immediate reunification with the homeland. In an analysis of the contest two days before the casting of ballots, the high commissioner reported the "race is too close to permit any reasonably accurate judgment on who will be a winner." Both candidates had a number of prominent Japanese political figures make campaign appearances, but Unger believed that their "impact of Okinawan voters has been slight." The general also observed that Yara was the candidate with the better-organized campaign. So, he was hardly surprised when Yara won the election with 53.4 percent of the vote.[26]

American and Japanese observers clearly saw the election as a watershed. Unger interpreted the outcome as a popular mandate for reversion. A year before, Wakaizumi had told Rostow that the actual return of the island could be delayed until as late 1980. Now, a NSC staff member informed Rostow that such delay was no longer possible. "The Yara victory can only be read as a vote to speed up reversion." In Tokyo, Kimura Toshio, chief cabinet secretary, agreed. On the other hand, the secretaries general of the LDP, both socialist parties, and the Clean Government Party warned Yara to pursue his goals with moderation. The U.S. effort to use the direct election of the chief executive as a way to deflect public attention away from reversion had backfired. Now, the pressure for the return of the island was even greater.[27]

In both countries, Okinawa began to grab more attention. In Japan the issue had grown significantly in importance since the Johnson-Sato summit meeting. Sato's new foreign minister, Aichi Kiichi, proclaimed 1969 to be the "year of Okinawa." An emotional issue, Okinawa, along with student riots over the implementation of the University Management Bill, was bleeding political support from Sato. There was open grumbling from opposition parties and rival factions in the Liberal Democratic Party about holding new parliamentary elections. If the security treaty was going to be in effect after 1970, or at least remain viable, the United States had to return the Ryukyu island chain. Returning the islands was the only thing Americans could do to influence domestic politics in Japan. While Okinawa was a critical issue in Japanese politics, such was not the case in the United States. William Loeb, publisher of the Manchester *Union Leader,* made a brief effort to make Okinawa a campaign issue during the New Hampshire primary in 1968, but little came of it.[28] Loeb's failure is important. Had he succeeded in making Okinawa a political issue, it would have been along lines of resisting reversion, making a diplomatic resolution much more difficult than was otherwise the case. American journalists, however, started to write more and more articles about the island.[29] In retirement from government service, Reischauer called Okinawa "an explosive problem of great magnitude and great danger to our country." Reischauer exaggerated a bit, Okinawa was not as important as ending the Vietnam War, the status of Berlin, or a nuclear nonproliferation treaty, but the essence of his message was true—Okinawa was a problem of real significance for the United States. Armin H. Meyer, the new ambassador in Tokyo, succinctly expressed this view in a telegram to Washington: "As Okinawa goes, so goes Japan."[30]

It was in this climate that Richard M. Nixon came into office with conflicting views about Japan. One aspect of Nixon's thinking was that he wanted the Japanese to take a more active role in international affairs.

As early as 1953 he had stated that Japan should rearm. (He made this remark at the request of Secretary of State John Foster Dulles). His biographer Stephen E. Ambrose wrote that "Japanese rearmament would become a standard Nixon theme for the next twenty years." In 1966 another biographer, Jonathan Aitken, witnessed a private meeting attended by Nixon, former British prime minister Sir Alec Douglas-Home, and former British foreign minister Selwyn Lloyd. Aitken called Nixon's comments on world affairs "dazzling" and "commanding." During the meeting, he said Japan was on the verge of becoming an economic superpower and the West had to make an effort to improve relations. He made much the same remarks in public. "Looking toward the future," he wrote in *Foreign Affairs*, "one must recognize that it simply is not realistic to expect a nation moving into the first rank of major powers to be totally dependent for its own security on another nation, however close the ties." He also believed Japan should develop a nuclear capacity. In a pre-election interview with a reporter from the *Asahi Shimbun*, he directly linked an increase in Japanese armament to reversion. These early views would soon coalesce as the Nixon Doctrine. According to this policy, the United States would pursue a more multilateral foreign policy and seek to have Asian nations assume more of the burden for their own defense. A scenario in which reversion forced the Japanese to assume more of the responsibility for its own defense burden was easy to imagine in 1969.[31]

The principle of the Nixon Doctrine clashed with another element in the new president's thinking about Japan. He still thought of the country as a valuable American asset that required careful attention to keep it from turning on the United States. As a result, Okinawa was in many ways a bad test of the new Nixon Doctrine. A continued American military presence on the island assured many nations in the Pacific that Japan would remain unarmed, which assured stability in the region. He expressed this view publicly and privately during his publicity drenched trip to China in 1972. These concerns undercut the desire to have the Japanese become more active in world affairs. As long as U.S. bases remained in Okinawa and metropolitan Japan, there was no reason for a greater burden on the part of the Japanese. Although Nixon would achieve a settlement on Okinawa that serviced basic American interests, he was confused about his own goals and that limited his effectiveness.[32]

Nixon made a number of good tactical decisions about Japan, including the appointment of talented and knowledgeable individuals. He made a spot for U. Alexis Johnson in his administration, which allowed the diplomat to remain the central figure in the Okinawa negotiations. John Welfield, in *An Empire in Eclipse*, argued that two NSC staff holdovers from the Johnson administration played the key roles in formulating reversion policy, but the diplomatic records make it clear that Alexis Johnson was the principal player.[33] The reason for his influence is simple. The president-elect trusted him and said so using that very word.[34] As a lawyer for Pepsi-Cola, Nixon had visited Tokyo in 1967. While there, the former vice president had lunch and a long conversation with Johnson. The ambassador found that he and Nixon shared similar views on Asia. Nixon firmly believed that Japan was becoming an economic superpower in its own right and deserved respect and equal treatment from the United States. Johnson's treatment of Nixon did not differ from that he accorded other distinguished American visitors, but it made a lasting impression on a man who distrusted bureaucracy in general and the Foreign Service in particular. After Nixon appointed his old friend William Rogers as secretary of state and selected Henry A. Kissinger of Harvard University to be his national security advisor, the secretary-designate asked Johnson to take the position of undersecretary of state for political affairs. Johnson was reluctant—he liked Tokyo and did not want to return to the grind of fourteen-hour days—but eventually agreed out of loyalty to the Foreign Service. He was the senior officer in the service and believed he had a duty to accept the senior career position.[35]

Kissinger, Nixon's closest foreign policy advisor, also understood the importance of the Okinawa issue. Edwin Reischauer was a major influence on him. Kissinger admitted, "When I first came into office, there was no major country I understood less than Japan." Just before the inauguration, though, Reischauer sent him a four-page memo on Japan. The former ambassador warned Kissinger that "this Japanese irredenta is rapidly mounting to explosive proportions" and recommended immediate reversion. These views fit well into Kissinger's global views. In his memoirs, he observed, "Important as Okinawa was strategically, our continuing occupation of it in the late sixties mortgaged our long-range relations with Japan."[36]

Work began on the Okinawa question almost immediately. Kissinger established an interagency study group to discuss Japan and Okinawa the day after Nixon's inauguration. It was also a subject at the NSC meeting held on the same day. Although Kissinger's contempt for the bureaucracy was legendary and Johnson later would savagely criticize him for ignoring the professionals in the State Department, the two of them, along with Nixon, were thinking alike on this issue. "For once," the presidential advisor remarked, "the United States government was united on an issue."[37]

The unity Kissinger fondly remembered stopped at the doors of the Pentagon. The military showed considerable reluctance about considering reversion. On March 8 Kissinger sent the president a JCS memo urging that the United States retain the right to store nuclear weapons in the Ryukyus. On March 18 he sent Nixon another memo—his own, this time—warning against delay. The political pressure in Japan was unstoppable. Increased agitation threatened the bases physically and risked the continued power of not only Sato but of the Liberal Democratic Party as well. Kissinger's view reflected a constant tendency on the part of American policymakers to project their understanding of American politics on to events in Tokyo. In the 1960s the LDP dominated Japanese political life. Even if one LDP faction fell into disrepute, the umbrella nature of the party made it impossible for groups to the left of political center to gain control of the government; if Sato fell from power, another LDP faction, not the Socialist or Communist parties, would replace him. Kissinger's ignorance of the political situation in Tokyo actual helped him in the bureaucratic struggle with the military, as strange as that may seem. He had essentially framed the issue as an "either-or" decision; the United States had to pick between Okinawa and Japan. Johnson had long talks with the Joint Chiefs trying to make them realize that Okinawa must be returned. The only question was whether it would take place in a manner that helped or hurt the United States. During these meetings, JCS chairman Earl Wheeler insisted that the military retain unrestricted free use of the islands. The chiefs said they accepted reversion, but there was little real difference between their new stand and the position they had taken earlier. They still wanted the right to store nuclear weapons and unrestricted use of the islands in the defense of Korea, Taiwan, and Vietnam. "It was difficult to imagine what areas we would want to defend from Okinawa other than those specified," responded Kissinger.[38]

Okinawa was the focus of an April 30 National Security Council meeting. The study Kissinger instructed the interagency group to prepare was ready. The paper declared, "Okinawan reversion is the most serious and potentially disruptive issue facing the United States and Japan." Postwar relations between the two countries had served U.S. interests well, "particularly in the provision of forward defense bases and the assurance that Japan's actual and potential power is primarily available to friendly, rather than hostile, forces." The paper stated that Okinawa reversion would eventually lead to one of three outcomes: the status quo, a full collective security partnership, or a break that would lead to a neutral Japan. The second possibility, which would entail a Japanese nuclear ability, was not realistic politically, while the third probable outcome would clearly be detrimental to U.S. interests. As a result, the group advised the NSC to pursue reversion on a "homeland level" basis. The Joint Chiefs and their staff dissented from this recommendation, noting that reversion on a "homeland level" basis would mean the removal of all nuclear weapons and cost the U.S. flexibility. Johnson warned the NSC that the United States should be sensitive to Japanese opinions on nuclear weapons.[39]

Nixon apparently agreed and decided to split the difference between the diplomats and the soldiers. If Japan would agree to allow the unrestricted use of Okinawa for the defense of its three Asian neighbors, he would drop the insistence on nuclear storage. In making this decision, the president accepted that the Japanese were not going to take a more active role in international affairs, much less its own nuclear capabilities. Kissinger signed a National Security Decision Memo that declared, "We shall continue our present policy of encouraging moderate increases and qualitative improvements in Japan's defense efforts." Afraid, however, that the JCS would raise a political firestorm over the nuclear issue, Nixon did not inform them of his decision. Nevertheless, this decision became public knowledge on the front page of *The New York Times* in a story H. R. Haldeman, the White House chief of staff, called "complete and accurate." The article infuriated Nixon. The only mention he makes of Okinawa in his memoirs is a complaint over this leak. He fumed that the paper had revealed America's negotiating strategy, doing great damage. Haldeman's notes of a meeting he had with the president indicate Nixon was concerned more about the military reaction than that of the Japanese. Haldeman oversaw an investigation to find the person responsible, with no apparent results. Years later, Morton Halperin claimed responsibility for the leak, stating that he was acting on instructions to give the Japanese a reassuring signal so Sato would agree to a meeting. The notes in Haldeman's hand, however, make it clear that Halperin was acting without the knowledge of the president, making his claims of authorized action suspect. Johnson for his part worried more about the ruckus the Pentagon might raise over nuclear storage than the Japanese. Kissinger told Johnson not to worry, he would tell Wheeler to "pipe down" and have Secretary of Defense Melvin Laird "keep quiet." Johnson observed later, "Whatever he said to them, they never raised any fuss."[40]

The Joint Chiefs remained suspicious until the end. The transcript of a conference phone conversation among three of the chiefs makes it clear they had concerns about reversion. The generals agreed to tell Congress that reversion would cost the military some flexibility, though it would not be an insurmountable problem. "The Japs recognize the importance of Korea and Taiwan to their national defense so this may give us greater freedom than we now have, Alexis Johnson believes," Wheeler said. But he feared that U.S. administration of the island was the last guarantee of Japanese dependability. After reversion the Japanese would be free to terminate the alliance and remove American bases. The commandant of the Marine Corps, Gen. Leonard F. Chapman, concurred. As far as the military was concerned, Japan had yet to prove itself as an ally, a partner, or even a friend. The Joint Chiefs had a highly pessimistic and legalistic view of reversion. The accord returning the island to Japan changed everything and nothing. Japan would have administrative authority over the island, but the bases and the American presence that assured so many other nations in the Pacific and Asia that Japan would not threaten them again remained.[41]

Since Sato had already announced his negotiating strategy, *The New York Times* leak had little impact on Japanese planning. Sato had always said that he intended to achieve reversion in a way that would not weaken the U.S.-Japanese alliance. He remained coy and vague when asked if the United States could store nuclear weapons on the island after reversion. The foreign ministry took the position that Japan should make an exception to the Japanese ban on nuclear weapons in the case of Okinawa. Sato instructed the Okinawa Problems Study Council, a quasi-official group affiliated with his faction, to study the issue. The council created a special subcommittee called the Okinawa Base Problems Research Council under the leadership of Kusumi Tadao, a former captain in the Imperial Japanese Navy, to report on the matter. Kusumi's commission studied U.S. strategy in the Pacific, trying to determine if the Americans really needed nuclear storage rights on Okinawa. In November, 1968, the group found that the United States had no need for such privileges and Japan could seek reversion for Okinawa on a basis equal with the rest of the country. Sato's leak on this matter was much worse than Nixon's had been. A member of Kusumi's group worked for the Central Intelligence Agency and reported the findings of the commission to the Americans. The CIA quickly sent a report to the White House. The Kusumi report became public in March, and Sato made a vague statement in the Diet that he would try to reach an agreement that was acceptable to the Okinawan people. When reporters asked Chief Cabinet Secretary Hori Shigeru to explain, he said a nuclear-free Okinawa was the prime minister's goal. Actually, Hori's clarification of Sato's remarks was nothing more than a guess. He had no idea what Sato was trying to do but observed that the prime minister never said anything to him on the matter. He took this silence to be an approval.[42]

Talks on reversion began shortly afterward. "The Okinawa negotiations that followed . . . demonstrated how much nervous strain could have been avoided and how much more effectively our government would have functioned if the White House and the State Department had managed to achieve the same compatibility on other subjects," Kissinger wrote in his memoirs. At Johnson's suggestion, negotiations focused on the language of the communiqué to be issued at the end of Nixon-Sato summit, making their meeting in November the deadline for completion of these talks. Johnson hoped the joint statement would announce the return of Okinawa; the more tedious talks on technical matters would follow. Ambassador Armin Meyer conducted negotiations in Tokyo while Assistant Secretary of State for East Asian and Pacific Affairs Marshall Green chaired an interdepartmental working group and Johnson acted as a troubleshooter. Kissinger had little interest in Japan, took a back seat during the negotiations, and let Johnson administer the talks. He occasionally discussed matters with Ambassador Shimoda Takezo, but Vietnam was a more pressing concern, and Kissinger disliked visiting with Shimoda. "Every time the Japanese Ambassador has me to lunch he serves me Weiner Schnitzel," he complained.[43]

The major issue of these negotiations was Okinawa's strategic role. American negotiators wanted Japan to assume more responsibility for its own defense. They also wanted effective bases on Okinawa after its return. Sato had stated during his 1965 visit that Japan needed to increase its role, and now the U.S. negotiators wanted the Japanese to acknowledged this new policy publicly. The Americans used the nuclear storage question as a lever to obtain this statement. Sato made two efforts to break this deadlock. First, he had Wakaizumi, still serving as his private diplomat, publish an article in *Foreign Affairs*. This essay served two purposes. First and foremost, it was an attempt to influence attentive American public opinion. Wakaizumi warned readers about the damage reversion could do to U.S.-Japanese relations. "The Japanese and American governments," he wrote, "must deal with already explosive issues such as Okinawa and trade restrictions in such a way as to prevent public outcries which might compel renunciation of the treaty by Washington or Tokyo." The article also functioned as a public *aide-mémoire*. Wakaizumi outlined three possible future scenarios for Japanese national security: Japan could end the U.S. alliance and enlarge its military establishment, which would include a nuclear force; the U.S.-Japanese alliance could continue on a very narrow basis, with the United States only providing nuclear protection; or the alliance could be continued on the "basis of equality and mutual interest." The last option was the preference of the Japanese government. In this scenario, Japan would have four goals for the 1970s and beyond: maintain friendly relations with the United States; contribute personnel, material, and funding to United Nations peacekeeping efforts; improve relations with its Pacific and Asian neighbors; and "make positive contributions to building the foundations for peace and security, especially in Asia, though cooperation with the developing nations in achieving growth and prosperity." These ideas were the same principal elements in Sato foreign policy.[44]

Sato also sent Foreign Minister Aichi to Washington in September, hoping he would break the formal deadlock. Not much happened in these "somber" meetings. The Wakaizumi piece represented the type of thinking that Johnson had wanted to see, but the article could easily be dismissed as the musings of one college professor, not a policy statement of the Japanese government. The meetings did not go well. "Nothing has been settled, nothing has been decided," a Japanese diplomat told a *New York Times* reporter. Nodding in the direction of the White House, he said, "It's all up to him."[45]

Shortly after these meetings, the Commerce Department added another wrinkle to the negotiations. Japan should make commercial concessions on textile imports in return for Okinawa. Kissinger wanted nothing to do with this mundane economic issue, but he was in a difficult position. The

National Security Decision Memo he signed contained a vague sentence that negotiations with Japan would include discussions about "other commitments to be sought from Japan." Nixon decided that textile concessions would be one of those "other commitments" and ordered Kissinger to address the issue during the negotiations. In response to a Japanese offer to reform foreign investment laws, the president wrote: "This capital liberalization is not important to us politically. We have to get something on textiles." Kissinger freely admitted in his memoirs that he did not understand the economic issues involved. He needed help and turned to U. Alexis Johnson. The undersecretary suggested that Kissinger link nuclear storage to textile concessions. Kissinger did so, and concessions on textiles followed shortly thereafter. The Joint Chiefs' continuing demand that some right be retained to reintroduce nuclear weapons made negotiations even more complex. Finding some compromise that satisfied the chiefs and assured Japan proved difficult. Johnson and Kissinger, in the words of the latter, "came up with a formula as ingenious as it was empty." The communiqué would refer the nuclear issue to a clause in the 1960 treaty about consultations prior to emergencies. This satisfied both sides. Sato could say that Okinawa was on a basis with the rest of Japan and the United States would need permission to bring nuclear weapons back onto the island, which was not likely to be granted ever. Nixon, on the other hand, was in a position to assert that while nuclear weapons had been removed, it was still possible to store them again in an emergency situation. Two days before Sato's arrival, Wakaizumi returned and informed Kissinger that Sato was facing "super partisan" pressure on textiles and asked him if it could be delayed until the formal trade talks scheduled for later in Geneva. Wishing to be rid of the textile matter and afraid the entire agreement might come apart, Kissinger agreed.[46]

When Sato left Tokyo for Washington, firebomb-throwing mobs saw him off. Witnesses described seeing a "sea of fire." Japanese antiwar protesters greeted him in Washington, but the meeting between Sato and Nixon went well. Nixon accurately described the importance of the U.S.-Japanese bilateral relationship when he greeted Sato: "whether we have peace and prosperity and progress in the Pacific will depend more than anything else upon the cooperation of the United States and Japan."[47]

Sato and Nixon met on November 19 at the White House in a showdown of two political masters witnessed only by their interpreters, James J.

Wickel and Akatani Genichi. As the host, Nixon initiated the conversation and raised the issue of emergency consultations. He observed that wars developed faster than they had in the past and would require decisions in hours instead of days. He carefully put the burden of resolution on his guest, explaining that this issue was of great concern to the Senate, diplomatically raising the specter that there might be difficulties in getting confirmation of the treaty returning the Okinawa to Japan. Sato gave an evasive response, saying emergency consultation was a difficult issue. Nixon agreed and asked him for suggestions on how to resolve the issue. Forced into a difficult position, Sato moved first on the issue of nuclear weapons, which Nixon said was the "key point." The prime minister handed his host proposed language for the communiqué. Nixon had the initiative. The president read the Japanese text in silence and declared that while the wording was agreeable to him, his "people" would require "more precise" language. He then handed his guest an American proposal. After silently reading the document, Sato said the language in this text was unacceptable. Nixon suggested the two might find a compromise position that would be acceptable. The implication was clear—Sato had to make his proposal first. Nixon had, once again, put the burden on Sato. The president had the luxury of accepting or rejecting Sato's idea and being able to make his own suggestion. Sato handed him the secondary Japanese proposal, which included the term "prior consultation." After reading the proposal, Nixon simply nodded in agreement and then asked how and in what form these consultations would take place. He was giving his guest no quarter, but Sato was prepared. He said reversion might weaken the utility of military forces stationed on the island—he personally doubted such a development—but the United States would have to endure some reduction. Then he suggested that the two nations establish a "hot line" between Tokyo and Washington. Nixon loved the idea, agreed, and shook Sato's hand. Okinawa would once again be Japanese and nuclear free. "The Okinawa nuclear issue turned out well," Sato later recorded in his diary.[48]

The two released a communiqué that announced the return of Okinawa and set 1972 as the goal for the end of technical negotiations and the actual transfer of administrative authority. The statement also announced that U.S. bases would fall under terms of the security treaty and ruled out the introduction of nuclear weapons. When negotiations were finished, Nixon surprised Foreign Minister Aichi when he presented him with a package of Japanese cigarettes; Aichi had vowed not to smoke again until Okinawa was Japanese again.[49]

Inside the White House, immediately after Nixon and Sato finished presenting the communiqué on the White House Lawn, Presidential Press Secretary Ron Ziegler introduced Alexis Johnson to the White House press corps for an off-the-record background press conference. He explained the dual importance of the just-released joint communiqué and Sato's coming speech at the National Press Club before fielding questions, which mostly focused on defense issues and nuclear storage.[50]

Thirty minutes later, Sato gave his speech and declared Japan's new active role in Asia. "Japan in cooperation with the United States, will make its contribution to the peace and prosperity of the Asian-Pacific region and hence to the entire world." A few minutes later he became more specific, explaining how Japan would achieve this task while adhering to its war-renouncing constitution. "Since the United States plays the central role in preserving global peace and also holds great responsibility for the security of Asia, I believe that it is Japan, rather than the United States, that should take the leading role in such fields as economic and technical assistance towards the nation-building efforts of the Asian countries." Sato also acknowledged that the security alliance with the United States played an important role in regional stability: "In the real international world it is impossible to adequately maintain the security of Japan without international peace and security of the Far East."[51]

In January of 1970, Johnson explained the importance of Sato's remarks to a subcommittee of the Senate Foreign Relations Committee. "Hitherto, the Japanese Government, the Japanese people in general, have tended to take the attitude that their security arrangements with the United States had significance only insofar as the security of Japan itself was concerned. That Japan was not interested in nor concerned with the security of other areas nor should it in any way get involved with security of other areas." The speech itself was representative of a "new stage of thinking in Japan, and it certainly represented a new stage of public statement by any authoritative Japanese spokesman."[52]

American and Japanese reaction to the communiqué was positive on the whole. In the United States most papers ran wire-service articles on their front pages and the bulk of editorial commentary was positive. Other issues, however, dominated the diplomatic settlement. These topics included the vote against Supreme Court nominee Clement F.

Haynsworth, Jr., in the Senate and the funeral of Joseph Kennedy.[53] A few provincial papers ignored the event altogether.[54] In Japan, Sato used the euphoria over the return of the island to hold parliamentary elections and take large majorities in the Diet.

Perhaps the oddest reaction to the settlement came from none other than Richard Nixon. He had extremely mixed views about returning Okinawa. In February he released his first foreign policy report and explained the reasons for Okinawa's return. Although largely written by Kissinger, the passages on Okinawa reflect Nixon's writing style. Okinawa was restored to Japan in order to strengthen U.S.-Japanese relations, which were key to Pacific stability; "This was among the most important decisions I have taken as President." In private, however, he was less enthusiastic. As the United States prepared to launch attacks on Vietnamese bases in Cambodia, White House Chief of Staff H. R. Haldeman recorded in his diary that Nixon told Kissinger: "we have been praised for all the wrong things: Okinawa, SALT, germs, Nixon Doctrine. Now finally doing the right thing."[55]

The long process that returned Okinawa to Japan was a diplomatic triumph for Japan *and* the United States. Both countries profited from reversion. The Japanese had reunification with Okinawa while the Americans preserved the regional political order. In fact, maintaining the security alliance with Japan, which was the foundation of regional stability, was the main reason the United States had agreed to return the island. U. Alexis Johnson played the key role not only in conducting the diplomatic negotiations, but also in getting the U.S. government to accept the reality of the situation in Japan and Okinawa. The Okinawa matter was far from over, though. Both countries had to resolve many technical issues and get the agreement ratified, which proved to be quite difficult.

CHAPTER 9

Aftermath, 1969–72

An anti-American riot broke out on Okinawa during the night of December 19–20, 1970. Protesters opposed to the Nixon-Sato agreement started burning an American-owned car and two military police vehicles in the city of Koza. The mob then split into two groups. One group stormed the gates of Kadena Air Force Base, throwing rocks and bottles. The crowd battled air police and burned a school before the Americans pushed them back. The second group stormed through Koza, burning American cars. Two lines of Okinawan police and American MPs in riot gear confronted the mob as it approached a military housing complex. The police used tear gas to break up the crowd. The next day, the riots were front-page news in the United States.[1] This riot was only one example of the discontent with reversion. There were many in the United States, Japan, and Okinawa who opposed the Nixon-Sato reversion agreement. The most intense opposition came not from Americans, who still harbored concerns about Japan, but from Japanese and Okinawan reversion activists. An important political concession from the Nixon administration, the political skill of a largely unknown general, and Japanese nationalism eventually overcame the resistance.

Opposition in the United States came from three distinct sources. Veterans organizations were the first element to object to reversion. This position was no surprise, but these organizations had the potential to turn reversion into an emotional political issue. The Veterans of Foreign Wars (VFW) had gone on record against returning the islands years before (but remained silent on Iwo Jima) and restated its view in a letter to Nixon just before his meeting with Sato.[2] Much of this resistance was emotional. "We won the war, they lost," was the attitude most veterans had toward Japan on this issue. One veteran working hard against reversion was Lt. Gen. Paul Caraway, the former high commissioner. "This is a subject about which I have very strong feelings," he wrote. "However, I find it a very difficult one to put into a logical convincing dissertation." His frustration soon exploded into an angry outburst: "If Mr. John Foster Dulles had kept his mouth firmly closed at the signing of the treaty of peace, act. 3; the question would never have arisen."[3]

Another reason for veteran resistance was institutional and economic in nature. Okinawa Memorial Post 9723 was the largest VFW post in the world. The veterans operated a two-floor club with 150 slot machines that brought in $100,000 a month, and alcohol sales produced another $120,000. The American Legion also maintained an extremely profitable club on the island. Under American rule this revenue was tax-exempt, the clubs were open to the public, and the management did most of its purchasing through the military commissary system. These establishments competed against both on-base clubs and local businesses. For understandable reasons, the Japanese wanted these practices terminated after reversion. The army agreed since regulations prohibited logistical support for private businesses anyway. The VFW appealed to the White House, talking about veterans' votes and the 1972 election. The Nixon administration, however, was unreceptive. This effort to protect its own institutional and economic position, rather than oppose reversion politically, doomed the VFW effort.[4]

A second American group working against returning Okinawa was the U.S. business community on the island. While the diplomats negotiated, businessmen worried about the capital they had invested in Okinawa and their uncertain future in a Japanese prefecture. "The civilian community has generally accepted defeat," the business manager of the English-language newspaper told Caraway. "The reaction to the Nixon-Sato communiqué here has been one of apathy and has been generally accepted as 'we have had it.'"[5]

The American Chamber of Commerce became the focal point for business concern, but a split in the chamber's membership diluted its influence. A number of member firms were large corporations with interests in Japan. Although concerned about their operations in Okinawa, these companies often had larger investments in Japan, which limited their resistance. Small businesses were a second group in the chamber. The owners and operators of these firms had all their operations in Okinawa and were adamantly opposed to reversion for fear of financial ruin.[6]

The result of these divergent interests was a carefully worded chamber statement on reversion. The nine-point paper declared that "American business interests in Okinawa must be present as a specific item on the agenda of the reversion negotiations." The paper made it clear that the chamber did not oppose reversion but wanted the U.S. government to protect American businesses before handing the island over to the Japanese. The chamber sent this paper to President Nixon, cabinet officers, and members of Congress.[7]

The Chamber of Commerce was quite successful on this matter. American diplomats made this paper the basis for their positions during the technical negotiations that followed the Nixon-Sato summit. Business matters took up the most amount of time during these talks. American businessmen remained suspicious, however. These expatriate merchants thought the State Department was "soft," blamed the diplomats for reversion in the first place, and became very worried when a foreign ministry spokesman said the chamber's paper contained "absurd" demands.[8]

In early 1971 American businessmen decided to take action. In a meeting with the high commissioner, Lt. Gen. James Lampert, Chamber of Commerce officials expressed their concerns and warned that they would take other actions if necessary. Lampert figured this would be a letter-writing campaign to Congress; he was exactly right. The chamber not only wrote letters but also sent officials to Washington to talk with senators and representatives. These members of Congress, in turn, wrote Nixon and Kissinger. The letters were moderate in tone, informing the Nixon administration of a matter in which they were interested. The replies were equally measured, reassuring the senators and representatives that the administration was working to protect American business interests.[9]

The ultimate product of these efforts was the Aichi-Meyer letter. In this document, the Japanese government agreed to honor foreign ownership of land; permit continued operation of businesses then in Okinawa, provided they obtained proper Japanese licenses; allow Okinawan banks to keep dollar-based accounts; license foreign lawyers currently practicing in the prefecture, but nowhere else in Japan; and let doctors take the Japanese national medical examination in English. The Chamber of Commerce expressed its satisfaction with the negotiated arrangement. "We are now talking on a regular basis with all Japanese ministries concerned," the executive director of the Okinawan Chamber of Commerce told the Senate Foreign Relations Committee. "Their understanding of what Minister Aichi said in his letter is not always the same as ours. This makes us apprehensive—but we are talking, and progress is being made." He suggested, though, that the Senate wait on ratification until the Japanese Diet passed the needed supporting legislation, which is exactly what the upper house decided to do.[10]

Objections from veterans and businessmen converged with resistance from the third and final source, Congress. Opposition in the legislature was institutional rather than politically or policy oriented. Simply put, Congress demanded a say in reversion. The whole matter started when two U.S. senators publicly rejected reversion. In May, 1969, Virginia Democrat Harry F. Byrd, Jr., told the Senate, "So long as the United States maintains its significant role in the Far East, the continued unrestricted use of our bases on Okinawa is vital and fundamental." Three months later, Republican Minority Leader Everett M. Dirksen of Illinois told the readers of his syndicated newspaper column that reversion would be "inimical to American security. Okinawa is the only Pacific base that we own outright. It is not a protectorate of ours. We own it."[11]

These statements garnered little attention until Byrd proposed a resolution on November 4 that the president submit any agreement with Sato to the Senate as a treaty. Byrd openly admitted that he opposed reversion but also believed the Senate should have a say in the resolution of the Okinawa issue. Since "the treaty governing control over the Ryukyus was ratified by the Senate, it is my view that any changes in the treaty should come to the Senate for approval or disapproval." Most of his colleagues agreed. A day later the Senate approved the following one-sentence resolution by a vote of 63-14: "It is the sense of the Senate that any agreement or understanding entered into by the President to change the status of any territory referred to in Article 3 of the Treaty of Peace with Japan shall not take effect without the advice and consent of the Senate."[12] The editorial board of the Washington *Evening Star* regarded the vote as political posturing: "The Senate has its proper place in the conduct of foreign relations. But to bring up the matter at the end of negotiations and two weeks before Sato's visit is to trifle with a delicate and crucial question." The reporter covering the vote for *The New York Times* was closer to the mark. "The move reflected a growing tendency in the Senate to reassert its prerogatives in the making of foreign policy."[13]

The Nixon administration treated congressional participation lightly at first. "There will be no need to submit the reversion agreement to the Senate," a National Security Council staff member informed Kissinger. The language of the Japanese peace treaty stated that the United States had "the right to exercise all powers of administration" over the Ryukyus. The administration believed that the treaty gave the United States authority over the treaty but no obligation to exercise that power. Since reversion required no modification of the original treaty, Senate ratification was unnecessary. "The Byrd amendment and the debate over it, however, indicate that the Senate will no longer accept such an interpretation," a researcher for the Legislative Reference Service observed. A number of editorials appeared in newspapers around the country supporting Byrd.[14]

The resolution concerned the Japanese. Foreign Minister Aichi, in an interview with the Mainichi newspapers, expressed concern about the Byrd resolution. "I felt very let down when I heard of it," he said.[15]

As a result of congressional sentiment, negotiators included language in the communiqué about obtaining "the necessary legislative support." When Byrd read the text of the communiqué, he was ecstatic. After reading the document, he decided it said very little. "No specific arrangements have been agreed to," he stated. "I am glad to state to the Senate that I support this communiqué." Byrd was also willing to take credit for this accomplishment: "I am especially pleased that the Senate's role in any final arrangements affecting Okinawa is specifically recognized in the text of the communiqué."[16]

Sen. Ernest Hollings of South Carolina was more skeptical. Standing on the floor of the Senate with Byrd, he said, "I do not necessarily enjoy the same assurance that this communiqué is crystal clear." Reading the same section of the text, he noted that "the word 'support' does not necessarily mean advice and consent." Hollings suspected that Nixon had no intention of submitting a treaty to the Senate and decided to do something about his concerns. He went back to his office and wrote the president a letter in an effort to have matters clarified. Hollings explained the differences in interpretation between himself and Byrd. "Please tell me whether or not Senator Byrd is correct in his understanding," he asked pointedly. Nixon took six weeks to respond while his NSC staff formulated a response. "Let me assure you that the Executive Branch will continue to maintain close contact with the Legislative Branch in order to work out mutually satisfactory arrangements for handling the problem of Okinawa reversion, including the appropriate form of Congressional participation in this matter," he replied. This language, Kissinger explained to Nixon, "avoids any commitment as to the precise nature of the consultation." Hollings did not make this distinction. "I am pleased that the President has erased any doubt as to the Senate's participation," he announced. It was Sen. Strom Thurmond, Hollings's colleague from South Carolina, who noticed that the president's letter said nothing about "advice and consent."[17]

Nixon wanted flexibility in dealing with Congress but knew he had to work with the legislature to some degree. On November 21, 1969, he briefed a number of key senators and representatives during a seventy-minute meeting. Included in this group were the majority and minority leadership, the chairmen and ranking minority members of the Joint Committee on Atomic Energy, and the foreign relations and armed services committees of each house. Nixon stressed the future: It was time to modify the relationship with Japan. The United States could no longer enjoy unlimited base rights. This presentation convinced Mississippi Democrat John Stennis, chairman of the Senate Armed Services Committee, to support reversion.[18]

Such briefings, however, impressive though they were, failed to satisfy the Senate. A commanding majority of the upper house wanted to reassert the legislative branch's role in foreign policy and vote on a treaty. The Senate remained silent on the issue during the technical negotiations, but on February 25, 1971, J. William Fulbright, the Democrat from Arkansas and chairman of the Senate Foreign Relations Committee, wrote Secretary of State William Rogers demanding the administration submit a treaty. Rogers wrote back six days later and agreed. Rogers had actually recommended a treaty format to Nixon three weeks before

Fulbright wrote his letter. He had a number of reasons for doing so. Foreign Service officers told Rogers that submitting a treaty to the Senate was good diplomacy. The Japanese were stalling on several issues, including the fate of American businesses, and congressional involvement would induce concessions. The Department of State legal advisor also recommended seeking the advice and consent of the Senate, since American rights on Okinawa were treaty based. If Congress challenged reversion in the courts, it "would leave the President exposed in a political confrontation." Finally and most important, the vote on the Byrd resolution made it clear that the Senate had strong and serious interest in this matter.[19]

The decision for a treaty format drew mixed responses. "I think it is the only appropriate course that can be taken," Senator Byrd said. The Rogers letter surprised Kissinger and his National Security Council staff. They knew nothing of the commitment to Fulbright until after the fact and believed that southern senators would try to tie reversion to concessions on textile imports. The editorial board of *The New York Times* agreed. In an April editorial the editors declared that the treaty format would allow southern senators to block the treaty, which would provoke anti-American riots in Japan and Okinawa and bring about the end of the U.S.-Japanese alliance. If these events occurred, "Japan ultimately might go 'Gaullist' and seek its own nuclear weapons." Somehow the editors managed to fix the blame for this pending crisis solely on Richard Nixon and his efforts to win southern votes in the coming presidential election.[20]

After reading this editorial, senators were, in their own words, "amazed" and "taken aback." Only months before the same paper had urged Congress to take a more active role in foreign policy. Fulbright penned a response. He did not know what Nixon's motivations were, but they were not important. The more significant consideration was that "the President acted in accord with the Constitution. The normal and proper means of altering a treaty is by means of another treaty." Byrd read the letter and told Fulbright it was "splendid."[21]

The *Times* editorial board continued to run editorials criticizing the treaty venue, always finding a way to put the blame on Nixon. One piece called the decision "a perversion of the treaty-making process." Montana Democrat Mike Mansfield, the majority leader, provided some hope that the reversion process would not go through the Senate. Mansfield knew Byrd was trying to use agitation about the format as a pretext to block reversion, and he told a reporter from the *Times* that he would try to get the matter handled through an executive order. A congressional staff member sent Fulbright a note when a story about Mansfield's efforts appeared in the *Times*. "J.W.F. I hope you can tone Sen. Mansfield down on this." Fulbright supported reversion but wanted Nixon to respect the congressional role in foreign policy formation, and to this end he was willing to make common cause with Byrd. "It is embarrassing to know that you wish the Committee and the Senate to be bypassed in regard to Okinawa," he told Mansfield in a letter.[22]

Nothing much came of the imagined textile threat to reversion. Hollings, Thurmond, and Rep. William Jennings Dorn, all from South Carolina, had made some harsh, demagogic statements on reversion and called for a tie between reversion and concessions on textiles, but little came from these statements. There was no uprising of southern senators against reversion in the defense of the southern textile industry, and Nixon White House documents show no real pressure on the matter coming from Congress. The technical talks and preparations on the island continued without pause.[23]

Although no actual effort was made to connect textiles and Okinawa, the specter of Senate ratification did help the United States. Kissinger and Johnson warned Japanese representatives that the dispute might jeopardize the treaty. David M. Kennedy, a former secretary of the treasury appointed by Nixon to resolve the textile problem, made similar statements.[24] A solution had to be found before the Senate began considering a treaty. Such tactics helped the United States resolve the issue on favorable terms. A number of other issues wracked U.S.-Japanese relations in the early 1970s; the opening to China without giving Tokyo any prior notice, ending the convertibility of dollars into gold, and several other issues became known in Japan as the "Nixon shocks." While these issues might have led to a rift or rupture in relations in other times, the fact that the United States still controlled Okinawa limited Japanese options. Okinawa was Nixon's trump card.

In the United States there was little to gain politically from blocking reversion. The American people had no deep interest in the issue. Two opinion polls conducted by Louis Harris and Associates produced conflicting results. A poll conducted in December, 1970, reported that 50 percent of the public opposed reversion (only 26 percent supported it). Yet, the same poll showed that 42 percent wanted the United States to encourage Japan to play a larger role in the Pacific (with 37 percent against this). A month later, another poll conducted for the *Asahi Shimbun*, found attitudes had reversed. According to this poll, Americans supported reversion 49 percent to 39 percent.[25] These contradictory findings from the same polling service only a month apart indicate that the numbers were hollow. Other polls from the Gallup organization actually showed that Americans had a positive image of Japan. A survey conducted in 1968 found that 72 percent of the public gave Japan a favorable rating. Four years later another poll reported that 64 percent of the public gave Japan either a highly or fairly favorable rating.[26]

The Senate had no interest in reversion beyond protecting its powers and gave its "advice and consent" quickly and without complication. Nixon submitted the treaty to the Senate on September 21, 1971. A month later, the Senate Foreign Relations committee scheduled two days of hearings. The first session lasted only two hours. "I do not think you need worry about the committee's attitude on the Okinawa reversion," Fulbright told Secretary of State Rogers at the end. The committee took testimony from interested parties on the second day, with only one Senator in attendance. The committee sent the treaty to the full Senate with its unanimous approval. The Senate Armed Services Committee also held hearings in executive session. Gen. William Westmoreland, the U.S. Army chief of staff, told the committee: "The Joint Chiefs of Staff understand and accept the judgment that political considerations in this case outweigh the partial loss of military flexibility entailed in reversion." Six weeks after receiving the treaty, the Senate approved the agreement 84-6.[27] The senators making comments about the treaty accepted Nixon's contention that a continuation of American administration was no longer realistic. Nor could a Democratic Senate make reversion a political issue since President Johnson had started the process with the return of the Bonins. The speed and overwhelming nature of the vote also indicated that Senate interest in Okinawa did not extend beyond protecting its institutional prerogatives.

In Japan and Okinawa, matters were less manageable. While a consensus for reversion existed among Japanese and Okinawan politicians and political activists, real and extreme differences existed on the conditions under which reversion would be acceptable. Individuals and organizations on the political Left had hoped to use reversion to remove American bases and end the U.S.-Japanese security alliance. In Japan these groups included the Socialists, Clean Government, and Communist parties, as well as Marxist-oriented student associations. In Okinawa these organizations included labor unions and the reversion council. These groups were unhappy that Sato had negotiated a settlement that preserved both the bases and the alliance. As a result, many reversion activists began looking for ways to scuttle the Nixon-Sato agreement and, ironically, reversion. The odds, however, were against their success.

In Okinawa an American, Lt. Gen. James Lampert, the high commissioner of the Ryukyu Islands, became the central figure as the island prepared for reversion. Fifty-five years old in 1969, Lampert graduated from West Point in 1936 and earned a master's degree from the Massachusetts Institute of Technology; he later returned to both his alma maters in administrative positions. At West Point he was the forty-sixth superintendent—a post equal to university president and previously held by the likes of Robert E. Lee, Douglas MacArthur, and William Westmoreland. During his tenure, the military academy nearly doubled in size. After his retirement from the army, he worked at MIT as a vice president in charge of alumni relations and fund raising. Lampert was a talented engineer, holding a number of assignments in both civil and nuclear engineering. He was also a skilled player at army politics. He had a tough, thick skin and could argue a point without letting it get personal. A good sense of political timing complemented these talents. He refined these abilities in the mid-1960s as deputy assistant secretary of defense for manpower. Lampert soon realized he would need all of his skills soon after he walked into the office of his old friend, William Westmoreland, then the U.S. Army chief of staff, and learned he would be the new (and last) high commissioner.[28] He had no illusions about his job: "It was . . . clear that the reversion of Okinawa was going to take place."[29]

The political atmosphere of the day demanded a new approach to governing the Ryukyus. Unger made this point clear in the briefing he gave Lampert. Unger said his main mission was to prepare Okinawa for reversion; Lampert later said Unger's briefing helped "10,000 percent." His new approach became clear from his weekend trips. He and his wife drove around the island and made unannounced visit to villages and the Naha market areas. On other occasions, they went out into the country, often pulling over to talk with farmers working in their fields. "Nothing of tremendous importance came from these visits," he recalled, but the visits "had a very good effect on the people in Okinawa. I think I was regarded as being unusual among the High Commissioners in the effort that my wife and I made to get out among the people."[30]

Lampert also developed close working partnerships with Armin Meyer, U.S. ambassador in Tokyo, and Yara. He always stayed with Meyer when he was in Tokyo. "It was clear to both of us that we had to work very, very closely together." He and Meyer actually began making reversion preparations before the Nixon-Sato summit. His relationship with Yara was, by necessity, more distant. "I always had a personal respect for Mr. Yara with a fair amount of affection mixed into it," he recalled, adding, "also a fair amount of exasperation at times."[31]

Lampert faced two major crises during his tenure as high commissioner. The social upheaval of reversion was the first. A number of American journalists found Okinawans uncertain about the future. "Reversion itself is a good thing, but there is uneasiness about some of its implications," Yara said. "Okinawans are getting night-before-the-wedding jitters," an American said in more colorful language. The United States and Japan formed a joint preparatory commission to handle many of these problems. (The Okinawan representative had observer status.)[32]

Economic matters were the most important of the technical issues this joint committee addressed. "Our biggest task will be to save the economy," Yara stated. Converting from a dollar- to a yen-based economy dominated negotiations. The Japanese wanted a yen-to-dollar ratio of 360:1, which was the exchange rate when dollars became the currency of the island. This position would bring about a capital windfall for the Japanese since this rate was better that the current ratio of ¥302:$1, which the Americans preferred. Progress on other economic-related issues, such as the conversion of loans and contracts to yen and the alteration of vending machines to accept Japanese coins, depended on a settlement of the exchange question. After much negotiation, the Americans conceded the matter to the Japanese. President Nixon's announcement on August 15, 1971, that dollars would no longer be convertible into gold ended fixed exchange rates, making the settlement moot.[33]

Reversion required a good deal of change on other everyday matters. Converting roads from right-hand to left-hand driving and signs from miles to kilometers were lengthy projects. Okinawans had always said they wanted equal status with the homeland, but there was a significant downside that went along with this equality. Okinawans enjoyed more power in local matters than they would under the political structure of a

Japanese prefectural government. Okinawans elected their school boards, which would not be the case after reversion, and Japanese law prohibited teachers from being politically active—when the Okinawan government tried passing a similar bill, Okinawan teachers took over the legislative building for a day. Japanese administration would also bring higher prices for meat and rice because of government subsidies.[34]

In a speech given early in 1971, Foreign Service officer Robert A. Fearey, the civil administrator, told an American audience that reversion was a difficult and confusing time for the Okinawans. It was also a dangerous time for the United States. "Radical leftist elements opposed to the U.S. presence here and in Japan seek to intensify these concerns and direct them against the United States," he warned. "If this effort were to succeed, if anti-American feelings were to develop and spread, we could still lose the Ryukyuan people's necessary acquiescence to our presence."[35] Americans should conduct themselves with restraint to prevent an event from being used as a pretext for anti-American protest.

Fearey's audience needed no convincing. Okinawa was in the middle of the second major crisis of Lampert's tenure. In July, 1969, a canister of nerve gas stored on Okinawa developed a leak. A telephone call in the middle of the night from Maj. Gen. Chuck Horner, commander of the Second Logistical Command, woke Lampert. Speaking in guarded words, Horner told Lampert: "I just want to let you know that we've got a leaker." Some soldiers, but no Okinawans, had been exposed, and Horner planned to dump the faulty canister in the ocean. Lampert said no, that he wanted to report the matter to Washington first. While messages traveled across the Pacific, a reporter for *The Wall Street Journal* learned of the leak and wrote a front-page story. The presence and location of chemical weapons was a closely guarded secret, and any leak from these munitions was a newsworthy item. Lampert described the article as "somewhat exaggerated." If it was overwrought or sensational, the general could only blame himself and the army; the article had no quotes or identified sources and little new information after the introductory paragraph. The body of the article was a history of chemical and biological weapons. "So after the publication of this story, rather quickly the decision was made to publicly acknowledge the presence of the munitions on Okinawa," Lampert said.[36]

Leaking chemical weapons offered political activists opposed to the alliance and American bases the perfect issue to attack the Nixon-Sato agreement. The assertion that the American bases put the average Okinawan at risk sounded extremely plausible. The U.S. decision to remove the weapons had little immediate impact, since it took over a year to find another storage location. The December, 1970, riots broke out after an anti-reversion, anti–nerve gas protest rally. An American in a car hit an Okinawan walking on foot, and when MPs arrived they sent the driver to the hospital but left the pedestrian in the street. A reporter for *The Washington Post* called this act "the crowning symbol of an arrogant 'occupation' mentality." The traffic congestion caused by the first accident caused a second, which provoked the crowd to riot. Lampert reacted immediately, sending out MPs and authorizing the use of tear gas. He also went on television and radio to calm the public and prevent the rioting from spreading.[37]

The disturbance showed how important Okinawan acquiescence to American rule had become and how easily it could be undone. Americans, however, downplayed the importance of the melee. An editorial in *The Honolulu Advertiser* asserted that the riots were not anti-American but rather a protest against the polarized society on Okinawa, where a small, foreign minority had most of the wealth and a different legal status. Lampert went even further, dismissing the riot as the result of the "anxieties and tension" accompanying reversion.[38]

Lampert needed the active support of Okinawans three weeks later when he removed the first portion of the chemical weapons. The stakes were quite high, and sensing a dramatic moment, reporters flocked to the island. Lampert reported briefing eighty-one journalists from news agencies such the BBC, ABC, CBS, NBC, AP, UPI, and Reuters. This big media contingent gave political activists a larger audience than usual. Leaders of the Okinawan Teachers' Association and the labor unions canvassed a village on the removal route, telling the residents that the Americans were putting them at great risk. If a canister started to leak, or if one of the trucks transporting the nerve gas had an accident, it could kill everyone in the village. The ploy worked. The evening before the removal was to begin, residents threatened to block the travel of trucks passing through their village. Lampert suspected a number of Okinawans wanted a confrontation for the media play. Yara met with Lampert and suggested a postponement of forty-eight hours. Yara had helped organize the Teachers' Association, was its first president, and owed his election to the work of the reversion council and the labor unions. He thought he could negotiate a settlement. Lampert agreed, and the undersecretary of the army approved a delay. The reversion council, unaware of the delay, held a rally along the convoy route that drew two thousand people.[39]

Yara spent the next day meeting with political activists from the reversion council. "Situation fluid with increasingly encouraging indications as time for initiation of shipment approaches," Lampert reported to Washington. He also made it clear he would hold off shipping the gas until he got a go-ahead signal from Yara. The general's decision was another example of American dependence on Okinawan support in the administration of the island.[40]

The two-day delay allowed passions to cool. The villagers used the time to evacuate the area. Yara told Lampert that Okinawan police could handle the situation. American drivers reported traveling through a ghost town of vacant houses and businesses with drawn shutters.[41]

Lampert drew wide acclaim for his handling of the episode. Columnists for *The Japan Times* wrote that protests over the gas shipments were "grossly overdone" and praised Lampert for his "cool and calm" judgment. U. Alexis Johnson sent Lampert a short note congratulating him on his peaceful resolution of the crisis. "I appreciate the difficult and frustrating circumstances in which you accomplished this," Johnson wrote. With little conflict or story beyond trucks passing through empty villages, reporters left the island.[42]

The crisis was far from over. The army had removed only 150 tons from a stockpile of approximately 100,000 tons. As media attention faded, though, shipping became easier. Negotiations continued immediately after the first shipment, and in order to avoid similar confrontations, Japanese government officials suggested building a road away from any population center for transporting the nerve gas. The Americans were willing to remove the gas, but thought building a special road was a bit absurd given the lethality of the gas and the length of time the United States had stored the weapons without incident. The Japanese offered to pay for the road if the Americans would build it. Lampert agreed to this compromise.[43]

Before the Americans and Japanese reached this agreement, politics intervened. Yamanaka Sadanori, director general of the prime minister's office but a member of a rival political faction, decided to get a little publicity. Over the objections of the foreign ministry, he traveled to Okinawa to propose that the United States and Japan each pay for half of the road.

The staff of the American embassy told Lampert that Yamanaka just wanted to go through the motions of making the proposal. Lampert met with Yamanaka on January 18 with only a translator present. Yamanaka made his proposal and Lampert refused. With gesture out of the way, construction on the road began in May and lasted throughout the summer. The army finished removing the gas in mid-September.[44]

In Japan, Sato returned to Tokyo from his conference with Nixon politically stronger than when he left. He faced a political landscape that was similar to that in Okinawa. The opposition parties, particularly the Communists and the Socialists, had hoped to use reversion to end the alliance with the United States. Sato had thwarted them, Okinawa would once again be Japanese and the alliance would endure. Many politicians from the minority parties started stalling the ratification in the hope that this would help terminate the security treaty.[45]

Political rivals in the LDP were suspicious of the price Sato had paid for Okinawa. Ohira Masayoshi, the minister of international trade and industry and the leader of a rival faction, suspected concessions on textiles. After the first cabinet meeting following Sato's return, Ohira asked him, "Apart from what you have told us, is there not anything else we should hear from you?"

"Not a thing," Sato replied curtly.

Ohira remained unconvinced. "I wonder what Sato promised," he remarked to a friend. "If for the return of Okinawa it was necessary to resolve the textile problem, there would have been some way to go about it. He might have frankly told me if he'd made such a promise."[46]

The Japanese public did not share this suspicion. In an act anticipated by journalists on both sides of the Pacific, Sato dissolved the Diet and called for new elections. The results were impressive. The Liberal Democrat Party won 300 seats out of 486, taking the largest parliamentary majority in Japan since the end of the war. "The campaign was won upon a foreign policy plank," Alex Johnson told a Senate subcommittee. Thomas R. H. Havens's careful examination of the 1970 election showed the election was not quite the mandate the Diet seats implied. The Liberal Democrats' vote percentage actually declined. One bitter opposition politician dismissed the elections results as a "victory of political tactics." Whatever the reasons behind the election's outcome, one thing was clear: Sato had gone from a position of weakness to command of his party and his government.[47]

During the campaign, his political opponents and reporters noticed the ambiguity in the communiqué about nuclear weapons and tried to focus public attention on this issue. The opposition claimed the vague language would allow the Americans to sneak nuclear weapons back into Okinawa. Sato responded at two different new conferences, saying he had achieved "homeland-level" reversion. "Are there nuclear weapons in the homeland?" he asked rhetorically. "There are not. As Okinawa will be the same as the homeland, there is no room to inject doubts," he said. Asked if the Japanese government would reject American requests to reintroduce nuclear weapons, he said, "yes." There was no political deceit in this statement. Sato had recorded in his diary after his meeting with Nixon that he and the president had settled on a reversion plan that gave Okinawa the same status as the rest of Japan.[48]

In a situation similar to the security treaty crisis of 1960, the political Left attempted to block ratification. Since the LDP controlled enough seats to ratify the agreement, the only chance the opposition parties had was to drag out debate and hope some event occurred that would turn the country against the settlement. On November 17 the LDP forced a vote during a special committee hearing. The Socialists quickly brought business in the Diet to a halt.[49]

Efforts to prevent ratification were even stronger than the crisis of 1960, according to Masumi Junnosuke—an observation that makes sense. Reversion was the last chance the Left had to undermine the alliance with the United States. Protest rallies and strikes started at the same time. On November 19 a riot or rally took place in every prefecture of Japan. The *chukaku* student organization, an extremist splinter faction of the Japanese Communist movement, organized a gathering in Yoyogi Park in Tokyo that drew seventy-eight thousand people, according to police reports. The mob threw firebombs, battled police, and burned down a restaurant in Hibiya Park.[50]

The country was spared a long and drawn out crisis similar to that of 1960 as a nationalist desire to see Okinawa returned to Japan overcame partisan politics, breaking the deadlock. Hori Shigeru, the LDP secretary-general, arranged a meeting on November 20 of the secretaries-general of the major Japanese political parties. Ishibashi Masashi, of the Japanese Socialist Party, attempted to scuttle any agreement, saying there was little use in meeting since every party was committed to its position. Afraid of press reaction to an early end to the meeting, Hori kept people talking. This effort produced results. The secretary-general of the Clean Government Party said his organization would support the Liberal Democrats if the LDP would pass a resolution calling for base reduction on Okinawa and a ban on the deployment of nuclear weapons in the Ryukyus after reversion. The Democratic Socialist Party agreed to support the treaty with these conditions as well. Hori immediately consented. With this agreement, ratification moved forward, although Diet members from the Japanese Socialist and Communist parties boycotted the final ratification sessions.[51]

When Lampert boarded his plane at Kadena Air Force Base at 12:15 A.M. on May 15, 1972, Okinawa became Japanese once again.[52] This transformation occurred only after Nixon, Sato, and Lampert overcame important opposition in the United States, Japan, and Okinawa. A number of influential Americans continued to express concerns about Japan, and many more Japanese still objected to the alliance with the United States. The actions of these three men, though, were critical in overcoming dissent and bringing about the end of twenty-seven years of American control over the Ryukyus.

CHAPTER 10

Conclusion

The occupation of Okinawa was the result of American policymakers' security concerns in Asia and their inability to answer one simple question: was Japan friend or foe? The United States therefore decided to retain Okinawa as a forward base against possible Communist *and* Japanese threats in the region. As the years passed, Americans could see that Japan had neither the power nor inclination to threaten the United States. Japanese politicians and their flirtation with neutrality, however, convinced many U.S. planners, particularly those with offices in the Pentagon, that Japan was an ally of dubious dependability. Counting on Japanese support and cooperation in a moment of crisis seemed unsound. The United States needed a base that it could use without question. Military leaders might have modified their reasoning over time, but the basic need for continued American rule remained fixed. Since generals and admirals repeatedly cited concerns about Japanese dependability for over twenty years—mainly in private—it is reasonable to accept these statements as representing their honest opinions. The leadership of several different administrations accepted these views until the Japanese forced Americans to act and resolve the Okinawa dispute. Politicians in Tokyo had accepted American administration because it helped meet their basic political goals for securing the country against external threat. In addition, the concept of "residual sovereignty" clearly implied that the United States would eventually return the Ryukyu Islands, providing enough legal cover for them to tolerate foreign control of an entire prefecture.

Three themes apparent during the American occupation of Okinawa support this analysis. First, Okinawa was an American colony in all but name for military reasons. After a period of indecision and internal debate, the U.S. government decided to remain in Okinawa. Located off the coast of Asia, the island had a strategic location that fit the operational plans of three armed services, allowing the United States to project its power onto the continent or block any Japanese initiative that ran counter to its interests. The air force could bomb targets in both Asia and Europe from airfields located on Okinawa. The Marine Corps had a forward base for rapid deployment while the army used the island as a logistical and supply center for sustained operations. Other than meeting military requirements, there were few reasons for American rule of the Ryukyus. Americans spent more in administrative costs than they received in revenue; Okinawans bought the majority of their goods from Japan, not the United States.

Second, while Okinawa was a political issue in Japan, it never generated much interest or controversy in America outside the federal bureaucracy. Reversion was the goal of all Japanese politicians with any standing, but there were significant differences on reunification within the context of the alliance with the United States. Politicians to the left of political center wanted to use the Okinawa issue to terminate the association, while those to the right hoped to find a way to preserve their relationship with the Americans. On the other side of the Pacific, policymakers in Washington debated U.S. relations with Japan and, in light of that issue, the proper American role in the Ryukyus. While all Japanese called for reversion and argued about an acceptable context for reunification, Americans debated a more fundamental issue—should reversion take place at all. The wide range of the American debate allowed those bureaucrats, mainly those in the Pentagon, who wished to delay and block movement toward reversion. The army also worked to keep the issue bureaucratic, limiting media access to the island and keeping congressional involvement to a minimum. The military feared that the American public or its representatives in Congress would turn against continued U.S. rule in a fit of anticolonialism. While successful in the short run, these actions worked against the U.S. military in the long run. Once the Japanese overcame their internal political differences—at least enough to establish a regular policy—and began pursuing reversion with strong effort, the ultimate return of the island was inevitable. American leaders had no public support to turn to against Japanese pressure on this matter.

Finally, Okinawans themselves did much to influence the course of events, and their strength grew during the occupation. Key American figures testified repeatedly that they could not have remained on the island without the acceptance and support of the Okinawan people. When the residents of the island objected to U.S. actions or decisions, they proved quite capable of using political pressure to force the Americans to reconsider and modify their policies. Outright opposition would have made the bases untenable. Okinawans proved this point when they prevented the air force from using the island as a bombing base in 1965. In 1968 a number of political developments transpired that ultimately overcame the American military's resistance to reversion. The Okinawans made their feelings on the issue clear at the ballot box and moved the timetable for reunification forward when they elected Yara Chobyo on the simple political platform of immediate reversion. That same month, Americans elected Richard Nixon as president of the United States. Nixon favored according American allies greater responsibility in defense and security, including Japan. This policy was a reaction, in part, to Vietnam but was also an acknowledgment on Nixon's part that Japanese power and economic might had grown. Reduced to one sentence, the thesis widely ascribed to in the Ryukyus that sees the Okinawans as passive victims of the Americans is grossly exaggerated.

This observation begs the question: was American rule good or bad for the Okinawan people? The answer, however, is more political than historical in nature and difficult to develop objectively. Clearly, Okinawans have reasons for *both* grievance *and* gratitude toward the United States. Measured against its own political ideology, the United States stumbled. It is difficult to explain how American administration was in keeping with the traditional American principle of self-determination. The removal of Senaga Kamejiro as mayor of Naha and the authority granted the high commissioner under Executive Order 10713 were undemocratic in nature. On the other hand, Americans unleashed their idealism on the island in full force. From 1945 to 1972 the Okinawan economy grew at a rate faster than any country in Asia except Japan. Okinawans also had access to education that was better than any they had ever known. Would Okinawa have been better under Japan during these years? This is a counterfactual question that is impossible to answer.

The American presence in Okinawa and the double-containment system are interesting subjects in their own right, but they also cast light on a larger issue about the nature of U.S.-Japanese relations and U.S. foreign policy in the postwar era in three ways. First, writers have used a good deal of ink trying to explain how two peoples as different as the Americans and Japanese could become and remain allies in a time span measured in multiple decades. Actually, these nations did not at first. When the alliance began, the United States considered it a control device over a suspect people as much as a way of combining its own strength with that of another sovereign nation. The basis for the partnership was the lowest common denominator: a shared threat. Unlike similar associations based on such small common ground, this one developed and became stronger over time. When American policymakers agreed to return Okinawa, they recognized and accepted that postwar Japan was different than its prewar incarnation.

Second, alliances constitute a voluntary association. National leaders choose to join in partnership with another country. There have been alliances in which one nation is stronger than the other and in which one nation pursues a course with which it has reservations, but this is only because the alternatives are even less ideal. Such was clearly the case during the Cold War with regards to the Washington-Tokyo connection. Leaders in both capitals accepted decisions and initiatives that they found distasteful, although it is abundantly clear that the Japanese made more concessions than the Americans.

Finally, with the advent of the Cold War, the United States found itself facing a new foe with resources far greater than those of its wartime enemies. Over the next forty years, the makers of U.S. foreign policy regularly designed their programs to counter the threat the nation faced from either the Soviet Union or the People's Republic of China. These factors molded U.S. interaction with the world in the postwar era. There was more to U.S. foreign policy after 1945 than simply doing battle with the disciples of Marx, though. Considerations other than anticommunism clearly shaped U.S. trade, immigration, and financial policies toward Japan and other nations, and this was also the case in the development of strategy. Even in the supposedly bipolar world, the United States realized it faced threats that originated from a number of different places, and it required strong allies throughout the world to help counter these problems. Such realizations are important to keep in mind as the United States faces the new, multipolar world.

Notes

Abbreviations Used in Notes

AFHRA	Air Force Historical Research Agency
CR	*Congressional Record*
DDEL	Dwight D. Eisenhower Presidential Library
DNZER	*Documents on New Zealand External Relations*
FRUS	*Foreign Relations of the United States*
HISU	Hoover Institute, Stanford University
HSTL	Harry S. Truman Presidential Library
JFKL	John F. Kennedy Presidential Library
LBJL	Lyndon Baines Johnson Presidential Library
MIT	Massachusetts Institute of Technology
NACP	National Archives, College Park, Md.
NADC	National Archives, Washington, D.C.
USAMHI	U.S. Army Military History Institute, Carlisle Barracks
USMCHC	United States Marine Corps Historical Center

Introduction

1. Douglas MacArthur, *Reminiscences;* Courtney Whitney, *MacArthur: His Rendezvous with History;* Charles A. Willoughby and John Chamberlain, *MacArthur, 1941–1951;* William J. Sebald, *With MacArthur in Japan: A Personal History of the Occupation;* William Manchester, *American Caesar: Douglas MacArthur, 1880–1964;* D. Clayton James, *The Years of MacArthur, 1880–1964,* 3 vols; Richard B. Finn, *Winners in Peace: MacArthur, Yoshida, and Postwar Japan;* Justin Williams, Sr., *Japan's Political Revolution under MacArthur: A Participant's Account;* Alfred C. Oppler, *Legal Reform in Occupied Japan: A Participant Looks Back;* Theodore Cohen, *Remaking Japan: The American Occupation as New Deal;* Dean Acheson, *Present at the Creation: My Years in the State Department;* Harry S. Truman, *Memoirs,* 2 vols.

2. Roger Buckley, *Occupation Diplomacy: Britain, the United States, and Japan, 1945–1952;* Thomas Burkman, ed., *The Occupation of Japan: The International Context.*

3. Roger Dingman, *Ghost of War: The Sinking of the* Awa maru *and Japanese-American Relations, 1945–1995.*

4. John Dower, "Reform and Reconsolidation," in *Japan Examined: Perspectives on Modern Japanese History,* ed. Harry Wray and Kilary Conroy, 347; idem, *Empire and Aftermath: Yoshida Shigeru and the Japanese Experience, 1878–1945;* idem, *Embracing Defeat: Japan in the Wake of World War II;* idem, "Occupied Japan in the American Lake, 1945–1950," in *America's Asia: Dissenting Essays on Asian-American Relations,* ed. Edward Friedman and Mark Selden; Michael Schaller, *The American Occupation of Japan: The Origins of the Cold War in Asia;* idem, *Douglas MacArthur: The Far Eastern General;* idem, "MacArthur's Japan: The View from Washington," *Diplomatic History* 10, no. 1 (winter, 1986); idem, "Securing the Great Crescent: Occupied Japan and the Origins of Containment in Southeast Asia," *Journal of American History* 69, no. 2 (Sept., 1982); Howard B. Schonberger, *Aftermath of War: Americans and the Remaking of Japan, 1945–1952.*

5. Joyce and Gabriel Kolko, *The Limits of Power: The World and United States Foreign Policy, 1945–1954.*

6. Michael Schaller, *Altered States: The United States and Japan since the Occupation,* 5; Walter LaFeber, *The Clash: U.S.-Japanese Relations throughout History,* xviii. I want to note that both writers cited earlier versions of this study in their books.

7. Benis M. Frank and Henry I. Shaw, *Victory and Occupation;* James H. and William Belote, *Typhoon of Steel: The Battle for Okinawa;* Gerald Astor, *Operation Iceberg: The Invasion and Conquest of Okinawa in World War II, An Oral History;* Roy Appleman, James M. Burns, Russell A. Gugeler, and John Stevens, *Okinawa: The Last Battle;* Samuel Eliot Morrison, *Victory in the Pacific, 1945,* vol. 14 of *History of United States Naval Operations in World War II;* George Feifer, *Tennozan: The Battle of Okinawa and the Atomic Bomb.*

8. Vern Sneider, *The Teahouse of the August Moon;* John Patrick, *The Teahouse of the August Moon, a Play by John Patrick; The Teahouse of the August Moon,* directed by Daniel Mann, screenplay by John Patrick; "The Teahouse of the August Moon," Television adaptation by John Patrick; John Patrick, Stan Freeman, and Franklin Underwood, *Lovely Ladies, Kind Gentlemen.*

9. Watanabe Akio, *The Okinawa Problem: A Chapter in Japan-U.S. Relations.*

10. Frederick L. Shiels, *America, Okinawa, and Japan: Case Studies for Foreign Policy Theory.*

11. Morton D. Morris, *Okinawa: A Tiger by the Tail;* Arnold G. Fisch, Jr., *Military Government in the Ryukyus Islands, 1945–50.*

12. Higa Mikio, *Politics and Parties in Postwar Okinawa.*

13. Feifer, *Tennozan;* L. Eve Armentrout Ma, "The Explosive Nature of Okinawa's 'Land Issue' or 'Base Issue,' 1945–1977: A Dilemma of United States Military

Policy," *Journal of American–East Asian Relations* 1, no. 4 (winter, 1992); Mark Selden, "Okinawa and American Security Imperialism," in *Remaking Asia: Essays on the American Uses of Power,* ed. Mark Selden.

Chapter 1. The Battle, 1945

1. Astor, *Operation Iceberg,* 129, 140; William Manchester, *Goodbye, Darkness: A Memoir of the Pacific War,* 352–56; Morrison, *Victory in the Pacific,* 146–47; David Nichols, ed. *Ernie's War: The Best of Ernie Pyle's World War II Dispatches,* 404–406; E. B. Sledge, *With the Old Breed at Peleliu and Okinawa,* 179–82; Lt. Gen. Simon B. Buckner, Jr., diary, Apr. 1, 1945, Papers of Simon B. Buckner, Jr., DDEL.

2. There are numerous accounts of the battle. Few authors examined the long-term impact of this engagement, most focusing on Marine Corps operations. Maj. Gen. John Hodge, commanding the XXIV Corps, even complained about media coverage in a four-page memo: "I have been able to find but little mention of Army troops fighting their hearts out in the last twelve days of the eighty-two-day battle." A brief examination of press coverage supports his assertion. A principal reason for Marine Corps dominance was that a navy captain in Hawaii, operating under orders from the secretary of the navy, provided the press with information and briefings emphasizing the actions of marine and naval units in the Pacific. Maj. Gen. John Hodge to Gen. Joseph Stilwell, June 30, 1945, box 28a, Papers of Joseph W. Stilwell, HISU; Townsend Hoopes and Douglas Brinkley, *Driven Patriot: The Life and Times of James Forrestal,* 192–93. See also Manchester, *Goodbye, Darkness;* Sledge, *With the Old Breed;* Henry Berry, *Semper Fi, Mac: Living Memories of the U.S. Marines in World War II;* Patrick O'Sheel and Gene Cook, eds., *Semper Fidelis: The U.S. Marines in the Pacific, 1942–1945;* and "The News Parade," World War II, part 23–24; "The News Parade," v.16, no. 262, 300, Hearst Newsreel Collection, Film and Television Archive Research and Study Center, University of California, Los Angeles.

  Both services later produced fine official histories on the battle that, by definition, are detailed and focused. All writers interested in the battle for Okinawa are in their debt. Frank and Shaw, *Victory and Occupation;* Appleman, Burns, Gugeler, and Stevens, *Last Battle.* The account herein differs from other histories by explaining the fighting's effect on Okinawa's future and utilizing previously unused sources, including the diaries of Buckner and his successor, Gen. Joseph Stilwell.

3. Lloyd J. Graybar, "The Buckners of Kentucky," *The Filson Club Quarterly* 58, no. 2, 202–14; Ronald H. Spector, *Eagle Against the Sun: The American War with Japan,* 178–82; Feifer, *Tennozan,* 237; Belote, *Typhoon,* 24; Gen. Joseph Stilwell diary, June 6, 1945, box 28, Stilwell Papers, HISU.

4. Russell Weigley, *Eisenhower's Lieutenants: The Campaign of France and Germany, 1944–1945,* 2–7, 26–28, 81.

5. Victor H. Krulak, *First to Fight: An Inside View of the U.S. Marine Corps*, 159–74; Russell Weigley, *The American Way of War: A History of United States Military Strategy and Policy*, 254–68.

6. Buckner diary, Sept. 2, Oct. 3, 1944, Apr. 23, 1945, Buckner Papers, DDEL.

7. Appleman, Burns, Gugeler, and Stevens, *Last Battle*, 19–27.

8. *New York Herald Tribune*, May 2, 1945.

9. Yahara Hiromichi, *The Battle for Okinawa*, 23; Belote, *Typhoon*, 17–18; Feifer, *Tennozan*, 94–97; Yahara Hiromichi to James Belote, n.d., Okinawa box, Papers of James and William Belote, USAMHI.

10. Frank and Shaw, *Victory and Occupation*, 45, 48, 51; Thomas M. Huber, *Japan's Battle for Okinawa, April–June, 1945*, 1–3, 6–8, 60, 63.

11. For this victimization thesis, see Kinjo Sihgeaki and Ota Masahide in Haruko Taya Cook and Theodore F. Cook, *Japan at War: An Oral History*, 364–66, 369–71.

12. Frank and Shaw, *Victory and Occupation*, 18, 47; Appleman, Burns, Gugeler, and Stevens, *Last Battle*, 91; Yahara, *Battle for Okinawa*, 8; Col. Shimura Tsuneo oral history, Belote Papers, USAMHI.

13. Buckner diary, Apr. 2, 1945, Buckner Papers, DDEL; Sledge, *With the Old Breed*, 192–95; Appleman, Burns, Gugeler, and Stevens, *Last Battle*, 138, 150; Belote, *Typhoon*, 72–74, 159–61, 172–83; Astor, *Operation Iceberg*, 217; Morrison, *Victory in the Pacific*, 152.

14. Appleman, Burns, Gugeler, and Stevens, *Last Battle*, 79–83.

15. Ibid., 181.

16. Chester W. Nimitz, foreword to *Brave Ship, Brave Men*, by Arnold S. Lott, x; Belote, *Typhoon*, 147; Morrison, *Victory in the Pacific*, 178–79, 235–36, 250–52, 389–92; Ugaki Matome, *Fading Victory: The Diary of Admiral Matome Ugaki, 1941–1945*, 589.

17. E. B. Potter, *Nimitz*, 375; Thomas B. Buell, *The Quiet Warrior: A Biography of Admiral Raymond A. Spruance*, 358; Buckner diary, Apr. 23–24, 1945, Buckner Papers, DDEL; Simon B. Buckner, Jr., to Adele Buckner, Apr. 27, 1945, Papers of Simon B. Buckner, Jr., USAMHI.

18. Belote, *Typhoon*, 120–33, 191, 200, 211.

19. Ibid., 218–26, 230–34; Lt. Gen. Merwin Silverthorn oral history, USMCHC, 353–54; *The New York Times*, May 11, 1945; *New York Herald Tribune*, June 19, 1945; Appleman, Burns, Gugeler, and Stevens, *Last Battle*, 283–302; "Prisoner of War Interrogation Report, 10th Army Interrogation Report #28," Aug. 6, 1945, in Yahara, *Battle for Okinawa*, 41, 207–16.

20. Appleman, Burns, Gugeler, and Stevens, *Last Battle*, 259; Belote, *Typhoon*, 212–14; Buckner diary, Apr. 27, 1945, Buckner Papers, DDEL.

21. Buckner diary, June 12, 1945, Buckner Papers, DDEL; *New York Herald Tribune*, May 29, 1945; Lawerence's syndicated column can be found in either the New York *Sun*, May 30 and June 4, 1945, or the Washington *Evening Star*, May 30 and June 4, 1945.

22. *New York Herald Tribune*, June 18, 1945. For the lack of coverage in other

major publications, see the following papers for June 18, 1945: Washington *Evening Star*, *The New York Times*, *The Washington Post*, *Chicago Daily Tribune*, and the *Los Angeles Times*.

23. *The New York Times*, June 17, 1945; *The Washington Post*, June 4, 1945; Richard Kluger, *The Paper: The Life and Death of the* New York Herald Tribune, 373.

24. *Newsweek*, July 2, 1945, 36; *Time*, June 16, 1945, 34.

25. *The New York Times*, June 17, 1945; *New York Herald Tribune*, June 17–18, 1945.

26. Belote, *Typhoon*, 267–70; Morrison, *Victory in the Pacific*, 178–79, 250–52, 270, 389–92; "The News Parade," World War II, part 23–24; "The News Parade," World War II, part 2324, Hearst Newsreel Collection, Film and Television Archive Research and Study Center, University of California, Los Angeles.

27. Belote, *Typhoon*, 247–49; Appleman, Burns, Gugeler, and Stevens, *Last Battle*, 375; Manchester, *Goodbye, Darkness*, 359.

28. Belote, *Typhoon*, 250; Manchester, *Goodbye, Darkness*, 363–65; Frank and Shaw, *Victory and Occupation*, 283.

29. Yahara, *Battle for Okinawa*, 81.

30. Ibid., 83; Sledge, *With the Old Breed*, 233; Manchester, *Goodbye, Darkness*, 361.

31. Frank and Shaw, *Victory and Occupation*, 286.

32. Buckner diary, Apr. 1, May 22, 26, 31, 1945, Buckner Papers, DDEL; New York *Sun*, May 2, 1945.

33. Stilwell diary, June 5, 6, 19, 1945; Buckner diary, June 3–7, 1945, Buckner Papers, DDEL.

34. Appleman, Burns, Gugeler, and Stevens, *Last Battle*, 463; *New York Journal-American*, June 12, 1945; Buckner diary, June 9, 1945, Buckner Papers, DDEL; Yahara, *Battle for Okinawa*, 136.

35. Appleman, Burns, Gugeler, and Stevens, *Last Battle*, 438–42, 455; Buckner diary, June 16, 1945, Buckner Papers, DDEL.

36. Astor, *Operation Iceberg*, 407; Brig. Gen. Fred Beans oral history, USMCHC, 90, 93.

37. J. Fred Haley, "The Death of Gen. Simon Bolivar Buckner," *Marine Corps Gazette*, Nov., 1982, 100–105.

38. Louisville *Courier-Journal*, June 20, 1945; *Los Angeles Times*, June 20, 1945; Cleveland *Plain Dealer*, June 20, 1945; *The Boston Daily Globe*, June 19, 1945; *Honolulu Star-Bulletin*, June 20, 1945; Baltimore *Evening Sun*, June 19, 1945, *The Washington Post*, June 21, 1945; *The Louisville Times*, June 19, 1945.

39. Portland *Oregonian*, June 20, 1945; *Honolulu Star-Bulletin*, June 20, 1945; Washington *Evening Star*, June 20, 1945.

40. Remarks in the Senate, *CR* (1945), 6264–65; *The New York Times*, June 19, 1945; *New York Herald Tribune*, June 19, 1945; *New York Journal-American*, June 19, 1945.

41. *The New York Times,* July 4, 7, Oct. 24, 1945, Feb. 9, 1949, July 20, 1954.

42. Buckner diary, Feb. 7, 1945, Buckner Papers, DDEL; Gen. Oliver P. Smith oral history, USMCHC, 155; Krulak, *First to Fight,* 30.

43. Silverthorn oral history, 375–76; "Assumption of Command" General Orders 101, June 19, 1945, box 1, Papers of Fred C. Wallace, USAMHI; "Assumption of Command" General Orders 101, June 23, 1945, box 1, Wallace Papers; *Ohio State Journal,* June 23, 1945; Washington *Times-Herald,* June 21, 1945; *New York Journal-American,* June 24, 1945; Carlo D'Este, *Patton: A Genius for War,* 397.

44. Beans oral history, 90–91; Morgan memoir manuscript, Morgan folder, box 4, Papers of James T. Watkins IV, HISU, 18.

45. Yahara, *Battle for Okinawa,* 154–56; Frank and Shaw, *Victory and Occupation,* 368; Feifer, *Tennozan,* 506–508; "Interrogation No. 45," June 26, 1945, G-2 Periodic Reports, June 19–30, 1945, box 801, 7th Infantry Division, U.S. Army Unit Records, DDEL.

46. Appleman, Burns, Gugeler, and Stevens, *Last Battle,* 471–73.

47. Stilwell diary, June 29, 1945.

48. The figures for the Tenth Army are based on numbers reported for total battle casualties and the number of assault troops unloaded as cited in Appleman, Burns, Gugeler, and Stevens, *Last Battle,* 490, 492. At Gettysburg, the Army of the Potomac suffered 23,000 casualties, equaling a quarter of its fighting force, while the Army of Northern Virginia had 28,000 casualties, which was roughly a third of its strength. James M. McPherson, *Battle Cry of Freedom: The Civil War Era,* 664.

49. Lester J. Foltos, "The New Pacific Barrier: America's Search for Security in the Pacific, 1945–47," *Diplomatic History* 13 (summer, 1989): 320, 323, 326, 336–37, 341.

Chapter 2. Occupation in a Vacuum, 1945–47

1. Patrick, *Teahouse of the August Moon, A Play,* 23; John Patrick, "The Teahouse of the August Moon script," Film Script Collection, Film Library, University of Southern California, 16; *Los Angeles Times,* Nov. 27, 1955.

2. The best-known account of postwar Okinawa is Vern Sneider's novel *The Teahouse of the August Moon,* which later became a stage play and a motion picture. Two other accounts focusing on the immediate postwar years are Morris, *Okinawa,* and Fisch, *Military Government.*

3. Buckner diary, Apr. 23, 1945, Buckner Papers, DDEL; Simon B. Buckner, Jr., to Adele Buckner, Apr. 22, 1945, Buckner Papers, USAMHI.

4. Buckner also added a warning about race: "We should not incorporate Okinawa into our country but control it as a 'mandate,' 'protectorate,' or some name that will keep the Okinawans from becoming Americans citizens and all coming to Anchorage." This position was similar to one he took against the introduction of black troops into Alaska: "Alaska is already

plagued with problems of Indians who are half Swede, half Chinese, or half something else. Certainly the Army has a responsibility in not further complicating the population characteristics of the Territory by leaving a trail of new racial mixtures." *Anchorage Times*, June 19, 1945.

5. Stilwell diary, Sept. 4, 1945, Stilwell Papers, HISU

6. George Kerr, *Okinawa: The History of an Island People.*

7. Stilwell diary, Sept. 1, 1945; Barbara Tuchman, *Stilwell and the American Experience in China, 1911–45*, 675.

8. Foltos, "New Pacific Barrier," 320, 323, 326, 336–37, 341.

9. Lester Foltos, "The Bulwark of Freedom: American Security Policy for East Asia, 1945–1950" (Ph.D. diss., University of Illinois, 1980), 28.

10. The Nansei Shoto and Nanpo Shoto are alternate names for the Ryukyu and Bonin Islands, which contain Okinawa and Iwo Jima, respectively. Nimitz to Joint Chiefs of Staff, Feb. 2, 1946, cited in Dwight D. Eisenhower, *The Papers of Dwight David Eisenhower*, vol. 7, *Chief of Staff*, 1098–1101 n. 3; Eisenhower to Joint Chiefs of Staff, June 4, 1946, in ibid., 1098–1101; JPS 785/3, May 10, 1946, JCS Files, box 7-3, Ryukyu Papers, USAMHI.

11. State Department paper SWNCC 59/1, June 24, 1946, Trusteeships–Pacific Islands folder, box 138, President's Secretary's File–General File, Papers of Harry S. Truman, HSTL, 7, 30.

12. JCS 1619/7, quoted in JCS 1619/24, Aug. 26, 1947, JCS Files, Ryukyu Papers.

13. Leahy to Truman, Sept. 10, 1946, William D. Leahy folder, box 126, President's Secretary's File–General File, Truman Papers; Lincoln to Handy, Sept. 25, 1946, and JCS to SWNCC, Oct. 18, 1946, both cited in Eisenhower, *Papers of Eisenhower*, 1100 n. 5.

14. JCS to SWNCC, Oct. 18, 1946, in Eisenhower, *Papers of Eisenhower*, 1100 n. 5.; Leahy to Truman, Oct. 19, 1946, Trusteeships–Pacific Islands folder, box 138, President's Secretary's File–General File, Truman Papers.

15. Handwritten note, Oct. 10, 1946, Foreign Relations–Pacific Islands folder, box 60, Harry S. Truman Administration–Subject File, Papers of George Elsey, HSTL.

16. Lincoln, memo for record, Oct. 22, 1946, cited in Eisenhower, *Papers of Eisenhower*, 1101 n. 5.

17. Deputy Commander for Military Government to Commandant, Naval Operation Base, Okinawa, and Chief Military Government Officer, Ryukyus, July 1, 1946, Report of Military Government Activities folder, box 1872, Liaison Department series, USCAR Records, Record Group [RG] 260, NACP; Appleman, Burns, Gugeler, and Stevens, *Last Battle*, 35, 415–19.

18. John Caldwell manuscript, Papers of John Caldwell, HISU, 3; Morgan manuscript memoir, box 4, Watkins Papers, 12–18; undated notes, The General folder, box 6, Watkins Papers; James T. Watkins war diary, June 25, 1945, box 22, Watkins Papers; Sneider, *Teahouse.*

19. Marius L. Bressoud, Jr., "The Way it Really Was, I Think. A Personal Account of the Okinawa Campaign, April 1 to June 21, 1945," Papers of

Marius L. Bressoud, Jr., USMCHC, vii; Astor, *Operation Iceberg*, 269, 452; Sledge, *With the Old Breed*, 192–93; Manchester, *Goodbye, Darkness*, 356; Henry Stanley Bennett, "The Impact of Invasion and Occupation on the Civilians of Okinawa," *U.S. Naval Institute Proceedings* (Feb., 1946): 272.

20. Belote, *Typhoon*, 186; Clelland S. Ford, "Occupation Experiences on Okinawa," *The Annals of the American Academy of Political and Social Sciences* (Jan., 1950): 179–80; T/3 Ralph Saito oral history, Aug. 21, 1945, Background Papers folder, box 5-1, Ryukyu Papers, USAMHI; PFC Takejiro Higa oral history, July 30, 1945, ibid.; Capt. Lowe Bibby oral history, Oct. 4, 1945, ibid.; Stilwell diary, June 25, 1945, Stilwell Papers.

21. *The Crossroads of the Corps* (newsletter of Marines' Memorial Association, San Francisco), Aug., 1948, box 24, Watkins Papers; Watkins to Davis, Jan. 14, 1949, General Correspondence folder, box 24, Watkins Papers; Wallace to Stilwell, July 20, 1945, box 1, Papers of Charles I. Murray, USMCHC.

22. Morris, *Okinawa*, 1, 53; Daniel D. Karasik, "Okinawa: A Problem in Administration and Reconstruction," *Far East Quarterly* 2 (May, 1948): 258–59; Bennett, "Impact of Invasion," 268–70.

23. "Col. Murray's Speech to Congressmen," July 25, 1945, box 4, Watkins Papers; Hana manuscript, box 6, Watkins Papers, 20; Appleman, Burns, Gugeler, and Stevens, *Last Battle*, 419–21.

24. John Ray Skates, *The Invasion of Japan: Alternative to the Bomb*, 195, 228–29.

25. Stilwell diary, July 20–22, 27, Aug. 3, 5, 8, 13, 1945; Skates, *Invasion of Japan*, 159, 202–204.

26. Watkins war diary, July 26, 30, Aug. 20, Sept. 2, 24, Dec. 20, 1945, Feb. 10, 13, 1946; memorandum by the Chief of Naval Operations, Mar. 6, 1946, JCS files, box 7-3, Ryukyu Papers; memorandum by the Chief of Staff, U.S. Army, Mar. 22, 1946, ibid.

27. Deputy Commander for Military Government to Commandant, Naval Operation Base, Okinawa, and Chief Military Government Officer, Ryukyus, July 1, 1946, 59, 65; Watkins war diary, July 20, 1945 (emphasis in original), Feb. 5, 1946; Paul Skuse to Margaret Skuse, June 20, 1945, box 23, Watkins Papers; Paul Skuse to Margaret Skuse, July 16, 1945, ibid.

28. John Caldwell manuscript, 16; *The Christian Science Monitor*, Aug. 1, 1945; Deputy Commander for Military Government to Commandant, Naval Operation Base, Okinawa, and Chief Military Government Officer, Ryukyus, July 1, 1946, 65.

29. John Caldwell, "A Political and Economic Plan for the Rehabilitation of Okinawa," Sept. 23, 1945, box 7, Watkins Papers.

30. Paul Skuse to Margaret Skuse, Mar. 21, 1946, box 23, Watkins Papers; John Caldwell manuscript, 10–13.

31. Watkins war diary, Mar. 31, 1946 (emphasis in original).

32. "Acceptance Address of Mr. Shikiya Koshin," Apr. 25, 1946, Murray Papers.

33. Memorandum by the Chief of Naval Operations, Mar. 6, 1946; memorandum by the Chief of Staff, U.S. Army, Mar. 22, 1946; Watkins war diary,

Oct. 12, 1945; Paul Skuse to Margert Skuse, Oct. 9, 1945, box 23, Watkins Papers; Watkins to Watkins, May 5, 1946, box 22, Watkins Papers.

34. Watkins war diary, June 11, 1946; J. M. Towers to Murray, July 5, 1946, The Colonel folder, box 6, Watkins Papers; Murray to Watkins, Feb. 11, 1949, General Correspondence folder, box 24, Watkins Papers; Wallace to Stilwell, July 20, 1945, Murray Papers; Rockey to Commandant of the Marine Corps, July 24, 1945, ibid.

35. Rockey to Commandant of the Marine Corps, July 24, 1945, Murray Papers; *Kosei Okinawa,* Apr., 1948.

36. *Daily Okinawan,* July 2, 1946; "Ceremony for Transfer of United States Military Government Ryukyu Islands from the United States Navy to the United States Army," program, July 1, 1946, box 5, Watkins Papers; Watkins war diary, July 4, 1946.

37. "Occupation Reports: Japan and Ryukyus," box 88, RG 5, MacArthur Memorial, Norfolk, Va.; "Summation of United States Army Military Government Activities in the Ryukyu Islands," No. 1, July–Nov., 1946, box 106, RG 6, MacArthur Memorial; U. Alexis Johnson oral history, HSTL, 22–23; *The New York World–Telegram and Sun,* July 11, 1947.

38. *Daily Okinawan,* Apr. 13, 30, May 6, 1947; Morris, *Okinawa,* 59–60; Eisenhower to Eda Wilhelmina Carlson, May 8, 1946, cited in Eisenhower, *Papers of Eisenhower,* 1056 n. 1.

39. Morris, *Okinawa,* 60–61.

40. Deputy Commander for Military Government to Commandant, Naval Operation Base, Okinawa, and Chief Military Government Officer, Ryukyus, July 1, 1946, Report of Military Government Activities folder, box 1872, International Activity subseries, Liaison Department Series, USCAR Records, 71; Watkins to Murray, Apr. 6, 1945, Fraternization folder, box 6, Watkins Papers; Fisch, *Military Government,* 82–86.

41. Ralph J. D. Braibanti, "Okinawa, the Church's Opportunity," *The Living Church,* June 7, 1953; Friends of Okinawa, "The Case for Okinawa," pamphlet, American Relief folder, box 10, Watkins Papers; Commanding General, RYKOM, to MacArthur, Dec. 12, 1947, box 68, RG 9, MacArthur Memorial.

42. Skuse to Hayden, May 22, 1947, Papers of Paul Skuse, HISU; memo for the record, n.d., folder 1, Skuse Papers.

43. "Summation of United States Army Military Government Activities in the Ryukyu Islands," No. 35, Sept., 1949, box 106, RG 6, MacArthur Memorial, 35.

44. "Ryukyus Command and Unit Historical Reports, 1949," Annual Command Historical Report, Feb. 2, 1951, Ryukyus Command History folder, box 8, Ryukyu Papers.

Chapter 3. Debate, Decision, and Diplomacy, 1947–51

1. Dean Acheson, "Crisis in Asia—An Examination of U.S. Policy," *Department of State Bulletin* (Jan. 23, 1950): 111–18.
2. There are many works on U.S. foreign policy for this time period, including studies of general policy for East Asia. Ronald McGlothlen, *Controlling the Waves: Dean Acheson and U.S. Foreign Policy in Asia;* Robert M. Blum, *Drawing the Line: The Origin of American Containment Policy in East Asia;* Marc S. Gallicchio, *The Cold War Begins in Asia: American East Asian Policy and the Fall of the Japanese Empire;* Akira Iriye, *The Cold War in Asia: A Historical Introduction;* and David Allan Mayers, *Cracking the Monolith: U.S. Policy against the Sino-Soviet Alliance.* There are also a number of works on the occupation of Japan: Finn, *Winners in Peace;* Schonberger, *Aftermath of War;* Dower, *Empire and Aftermath;* Schaller, *American Occupation of Japan;* Schaller, *Douglas MacArthur;* James, *Years of MacArthur,* vol. 3; and Manchester, *American Caesar.* A number of other works also exist on the Japanese peace treaty and the ANZUS alliance treaty, the latter also discuss concerns about a remilitarized Japan: Ronald Pruessen, *John Foster Dulles: The Road to Power;* John Allison, *Ambassador from the Prairie, or Allison in Wonderland;* Percy Spender, *Exercises in Diplomacy: The ANZUS Treaty and the Colombo Plan;* W. David McIntyre, *Background to the ANZUS Pact: Policy-Making, Strategy, and Diplomacy, 1945–55;* and Glen St. J. Barclay, *Friends in High Places: Australian-American Diplomatic Relations since 1945.*
3. John Lewis Gaddis, *Strategies of Containment: A Critical Appraisal of Postwar American National Security Policy,* 58–62, 77–78, 83–91.
4. Finn, *Winners in Peace,* 156–58; George F. Kennan, *Memoirs, 1925–1950,* 375.
5. Eisenhower to Patterson, Mar. 15, 1947, Eisenhower, *Papers of Eisenhower,* 1602–1604, 1603 n. 1, 1604 nn. 4, 5.
6. Memorandum by the Director of the Policy Planning Staff, Oct. 14, 1947, U.S. State Department, *FRUS, 1947,* 6:540.
7. Kennan, *Memoirs, 1925–1950,* 377.
8. Ibid., 387–88; conversation between General of the Army MacArthur and Mr. George F. Kennan, Mar. 5, 1948, attached to "Recommendations with Respect to U.S. Policy toward Japan" (PPS 28), Mar. 25, 1948, *FRUS, 1948,* 6:700–702. I made an effort to document the idea that the Emperor gave MacArthur the suggestion that Japan would accept U.S. retention of Okinawa after the occupation ended. It is difficult to prove a negative, however, and no documents have surfaced that would support this contention.
9. Conversation between General of the Army MacArthur and Mr. George F. Kennan, Mar. 5, 1948, attached to "Recommendations with Respect to U.S. Policy toward Japan" (PPS 28), Mar. 25, 1948, *FRUS, 1948,* 6:691–92; "Recommendations with Respect to U.S. Policy toward Japan, PPS 28/2," Mar. 25, 1948, in *The State Department Policy Planning Staff Papers, 1948,* ed. Anna

Kasten Nelson, 2:210; Kennan, *Memoirs, 1925–1950*, 393; idem, *Memoirs, 19501963*, 52–53.

10. Kennan, *Memoirs, 1925–1950*, 394.

11. Central Intelligence Agency, "The Ryukyu Islands and their Significance," box 225, President's Secretary's File–Intelligence File, Truman Papers.

12. "The Acting Secretary of State to the Executive Secretary of the National Security Council," Oct. 26, 1948, *FRUS, 1948*, 6:876–77.

13. *New York Herald Tribune*, Nov. 2, 1949. With this inaction in mind, the emphasis Shiels placed on the meeting between General of the Army Douglas MacArthur and George F. Kennan as a critical turning point in the formation of NSC 13/3 seems incorrect—the fact that a year passed between these events also makes it difficult to accept this assertion.

14. CSCAD to CINCFE, Dec. 19, 1948, Ryu 1-61 folder, box 154, Blue Binder Series, RG 9, MacArthur Memorial.

15. Ibid.; William H. Draper, Jr., to Charles E. Saltzman, Aug. 18, 1948, Memorandum to JCS & Others folder, box 8, Ryukyu Papers, USAMHI.

16. "Report by the National Security Council on Recommendations with Respect to United States Policy toward Japan," May 6, 1949, U.S. State Department, *FRUS, 1949*, 7:730–31.

17. Edgar Erskine Hume, "Gloria on Okinawa," *The Military Engineer* 42, no. 287 (May–June, 1950): 167–70; *The New York Times*, July 25, 1949; The Director of the Office of Far Eastern Affairs (Butterworth) to Mr. Robert R. West, Deputy to the Assistant Secretary of the Army, July 29, 1949, *FRUS, 1949*, 7:815–16; memorandum by the Assistant Secretary of State for Far Eastern Affairs to the Secretary of State, Dec. 12, 1949, ibid., 7:912–13; *Life*, Dec. 19, 1949, 19; House Committee on Appropriations, *Foreign Aid Appropriation Bill for 1950, Hearings before the Subcommittee of the Committee on Appropriations*, 81st Cong., 1st sess., 919.

18. Senate Committee on Armed Services, Nomination of John T. McNaughton and Development of the Ryukyu Islands, 87th Cong., 2nd sess., *CR* (n.d.), 30; Witsell to MacArthur, Feb. 23, 1951, SHE folder, box 53, RG 5, MacArthur Memorial; Back to Bunker, Jan. 26, 1950, Personal for No. 1 folder, box 112, Blue Binder Series, RG 9, MacArthur Memorial; CINNCFE to CG RYCOM, Sept. 22, 1949, RYCOM folder, box 71, Blue Binder Series, RG 9, MacArthur Memorial; Voorhees to MacArthur, Oct. 6, 1949, Ryu 1-61 folder, box 154, Blue Binder Series, RG 9; Sheetz to MacArthur, Nov. 25, 1949, Sheetz folder, box 10, VIP Correspondence, RG 10, MacArthur Memorial; Voorhees to Cannon, Jan. 16, 1950, Papers from the MacArthur Memorial, box 5-2, Ryukyu Papers; *Time*, Nov. 28, 1949, 24.

19. Nold to Pick, Oct. 28, 1949, Nold Mission folder, box 7-2, Ryukyu Papers; "Agriculture and Economic Reconstruction in the Ryukyus: A Report," Nov., 1949, Vickery Report, box 6-2, Ryukyu Papers, ii.

20. Pruessen, *John Foster Dulles*, 22–24, 29–57.

21. Spender, *Exercises in Diplomacy*, 85

22. Mark Toulouse, *The Transformation of John Foster Dulles: From Prophet of Realism to Priest of Nationalism*, xxi; Leonard Mosley, *Dulles: A Biography of Eleanor, Allen, and John Foster Dulles and their Family Network*, 255; Pruessen, *John Foster Dulles*, 205–206, 209–10; Richard H. Immerman, introduction to *John Foster Dulles and the Diplomacy of the Cold War*, 18.

23. Allison, *Ambassador*, 126; Maj. Gen. C. Stanton Babcock oral history, John Foster Dulles Oral History Collection, Seely-Mudd Library, Princeton University, 12, 15; Sir Carl Berendsen oral history, Dulles Oral History Collection, 1, 14, 20–21; William J. Sebald oral history, Dulles Oral History Collection, 117–22.

24. Acheson, *Present at the Creation*, 432.

25. McGlothlen, *Controlling the Waves*, 44–45; Pruessen, *John Foster Dulles*, 434–37.

26. Vandenberg to Acheson, Mar. 31, 1950, box 66, Memos of Conversation Series, Papers of Dean Acheson, HSTL; Princeton seminar transcript, Mar. 14, 1954, box 90, Princeton Seminars Series, Acheson Papers, 1475; Lucius D. Battle oral history, HSTL, 63–65; W. Walton Butterworth oral history, Dulles Oral History Collection, 5–9.

27. Walter Isaacson and Evan Thomas, *The Wise Men: Six Friends and the World They Made Acheson, Bohlen, Harriman, Kennan, Lovett, McCloy*, 563, 581.

28. Memorandum of phone conversation, Apr. 5, 1951, box 65, Memorandum of Conversation Series, Acheson Papers; Princeton seminar transcript, Mar. 14, 1954, 1475–76.

29. Acheson, *Present at the Creation*, 429; Dulles to Butterworth, Mar. 9, 1950, U.S. State Department, *FRUS, 1950*, 6:1141.

30. Memo by Robert Fearey, n.d., *FRUS, 1950*, 6:1329–30.

31. Allison, *Ambassador*, 140, 145–46.

32. Isaacson and Thomas, *Wise Men*, 469, 500; McIntyre, *ANZUS Pact*, 252–56, 264–67; Memorandum of Conversation, by the Special Assistant to the Secretary, Apr. 24, 1950, *FRUS, 1950*, 6:1175–78; Dulles to Acheson, Jan. 4, 1951, U.S. State Department, *FRUS, 1951*, vol. 6, pt. 1, 781–83.

33. Sebald, *With MacArthur*, 250; Sebald oral history, Dulles Oral History Collection, 7. The evidence in this matter is ambiguous. On the one hand, General of the Army Omar Bradley, the JCS chairman at the time, stated in his posthumously published memoirs that the two groups met collectively and individually with MacArthur. (Omar N. Bradley, *A General's Life*, 529–30.) Dulles implied in a report that he sent to Acheson the two groups did meet. (Dulles to Acheson, Dec. 28, 1951, box 3, JFD-JMA Chronological Series, Papers of John Foster Dulles, DDEL.) On the other hand, Dulles stated in a briefing with Lt. Gen. Matthew Ridgway on the progress of the treaty that the two groups met separately with MacArthur. (Memorandum of record, Apr. 17, 1951, box 20, Papers of Matthew B. Ridgway, USAMHI. Bradley and Clay Blair, his coauthor, cite this document in the general's memoirs.) Historian

Michael Schaller presented Sebald's observation without comment in *American Occupation of Japan*, 273. In *Douglas MacArthur: The Far Eastern General*, 178, 287, Schaller, citing volume six of the *FRUS* series, noted that there was "some minimal contact" between the two groups.

34. Memo by MacArthur, June 14, 1950, *FRUS, 1950*, 6:1213–21; memo by MacArthur, June 23, 1950, ibid., 6:1227–28; memo by Dulles, June 30, 1950, ibid., 6:1229–30.

35. Allison, *Ambassador*, 150; Bradley to Johnson, Aug. 22, 1950, attached to Acheson to Jessup, Aug. 22, 1950, *FRUS, 1950*, 6:1278–82; Allison to Acheson, Sept. 4, 1950, ibid., 6:1290–93; memorandum for the president, Sept. 7, 1950, attached to Acheson to Johnson, Sept. 7, 1950, *FRUS, 1950*, 6:1293–96.

36. Pruessen, *John Foster Dulles*, 462; John Foster Dulles, "The San Francisco Conference on Proposed Japanese Peace Treaty," Aug. 15, 1951, *Department of State Bulletin* 25 (Aug. 27, 1951): 347; Princeton seminar transcript, Mar. 14, 1954, box 90, Princeton Seminars Series, Acheson Papers, 1494.

37. Unsigned memo prepared in the Department of State, Sept. 11, 1950, *FRUS, 1950*, 6:1296–97; memo of conversation, Oct. 26–27, 1950, ibid., 6:1332–36; Allison, *Ambassador*, 151–52; Official Secretary, Office of the High Commissioner for New Zealand, Canberra, to the Secretary for External Affairs, Oct. 27, 1951, Department of External Affairs, Historical Publications Branch, *DNZER*, vol. 3, *The ANZUS Pact and the Treaty of Peace with Japan*, 549.

38. Dulles to MacArthur, Nov. 15, 1950, *FRUS, 1950*, 6:1351.

39. Barclay, *Friends in High Places*, 32–33. Lady Spender wrote murder mysteries: Jean Spender, *The Charge is Murder!*

40. Sir Howard Beale oral history, Dulles Oral History Collection, 6; Barclay, *Friends in High Places*, 32–55; Sir Robert Gordon Menzies, *The Measure of the Years*, 51; summary report by John Foster Dulles, July 3, 1950, *FRUS, 1950*, 6:1261–62; memorandum of conversation, July 29, 1950, ibid., 6:1235.

41. McIntyre, *ANZUS Pact*, 290–91, 304–307; Sir Walter Nash oral history, Dulles Oral History Collection, 2–3; Berendsen oral history, 3–4; McIntosh to Berendsen, Apr. 12, 1950, *Undiplomatic Dialogue: Letters between Carl Berendsen and Alister McIntosh, 1943–1952*, ed. Ian McGibbon, 225.

42. In his memoirs Spender claimed that negotiations started the day Dulles arrived and continued until February 18. He produced a detailed account based, no doubt, on Australian records of these conversations. The editors of the *FRUS* series cast doubt on this claim, finding no record of any conversation on February 14–15 or 18. The New Zealand records of these meetings revealed that the conference Spender describes taking place on February 14 actually occurred on the fifteenth. American documents and New Zealand documents agree that there was one meeting on the sixteenth and two meetings on February 17 but none on February 18. Spender appears to have confused the date for the second meeting on the seventeenth. All told there

were four meetings in three days with no conference on either the first or last day of Dulles's stay. Spender, *Exercises in Diplomacy*, 112; memorandum by Fearey, *FRUS, 1951*, vol. 6, pt. 1, 156 n. 1; notes on the Australian–New Zealand–United States talks in Canberra, Feb. 15–17, 1951, *DNZER*, 3:593–613.

43. Spender, *Exercises in Diplomacy*, 45–47, 54–55, 112, 116–17, 121–22, 148; Sir Robert Gordon Menzies, "The Pacific Settlement Seen From Australia," *Foreign Affairs* 30 (Jan., 1952): 190, 193; notes on the Australian–New Zealand–United States talks in Canberra, Feb. 15–17, 1951, *DNZER*, 3:593–613.

44. Sir Alan Watt, *Australian Diplomat: Memoirs of Sir Alan Watt*, 175–85.

45. McIntosh to Berendsen, Mar. 16, 1951, *Undiplomatic Dialogue*, 254; memorandum by Fearey, Feb. 2, 1951, *FRUS, 1951*, vol. 6, pt. 1, 891; memorandum by Fearey, Feb. 17, 1951, ibid., vol. 6, pt. 1, 169–72; Dulles to the Minister for External Affairs of New Zealand, Feb. 18, 1951, ibid., vol. 6, pt. 1, 175–76; memorandum on the substance of discussions at a Department of State–Joint Chiefs of Staff meeting, Apr. 11, 1951, ibid., vol. 6, pt. 1, 195, 199; notes on the Australian–New Zealand–United States talks in Canberra, Feb. 15–17, 1951, *DNZER*, 3:593–613.

46. Martin E. Weinstein, *Japan's Postwar Defense Policy, 1947–1968*, 15–43; Watanabe, *Okinawa Problem*, 22–24; Yoshida Shigeru, *The Yoshida Memoirs: The Story of Japan in Crisis*, trans. Yoshida Kenichi, 250–51.

47. Yoshida Shigeru, *Kaiso Junen*, 3:120–21; Acheson to Sebald, Jan. 3, 1951, *FRUS, 1951*, vol. 6, pt. 1, 778–79; memorandum of conversation by Robert Fearey, Jan. 27, 1951, ibid., 822 n. 3; Fearey to Dulles, Jan. 25, 1951, ibid., 810–11; memorandum by the prime minister of Japan, n.d, ibid., 833–35.

48. Fearey to U. Alexis Johnson, Nov. 14, 1950, *FRUS, 1950*, 6:1346–47; Acheson to Marshall, Dec. 13, 1950, ibid., 6:1363–67; MacArthur to the Department of the Army, Dec. 28, 1950, ibid., 6:1383–85; report by the Joint Strategic Survey Committee to the JCS, Dec. 28, 1950; ibid., 1385–92; memorandum by Robert Fearey, Feb. 1, 1951, *FRUS, 1951*, vol. 6, pt. 1, 838–39. Dulles gave the Overseas Writers' Club in Washington a brief version of this meeting in an off-the-record briefing. The New Zealand embassy obtained a summary of this meeting. First Secretary, New Zealand Embassy, Washington, to Secretary of External Affairs, Mar. 9, 1951, *DNZER*, 3:819.

49. Memorandum by Robert Fearey, Jan. 31, 1951, *FRUS, 1951*, vol. 6, pt. 1, 835–37; memorandum of conversation by Robert Fearey, Jan. 27, 1951, ibid., 818–22; memorandum by Robert Fearey, Mar. 19, 1951, ibid., 933.

50. Memorandum of conversation by the Second Secretary of the Embassy in the United Kingdom, Mar. 21, 1951, *FRUS, 1951*, vol. 6, pt. 1, 937; memorandum on the substance of discussions at a Department of State–Joint Chiefs of Staff meeting, Apr. 11, 1951, ibid., 970; Johnson to Rusk, Mar. 22, 1951, Japanese Peace Treaty Files of John Foster Dulles, RG 59, NACP (microfilm reel 6).

51. Memorandum by Dulles, June 27, 1951, *FRUS, 1951*, vol. 6, pt. 1, 1152–53; memorandum of conversation by Witman, Aug. 14, 1951, ibid., 1269–70.

52. Memorandum, Oct. 19, 1951, *FRUS, Memoranda of the Secretary of State, 1949–1951, and Meetings and Visits of Foreign Dignitaries, 1949–1952*, microfiche 31, no. 2068; *Newsweek*, Sept. 10, 1951; *Time*, Sept. 10, 1951; U.S. Department of State, *Conference for the Conclusion and Signature of the Treaty of Peace with Japan. San Francisco, California September 48, 1951: Record of Proceedings*, 78, 277.

Chapter 4. The Making of an American Colony, 1950–56

1. "Remarks upon Arrival at Kadena Air Force Base, Okinawa," June 19, 1960, in Eisenhower, *Public Papers of the President of the United States: Dwight D. Eisenhower, 1960–61*, 197; Booth to Department of the Army, June 20, 1960, U.S. State Department, *FRUS, 1958–1960*, vol. 17/18 microfiche supplement; *New York Post*, June 18, 1960; *New York Journal-American*, June 19, 1960; *Okinawa Taimusu*, June 20, 21, 1960; *Ryukyu Shimpo*, June 20, 21, 1960; *The New York Times*, June 20, 28, 1961; *The Honolulu Advertiser*, Sept. 3, 1961; Booth to Herter, Feb. 4, 1960, Okinawa folder, box 11, International Series, Papers of Dwight D. Eisenhower, DDEL; Eisenhower to Booth, June 20, 1960, Ryukyu Islands folder, box 46, ibid.

2. Historiographically, there is little on Okinawa or U.S.-Japanese relations in the period immediately following the occupation. While Eisenhower revisionism has made the 1950s a popular decade for historical study, there are few studies on U.S.-Japanese relations during these years in comparison to other topics of the era. Schaller, *Altered States*; LaFeber, *The Clash*; Dingman, *Ghost of War*; Roger Buckley, *U.S.-Japan Alliance Diplomacy, 1945–1990*; John Welfield, *An Empire in Eclipse: Japan in the Postwar American Alliance System—A Study in the Interaction of Domestic Politics and Foreign Policy*; Watanabe, *Okinawa Problem*; Roger Dingman, "Alliance in Crisis: The Lucky Dragon Incident and Japanese-American Relations," in *The Great Powers in East Asia, 1953–1960*, ed. Warren I. Cohen and Akira Iriye. Even the essays in Immerman, ed., *John Foster Dulles* do not examine his handling of Japan during the 1950s.

3. Memorandum of discussion at the 177th meeting of the National Security Council, Dec. 23, 1953, U.S. State Department, *FRUS, 1952–1953*, 14:1567–69.

4. *Time*, Aug. 15, 1955, 19; *Newsweek*, Mar. 5, 1962, 42; *CR*, (1957), 11322; *The Economist*, Dec. 8, 1956, 893; Okinawa *Morning Star*, Apr. 11, 1957.

5. "The Ryukyus—the Cyprus of the United States?" Jan. 30, 1958, box 3978, 794c.00 Mayday/5-257, State Department Central Decimal File, 1955–59, RG 59, NACP.

6. Watanabe, *Okinawa Problem*, 101, 131; Reischauer to Rusk, Feb. 15, 1962, 794c.02211/1-362, box 2176, State Department Central Decimal Files, 1960–63, RG 59, NACP; Reischauer to Rusk, Apr. 30, 1962, 794c.0221/4362, box 2177, State Department Central Decimal Files, 1960–63; Lt. Gen. Paul W. Caraway oral history, Senior Officers Debriefing Program, USAMHI,

vol. 3, sect.8, pt. 2, 51; Caraway to Julian A. Gascoigne, July 25, 1962, box 1962, Papers of Paul Caraway, USAMHI.

7. Ridgway to Pace, Apr. 29, 1951, Special File folder, box 20, Ridgway Papers, USAMHI; Watanabe, *Okinawa Problem*, 3132.

8. CINCFE to JCS, Dec. 5, 1951, JCS Files folder, box 7-3, Ryukyu Papers, USAMHI.

9. Report by the Joint Strategic Survey Committee, Jan. 14, 1952, JCS Files folder, box 7-3, Ryukyu Papers.

10. Cowen to Acheson, Jan. 25, 1952, *FRUS, 1952–1954*, vol. 14, pt. 2, 1116–20; Murphy to Allison, Mar. 31, 1952, ibid., 1222–23; Young to Allison, June 10, 1952, ibid., 1271–72; Foster to Acheson, Aug. 29, 1952, ibid., 1318–19.

11. JCS to Secretary of Defense Robert Lovett, Aug. 15, 1952, *FRUS, 1952–1954*, vol. 14, pt. 2, 1319–27.

12. Memorandum of conversation by McClurkin, Sept. 22, 1952, *FRUS, 1952–1954*, vol. 14, pt. 2, 1333–35; Young to Allison, Jan. 12, 1953, ibid., 1376–78, 1377–78 n. 1; Joseph W. Ballantine, "The Future of the Ryukyus," *Foreign Affairs* (July, 1953): 663–74.

13. Allison to Dulles, Mar. 18, 1953, *FRUS, 1952–1954*, vol. 14, pt. 2, 1397–1400.

14. Memorandum of discussion at the 151st meeting of the NSC, June 25, 1953, *FRUS, 1952–1954*, vol. 14, pt. 2, 1438–45.

15. Dulles to Rusk, Dec. 29, 1953, box 6, Chronological Series, Dulles Papers Dulles, DDEL. For later examples of this view, see CINCFE to Department of the Army, May 20, 1957, Japan sec. 23 folder, box 11, 1957 Okinawa Geographic File, JCS Files, RG 218, NACP; JCS to the Secretary of Defense, May 1, 1958, Japan sec. 27, box 8, 1958 Okinawa Geographic File, ibid.; Martin E. Weinstein, *Japan's Postwar Defense Policy*, 64–86.

16. Washington *Evening Star*, Aug. 15, 1953; *The New York Times*, Aug. 9, Dec. 19, 25, 26, 1953.

17. Watanabe, *Okinawa Problem*, 34; "State of the Union," Jan. 7, 1954, Eisenhower, *Public Papers of the Presidents of the United States: Dwight D. Eisenhower, 1954*, 8; *The San Francisco Chronicle*, Jan. 9, 1954; *Ryukyu Shimpo*, Jan. 8, 1954.

18. *Saturday Evening Post*, Mar. 30, 1957, 27; Lt. Gen. Ferdinand Unger oral history, Senior Officers Debriefing Program, 32; *Palo Alto Times*, Apr. 30, 1964.

19. *The Wall Street Journal*, July 15, 1963; Selden, "Okinawa and American Security Imperialism," 288.

20. John Foster Dulles, "Policy for Security and Peace," *Foreign Affairs* (Apr., 1954): 360; transcript, Mar. 25, 1965, box 287, High Commissioner–Chief Executive Meetings subseries, Liaison Department Series, USCAR Records, RG 260, NACP; Watanabe, *Okinawa Problem*, 125.

21. *The New York World–Telegram and Sun*, Mar. 15, 1952; New York *Daily News*, June 19, 1960; transcript, June 22, 1965, box 287, High Commissioner–Chief Executive Meetings suberies, Liaison Department Series, USCAR

Records; Walter Robertson oral history, DDEL; Caraway oral history, vol. 3, sect. 8, pt. 2, 52, Senior Officers Debriefing Program; memorandum of conversation by McClurkin, Sept. 22, 1952, *FRUS, 1952–1954*, vol. 14, pt. 2, 1333–34; "History of the Twentieth Air Force: 1 July through 31 Dec. 1950," Mar. 24, 1951, K760.01, AFHRA, 1.

22. Conversation between General of the Army MacArthur and Mr. George F. Kennan, Mar. 5, 1948, attached to "Recommendations with Respect to U.S. Policy toward Japan" (PPS 28), Mar. 25, 1948, *FRUS, 1948*, vol. 6, 700–702; George Barrett, "Report on Okinawa: A Rampart We Built," *The New York Times Magazine*, Sept. 21, 1952, 9; *U.S. News and World Report*, June 22, 1951, 26.

23. *Saturday Evening Post*, Aug. 5, 1950; "History of the Twentieth Air Force," Mar. 24, 1951, 39–42.

24. "History of the Twentieth Air Force," 39–42 and CS-1; Stearley to Volandt, Mar. 24, 1952, 168.7045-147-170, box 6, Papers of Ralph Stearley, AFHRA.

25. Richard Rhodes, *Dark Sun: The Making of the Hydrogen Bomb*, 450–51; "Southeast Asia, 1953" (brochure), Pamphlets, K730.6101(s), AFHRA.

26. T. A. Lane, "Construction on Okinawa," *The Military Engineer* 44, no. 302 (Nov.–Dec., 1952): 418–20; Stearley to McClure, Feb. 28, 1952, box 6, Stearley Papers; Stearley to Smith, Mar. 14, 1952, ibid.; Far East Air Forces, "Special Construction Program for Kadena Air Force Base, Okinawa," Aug. 20, 1949, 720.935A, AFHRA.

27. Caraway oral history, vol. 3, sect. 8, pt. 2, 6, 13; Unger oral history, Senior Officers Debriefing Program, 27; *Army*, Oct. 1969, 52.

28. *The San Francisco Chronicle*, May 11, 1962; *The New York Times*, May 20, 1956; *The Christian Science Monitor*, July 25, 1962; Lt. Gen. Ormond Simpson oral history, USMCHC, 340.

29. Gen. Randolph Pate, "Remarks to the Senate Armed Services Committee," Feb. 28, 1956, General Pate's Speeches folder, 78-0022, box 3, RG 127, USMCHC; Commanding General, 3rd Marine Division, to CINCPAC Ryukyuan Representative, Dec. 25, 1958, 9147/8920, box 135, Central Decimal File, 1959, JCS Files, RG 218, NACP.

30. Bradley to Lovett, Dec. 22, 1951, enclosure to Lovett to Truman, Jan. 15, 1952, Misc. folder, box 3, Papers of Robert Denninson, HSTL; Operational Plan 4-5, Oct. 14, 1957, 65A-0097, box 79, RG 127, USMCHC; *Fort Worth Star-Telegram*, June 13, 1960.

31. Lane, "Construction on Okinawa," 418–20; Peter Kalischer, "Our Gibraltar in the Pacific," *Collier's*, Oct. 11, 1952, 22–26; Senate Committee on Armed Services, Nomination of John T. McNaughton and Development of the Ryukyu Islands. 87th Cong., 2nd sess., 30; "Value of U.S. Physical Assets in the Ryukyu Islands," May 3, 1971, Ryukyuan Affairs Division–Directorate of International and Civic Affairs folder (ODCSOPS), Ryukyus Internal and Civic Affairs box, Ryukyus Papers; memorandum for record, Sept. 14, 1961, box 287, High Commissioner–Chief Executive Meetings subseries, Liaison

Department Series, USCAR, RG 260, NACP; memorandum of conversation, Apr. 11, 1956, 794c.0221/1-356, box 3979, State Department Central Decimal File, 1955–59, RG 59, NACP; "Okinawa Construction Program" pamphlet, 168.7045 85, box 21, Stearley Papers, AFHRA.

32. *The New York Times,* Aug. 30, 1961; *The Christian Science Monitor,* July 25, 1962; New York *Daily News,* June 19, 1962; *U.S. News and World Report,* June 22, 1951, 25–26; Richard H. Lamb, "Trip to Okinawa," May, 1956, 794c.00/4-556, box 3977, State Department Central Decimal File, 1955–59, RG 59, NACP.

33. William J. Sebald diary, June 8–9, 1956, box 49, Papers of William J. Sebald, U.S. Naval Academy; William J. Sebald oral history, box 22, Sebald Papers, 9.

34. *Time,* Aug. 15, 1955, 18–20; *The New York Times,* Feb. 21, 1960; *The New York World–Telegram and Sun,* May 9, 1958; Far East Air Forces, "Special Construction Program for Kadena," Aug. 20, 1949; Stearley to McClure, Feb. 28, 1952, box 6, Stearley Papers; Stearley to Cassidy, Mar. 14, 1952, ibid.

35. *The New York World–Telegram and Sun,* May 9, 1958; Lt. Gen. Alan Shapley oral history, USMCHC, 139–40; Col. James R. Aichele oral history, USMCHC, 16–17; Maj. Gen. August Larson oral history, USMCHC, 162–63; Maj. Gen. William P. Battell oral history, USMCHC, 211–15; Barton M. Biggs, "The Outraged Okinawans," *Harper's Magazine,* Dec., 1958, 58–59; Commanding General, 3rd Marine Division, to CINPAC, Ryukyuan Representative, Dec. 25, 1958, 9147/8920, box 135, Central Decimal File, 1959, JCS Files, RG 218, NACP.

36. The marine housing shortage became a major public-relations disaster in the 1960s, when the wife of Maj. Nathaniel Reich refused to leave Okinawa after a vacation with her husband came to an end. She surprised and confronted Lt. Gen. Victor Krulak, the commanding general of Pacific Fleet marines, about housing policies as he arrived at the airport on an inspection trip. Major Reich was reassigned to a remote post in northern Okinawa after he refused to talk her into leaving. Mrs. Reich eventually had Robert Kennedy, her senator, intervene to keep the marines from forcing her to leave. After the episode at the airport, the stringer for *The New York Times* on the island described her as "obviously neurotic," but also added that "the whole thing was handled so clumsily to begin with that the Division is really getting its just due." *The New York Times,* Jan. 27, Feb. 2, Mar. 2, 14, 1965; Grubnick to Caraway, July 30, 1964, Selected letters from Okinawa *Morning Star* Reporters folder, box 1968, Caraway Papers; Paige to Chief of Staff, Sept. 23, 1957, Staff Trip to Far East folder, 78-0022, box 4, RG 127, USMCHC; memorandum by William C. Chip, Feb. 16, 1972, C.G. FMF PAC HQMC Visit folder, 78-0053, box 2, RG 127, USMCHC.

37. *Weekly Okinawa Times,* Feb. 18, 1967; *Palo Alto Times,* Apr. 10, 1952; *Honolulu Advertiser,* Sept. 3, 1961; Robert F. McKeta, "Youth Activities on Okinawa," *Parks & Recreation,* Feb., 1966, 156–58; Faubion Bowers, "Letter from Okinawa," *The New Yorker,* Oct. 23, 1954, 139; Gladys Zabilka, *Customs and Culture of Okinawa,* rev. ed.; Fuchaku Isamu, and Mitsugu Miyagi, *Okinawa*

at Work; Fuchaku Isamu, Mitsugu Miyagi, Gasei Higa, and Zenkichi Toyama, *Tours of Okinawa; Time,* Aug. 15, 1955; George Barrett, "Report on Okinawa: A Rampart We Built," *The New York Times Magazine,* Sept. 21, 1952, 9; Marian Chapple Merritt, *Is Like Typhoon: Okinawa and the Far East;* "U.S. Lady-of-the-Month: Mrs. Robert Merritt," *U.S. Lady,* Apr., 1956, 30–31, 53.

38. *The New York Times,* Apr. 4, 1970; *Time,* Aug. 15, 1957, Feb. 22, 1960, 31–32; *The New York World–Telegram and Sun,* May 9, 1958; Bowers, "Letter from Okinawa," 139.

39. Smith to Risher, Dec. 22, 1958, 9147.8920-(59), box 136, Central Decimal File, 1959, JCS Files, RG 218; *Honolulu Advertiser,* Sept. 8, 1961; Rupert D. Graves diary, Feb. 18, 1951, Papers of Rupert D. Graves, USAMHI.

40. Military and diplomatic historians have recognized that the sexual interaction between Americans on garrison duty and members of the host society has had an impact on policy matters. For examples, see Brian McAllister Linn, *Guardians of Empire: The U.S. Army in the Pacific, 1902–1940,* 126–29; Katharine H. S. Moon, *Sex among Allies: Military Prostitution in U.S.-Korean Relations;* David Reynolds, *Rich Relations: The American Occupation of Britain, 1942–1945,* 200–15, 413–28; Dower, *Embracing Defeat,* 123–39.

41. Yehudi A. Cohen, "The Sociology of Commercialized Prostitution in Okinawa," *Social Forces,* 37, no. 2 (Dec., 1958): 160–68; Reynolds, *Rich Relations,* 76–81, 148–54, 247–50.

42. *Triad,* Aug. 5, 12, Sept. 16, Nov. 4, 1955, Jan. 20, Mar. 9, 16, May 4, 1956, July 6, 1962.

43. Ibid., Sept. 23, 1955, Jan. 18, 1957.

44. USCAR, *The Final Civil Affairs Report, 30 June 1971–15 May 1972,* 80; Selden, "Okinawa and American Security Imperialism," 295.

45. Selden, "Okinawa and American Security Imperialism," 295; Senate Appropriations Committee, The Supplemental Appropriation Bill for 1955. Hearings before the Committee on Appropriations, 83rd Cong., 2nd sess., pt. 2, 609, 615; House Appropriations Committee, The Supplemental Appropriation Bill for 1956. Hearings before Subcommittees of the Committee on Appropriations, 84th Cong., 1st sess., 66.

46. USCAR, *The Final Civil Affairs Report,* 82; idem, *Report for Period 1 July 1966 to 30 June 1967,* 390; idem, *Report for Period 1 July 1967 to 30 June 1968,* 345; idem, *Report for Period 1 July 1968 to 30 June 1969,* 330; *Time,* Aug. 8, 1960; *Kosei Okinawa,* July 7, 1947; Press Release, Dec. 7, 1971, Stanley S. Carpenter, "Time of Change," May 17, 1969, Scholarship folder, box 2938, Public Affairs Department Series, USCAR Records, RG 260, NACP; House Committee on Appropriations, The Supplemental Appropriation Bill for 1957: Hearings before Subcommittee of the Committee on Appropriations. 84th Cong. 2nd sess., 76.

47. "University of the Ryukyus, 1968–1969" pamphlet, University of the Ryukyus folder, box 2943, Public Affairs Department Series, USCAR Records; "Report of Observations of Problems and Conditions on Okinawa Relative to

Michigan State College 'Adoption' of University of the Ryukyus," July 28, 1951, box 6-2, Ryukyus Papers.

48. Averages from calculations done by the author based on figures in "University of the Ryukyus, 1968–1969" pamphlet.

49. "University of the Ryukyus Celebrates its Tenth Anniversary," 894c.43/5-1860, box 2903, State Department Central Decimal File, 1960–63, RG 59.

50. Senate Appropriations Committee, The Supplemental Appropriation Bill for 1957. Hearings before the Committee on Appropriations, 84th Cong., 2nd sess., 6.

51. Senate Appropriations Committee, Supplemental Appropriation Bill for 1955, 620; *The San Francisco Chronicle*, Aug. 6, 1952.

52. Senate Appropriations Committee, Supplemental Appropriation Bill for 1955, 610.

53. USCAR, *Civil Affairs Activities in the Ryukyu Islands for the Period Ending 31 March 1957* vol. 5, no. 1, 92; House Appropriations Committee, The Supplemental Appropriation Bill, 1955. Hearings before Subcommittee of the Committee on Appropriations, 83rd Cong., 2nd sess., pt. 2, 93, 113.

54. J. W. Fulbright to John Foster Dulles, July 1, 1954, 749c.00(w)/4-2853, box 4260, State Department Central Decimal File, 1950–54, RG 59.

55. Memorandum of discussion at the 151st meeting of the National Security Council, June 25, 1953, *FRUS, 1952–1954*, vol. 14, pt. 2, 1438–45.

Chapter 5. The Difficult Years, 1956–60

1. MacArthur to Herter, May 8, 1960, *FRUS, 1958–1960*, vol. 17/18 microfiche supplement; Welfield, *Empire in Eclipse*; George R. Packard III, *Protest in Tokyo: The Security Treaty Crisis of 1960*.

2. Although the events of the time drew considerable contemporary public attention, few scholars have attempted to look at these crises and their collective impact on American foreign policy. Ma, "Okinawa's 'Land Issue' or 'Base Issue,'" 435–63; Higa, *Politics and Parties;* see also Watanabe, *Okinawa Problem*.

3. House Committee on Armed Services, Report of a Special Committee of the Armed Services Committee, Following an Inspection Tour Oct. 14–Nov. 23, 1955, 7654–55.

4. Ibid., 7655–56; House Committee on Armed Services, Okinawan Lands: Hearings before a Subcommittee of the Committee on Armed Services, 84th Cong., 1st sess., 3.

5. House Committee on Armed Services, Okinawan Lands, 21.

6. Ibid., 7; idem, Report of a Special Committee, 7656.

7. House Committee on Armed Services, Report of a Special Committee, 7659, 7664.

8. *The Christian Century*, July 4, 1956; *The Commonweal*, Dec. 28, 1956; Higa, *Politics and Parties*, 46.

9. Dispatch, July 23, 1956, 794c.0221/7-156, box 3979, State Department Central Decimal File, 1955–59, RG 59, NACP.

10. Dulles to Wilson, June 22, 1956, U.S. State Department, *FRUS, 1955–1957,* vol. 23, pt. 1, 180–81.

11. Allison to State Department, Aug. 14, 1956, *FRUS, 1955–1957,* vol. 23, pt. 1, 200–201.

12. Robertson to Dulles, Sept. 21, 1956, *FRUS, 1955–1957,* vol. 23, pt. 1, 232–33; Department of State to Embassy in Japan, Sept. 19, 1957, ibid., 476–79; Dulles to Wilson, Jan. 8, 1957, ibid., 244–46.

13. Robertson to Dulles, Sept. 21, 1956, *FRUS, 1955–57,* vol. 23, 232–33; Department of State to Embassy in Japan, Sept. 19, 1957, Ibid., 476–79; Dulles to Wilson, Jan. 8, 1957, Ibid., 244–46.

14. Ma, "Okinawa's 'Land Issue' or 'Base Issue,'" 449; Higa, *Politics and Parties,* 47; record of meeting, June 30, 1958, *FRUS, 1958–1960,* vol. 17/18 microfiche supplement.

15. L. Eve Armentrout Ma, using Army Corps of Engineer and congressional documents, argued that the land issue continued to plague the United States and ultimately forced reversion. Ma was correct in her argument that disagreements about land use continued, but the issue lost its punch as a diplomatic issue between the United States and Japan after 1958, when other issues moved to the forefront. Ma, "Okinawa's 'Land Issue' or 'Base Issue,'" 449; memorandum from Dulles to Eisenhower, Aug. 11, 1958, U.S. State Department, *FRUS, 1958–1960,* 18:50–51, 51 n. 3.

16. Packard, *Protest in Tokyo,* 42–46.

17. Ito Takashi, "Shigemitsu Mamoru and the 1955 System," in *Creating Single-Party Democracy: Japan's Postwar Political System,* ed. Katakoa Tetsuya, 101, 115–16; memorandum of conversation, Aug. 19, 1956, *FRUS, 1955–1957,* vol. 23, pt. 1, 202 n. 3.

18. Memorandum of conversation, Aug. 19, 1956; Secretary of State to the Department of State, Aug. 22, 1956, *FRUS, 1955–1957,* vol. 23, pt. 1, 202–204; *The New York Times,* Aug. 28, 1956; LaFeber, *The Clash,* 313.

19. LaFeber, *The Clash,* 314; Ito, "Shigemitsu Mamoru," 116.

20. *The New York Times,* Jan. 10, 1957; *The Christian Science Monitor,* Dec. 28, 1956; *U.S. News and World Report,* Feb. 22, 1957, 20; Vern Sneider, *The King from Ashtabula.*

21. *Okinawa Taimusu,* Dec. 28, 1956; Steeves to Parsons, Jan. 7, 1957, 794c.0221/1357, box 3980, State Department Central Decimal File, 1955–59.

22. *Okinawa Taimusu,* Dec. 28, 1956; *The New York Times,* Oct. 9, 1994; *U.S. News and World Report,* Feb. 22, 1957; Roderick Gillies oral history, Ryukyus Papers, USAMHI.

23. *U.S. News and World Report,* Aug. 16, 1957, 7677; Higa, *Politics and Parties,* 80.

24. *Time,* Dec. 9, 1957, 32, 35.

25. Parsons to Robertson, Apr. 19, 1957, *FRUS, 1955–1957*, vol. 23, pt. 1, 281; Parsons to Robertson, May 24, 1957, ibid., 318–20.

26. Olcott H. Deming oral history, Foreign Service Oral History Program, Georgetown University Library, 1921; memorandum of conversation, Nov. 27, 1957, 794c.00/1757, box 3977, State Department Central Decimal File, 1955–59; Robertson to Sprague, Dec. 11, 1957, *FRUS, 1955–1957*, vol. 23, pt. 1, 544–46.

27. "Special Study of the Subversive Situation in Ryukyu Islands (Okinawa)," July 1, 1958, K-717.6243-5, AFHRA.

28. Biggs, "Outraged Okinawans," 60.

29. Higa, *Politics and Parties*, 80–81; *The New York Times*, Nov. 26, 1957; Martin to Parsons, Dec. 6, 1957, box 1.3, Lot File 61 D69, RG 59, NACP; Robertson to Sprague, Dec. 11, 1957, *FRUS, 1955–1957*, vol. 23, pt. 1, 544–46.

30. Robertson to Roderick, Jan. 28, 1958, 794c.001/1-758, box 3977, State Department Central Decimal File, 1955–59; Higa, *Politics and Parties*, 81.

31. *Time*, Jan. 27, 1958, 29; *The Christian Science Monitor*, Jan. 14, 15, 1958; *New York Herald Tribune*, Jan. 14, 17, 1958; *The New York Times*, Jan. 12, 14, 15, 19, 1958; *Honolulu Star-Bulletin*, Jan. 18, 1958; *The Christian Century*, Jan. 28, 1958; *Newsweek*, Jan. 27, 1958, 38.

32. New York *Daily Mirror*, Jan. 14, 1958.

33. Other mayors had died in office or resigned to become the chief executive of the Ryukyu Islands: Higa, *Politics and Parties*, 81; *The Christian Science Monitor*, Jan. 13, 1958; Roderick to Robertson, Feb. 2, 1958, *FRUS, 1958–1960*, vol. 17/18 microfiche supplement.

34. Robertson to Dulles, Sept. 27, 1958, 794c.00/4-158, box 3978, State Department Central Decimal File, 1955–59; *The Christian Science Monitor*, Mar. 18, 1958; *Time*, Mar. 31, 1958, 20–21; *The New York Times*, Mar. 18, 1958.

35. *New York Herald Tribune*, Sept. 11, 1958.

36. Douglas MacArthur II oral history, pt. 3, 1, 4, 18, 50, Foreign Service Oral History Program, Georgetown University Library; Philip Tresise oral history, Foreign Service Oral History Program, 7.

37. Fujiyama Aiichiro, *Seiji waga michi* (Politics, my way), 86

38. Ulrich Straus oral history, Foreign Service Oral History Program, 19; Edwin Reischauer, *My Life between Japan and America*, 154; idem, "The Broken Dialogue with Japan," *Foreign Affairs* (Oct., 1960): 11–26.

39. Ryukyu Island Fact Sheet, Army folder, box 2, Office of the Staff Secretary, International Series, Papers of Dwight D. Eisenhower, DDEL, 4.

40. "Talking Paper: Introduction of U.S. Currency in the Ryukyu Islands," Aug. 12, 1958, Japan folder, box 8, International Series, Eisenhower Papers.

41. Memo of phone conversation, May 23, 1958, Phone Calls folder, box 33, Diary Series, Eisenhower Papers.

42. MacArthur to Dulles, May 23, 1958, *FRUS, 1958–1960*, vol. 17/18 microfiche supplement; Booth to Dulles, May 26, 1958, ibid.

43. Memorandum of conversation with the President, June 4, 1958, box 6,

White House Memorandum Series, Dulles Papers, DDEL; Eisenhower to Dulles, June 4, 1958, *FRUS, 1958–1960*, 18:31; memorandum for the president from Dulles, June 3, 1958, *FRUS, 1958–1960*, vol. 17/18 microfiche supplement; memorandum of telephone conversation between Dulles and Robertson, June 4, 1958, ibid.; memorandum of telephone conversation between Dulles and Secretary of the Army Wilber M. Brucker, June 5, 1958, ibid.

44. Memorandum of conversation with the President, June 4, 1958; memorandum of telephone conversation between Dulles and Robertson, June 4, 1958; Dulles to MacArthur, June 16, 1958, Japan folder, box 8, International Series, Office of the Staff Secretary, Eisenhower Papers.

45. MacArthur to Dulles, June 19, 1958, *FRUS, 1958–1960*, vol. 17/18 microfiche supplement; Robertson to Dulles, Aug. 2, 1958, Japan Ryukyu Islands folder, box 2, lot 60 D90, Correspondence Files of Far Eastern Affairs, RG 59, NACP; Dulles to Eisenhower, Japan (1957–58) folder, box 34, International Series, Office of the Staff Secretary, Eisenhower Papers; Eisenhower to Kishi, Aug. 12, 1958, Japan folder, box 8, International Series, Office of the Staff Secretary, Eisenhower Papers.

46. Gillies oral history; Gillies Speech to Golden Gate Club, Dec. 13, 1958, Roderick Gillies Ryukyu Papers folder, box 5-2, Ryukyu Papers; Parsons to Robertson, Sept. 26, 1958, Japan Ryukyu Islands, box 2, lot 60 D90, Correspondence Files of Far Eastern Affairs, RG 59, NACP; "Currency Conversions in the Ryukyus," K-DIV 313 SU-RE 1958, AFHRA, 58.

47. Biggs, "Outraged Okinawans," 56–60; *The Washington Daily News*, Nov. 26, 1958.

48. Biggs, "Outraged Okinawans," 56–60.

49. Risher to Booth, Jan. 12, 1959, 9147/8920-(59), box 136, Central Decimal File, JCS Files, RG 218, NACP; Booth to CINCPAC, Jan. 27, 1959, ibid.

50. Steele to Risher, Dec. 23, 1958, 9147/8920-(59), box 136, Central Decimal File, JCS Files, Record Group 218, NACP; Commanding General, 3rd Marine Division, to Booth, Dec. 25, 1958, ibid.

51. Risher to Booth, Jan. 12, 1959; Commanding General, 3rd Marine Division, to Booth, Dec. 25, 1958.

52. Senate Committee on Appropriations, Foreign Assistance and Related Agencies Appropriations for 1964, 88th Cong., 1st sess., 107–10; Allan R. Millett, *Semper Fidelis: The History of the United States Marine Corps*, 522, 527–28, 543–44.

53. Risher to Booth, Jan. 12, 1959.

54. Ibid.; Booth to CINCPAC, Jan. 27, 1959, 9147/8920-(9 Feb., 59), box 136, Central Decimal File, JCS Files, RG 218, NACP; "Message of the High Commissioner to the 23rd Session of the Legislature of the Government of the Ryukyu Islands," Feb. 1, 1963, USCAR, *Civil Administration of the Ryukyu Islands, Report for Period 1 July 1962 to 30 June 1963*, 218; USCAR, *Civil Administration of the Ryukyu Islands, Report for Period 1 July 1964 to 30 June*

1965, 226; Camp Smedly D. Butler command chronology, July–Dec., 1968, II6, Archives, USMCHC; Camp Smedly D. Butler command chronology, July–Dec., 1970, II9, Archives, USMCHC.

55. The influence of the briefing is readily apparent from stories in the following publications: *The New York World–Telegram and Sun,* Mar. 15, 1952; New York *Daily News,* June 19, 1960, June 19, 1962; *U.S. News and World Report,* June 22, 1951, 26; *The Christian Science Monitor,* May 26, 1955; Denis Warner, "Our Fire Brigade on Okinawa," *The Reporter,* Oct. 13, 1960, 37–38. The control of reporters is discussed in David S. Grubnick to Caraway, Mar. 11, 1965, Selected letters from Okinawa *Morning Star* Reporters file, box 1968, Caraway Papers, USAMHI, and *The Honolulu Advertiser,* Sept. 3, 1961. For a sampling of Trumbell's articles see the following: *The New York Times,* Apr. 14, 15, 1956, Jan. 10, 1957, Jan. 14, 19, 1958, Nov. 14, 15, 1960; "Okinawa: 'Sometimes Painful' Lesson for Us," *The New York Times Magazine,* Apr. 7, 1957, 29, 60, 62.

56. Okinawa *Morning Star,* Apr. 11, 1957, Apr. 12, Aug. 15, 1958, Jan. 13, 1962; *The Washington Post,* Jan. 7, 1962; *The Honolulu Advertiser,* Sept. 3, 1961.

57. MacArthur to Dulles and Robertson, Feb. 12, 1958; MacArthur to Dulles, Feb. 18, 1958, MacArthur to Robertson, Apr. 18, 1958; MacArthur to Dulles, Apr. 18, 1958, *FRUS, 1958–1960,* 18:4–10, 22–24.

58. MacArthur to Dulles, Feb. 1, 1958, *FRUS, 1958–1960,* vol. 17/18 microfiche supplement (emphasis in the original).

59. Dulles to MacArthur, Feb. 10, 1958, 794c.0221/2-158, box 3981, State Department Central Decimal File, 1955–59, RG 59, NACP.

60. Memorandum for the record by Eisenhower, Apr. 9, 1958, *FRUS, 1958–1960,* 18:16–17.

61. Howe to Reinhardt, Mar. 4, 1958, 794c.0221/3-358, box 3982, State Department Central Decimal File, 1955–59; "Problems and Issues Affecting the U.S. Civil Administration of the Ryukyu Islands," Feb. 2, 1958, *FRUS, 1958–1960,* vol. 17/18 microfiche supplement; "An Immediate Program for the Ryukyus," Mar. 31, 1958, ibid.

62. Telephone call from the President, Apr. 9, 1958, box 13, Telephone Call Series, Dulles Papers, DDEL; Telephone calls, Apr. 9, 1958, box 31, Diary Series, Eisenhower Papers.

63. Joint Chiefs of Staff to Secretary of Defense, May 1, 1958, *FRUS, 1958–1960,* 18:29–31.

64. U. Alexis Johnson, *The Right Hand of Power: The Memoirs of an American Diplomat,* 171; memorandum of telephone conversation between Eisenhower and Dulles, Apr. 17, 1958, *FRUS, 1958–1960,* 18:21–22; Robertson to Dulles, Apr. 11, 1958, 794c.0221/3-358, box 3982, State Department Central Decimal File, 1955–59; MacArthur to Robertson, Apr. 30, 1958, 794c.0221/4-1558, ibid.

65. Packard, *Protest in Tokyo,* 70–71; MacArthur oral history, pt. 3, 21–24.

66. CINCFE to Department of the Army, May 20, 1957, Japan sec. 23 folder,

box 11, 1957 Okinawa Geographic File, CS Files, RG 218, NACP; JCS to the Secretary of Defense, May 1, 1958, Japan sec. 27 folder, box 8, 1958 Okinawa Geographic File, ibid.

67. Joint Chiefs of Staff to the Secretary of Defense, Dec. 1, 1958, *FRUS, 1958– 1960,* 18:104–105, 126–127.

68. *Asahi Shimbun,* Oct. 23, 1958.

69. Memorandum of meeting with the President, Apr. 16, 1959, box 4, Special Assistant Series, Eisenhower Papers.

70. Picher to Twining, Feb. 11, 1959, 9147/4920, box 135, Central Decimal File, JCS Files, RG 218, NACP; Booth to CINCPAC, June 5, 1959, ibid.

71. Joint Chiefs of Staff to the Secretary of Defense, Oct. 1, 1959, 9147/4920, box 135, Decimal File, JCS Files.

72. Memorandum of meeting with the President, Nov. 30, 1959, box 4, Special Assistant Series, Eisenhower Papers.

73. Welfield, *An Empire in Eclipse,* 150–51, 154–55; Masumi Junnosuke, *Contemporary Politics in Japan,* trans. Lonny E. Carlise, 24–26; MacArthur to the Department of State, Apr. 29, 1958, *FRUS, 1958–1960,* 18:126–27

Chapter 6. Reischauer vs. Caraway, 1961–64

1. Edwin O. Reischauer oral history, JFKL, 1–5.

2. MacArthur oral history, Foreign Service Oral History Program, pt. 3, 46.

3. *The Washington Post,* May 7, 1964; Shiels, *America, Okinawa, and Japan,* 149–76

4. Reischauer, *My Life,* 204–206, 248–49, 276, 299.

5. Caraway oral history, Senior Officers Debriefing Program, vol. 3, sect. 8, pt. 2, 18, 62.

6. Edwin O. Reischauer, *The United States and Japan;* idem, *Wanted: an Asian Policy;* idem, *Beyond Vietnam: The United States and Asia.*

7. Reischauer, *My Life,* 1–29, 97–103.

8. Ibid., 116–17.

9. For literary works, see Edwin O. Reischauer, *Ennin's Travels in T'ang China;* idem, ed., *Ennin's Diary: The Record of a Pilgrimage to China in Search of the Law;* and Reischauer and Joseph Yamagiwa, *Translations from Early Japanese Literature.*

10. In addition to the previously cited works, see Edwin O. Reischauer, *Japan Past and Present;* Reischauer and John K. Fairbank, *A History of East Asian Civilization.*

11. Haru Matsukata Reischauer, *Samurai and Silk: A Japanese and American Heritage,* 1–17.

12. Reischauer, *My Life,* 161–63; Matsukata Reischauer, *Samurai and Silk,* 16; *New York Journal-American,* Mar. 25, 1961.

13. *Mainichi Shimbun,* Mar. 14, 1961; *The Japan Times,* May 20, 1961; Reischauer, *My Life,* 166–71.

14. Lecture notes on Japan for War College, Mar. 17, 1961, Ambassadorial Pa-

pers, 1961–66, Papers of Edwin Reischauer, Harvard University; Reischauer, *The United States and Japan*, 238, 335. The Bonin Islands include Iwo Jima and were administered by the U.S. Navy. The Kurile Islands were to the north and controlled by the Soviet Union.

15. Bidwell to Dulles, Oct. 9, 1950, Japan and the Japanese Peace Treaty folder, box 48, Papers of John Foster Dulles, Princeton University; Bidwell to Dulles, Oct. 24, 1950, ibid.; Franklin to Dulles, Oct. 24, 1950, ibid.; "Study Group Reports: Japanese Peace Treaty Problems—Digest of Discussion," Oct. 23, 1950, ibid.; LaFeber, *The Clash*, 335.

16. Caraway oral history, vol. 3, sect. 8, pt. 2, 6; Okinawa *Morning Star*, Feb. 16, 1961.

17. David Malone, *Hattie and Huey: An Arkansas Tour*; Diane D. Kincade, ed., *Silent Hattie Speaks: The Personal Journal of Senator Hattie Caraway*.

18. Biographical essay, box 1962, Caraway Papers, USAMHI.

19. Ibid.

20. Ibid.; Bean to Oblinger, Jan. 11, 1962, box 1962, Caraway Papers.

21. Ibid.

22. Caraway to Mrs. Joseph Little, n.d., Personal Correspondence (Jan.–Oct., 1961), box 1962, Caraway Papers.

23. Caraway oral history, vol. 3, sect. 8, pt. 2, 21.

24. Ibid., 54; "Okinawa, An Overview from the United States of America," n.d., box 1970, Caraway Papers; "Memorandum for General [Albert] Wedemeyer," n.d., ibid.

25. Memorandum of conversation, June 21, 1961, U.S. State Department, *FRUS, 1961–1963*, 22:698–700.

26. Reischauer, *My Life*, 202–203; memorandum of conversation, June 21, 1961, *FRUS, 1961–1963*, 22:698; Scope Paper, June 16, 1961, Briefing Book Ikeda Visit folder, box 120, President's Office File Papers of John F. Kennedy, JFKL; National Security Action Memorandum No. 68, NASM 68 folder, box 330, National Security File–Meetings and Memorandum, Kennedy Papers.

27. Caraway to Mrs. Joseph Little, July 10, 1961, Personal Correspondence folder, box 1962, Caraway Papers.

28. National Security Action Memorandum No. 68; Rusk to Reischauer, Aug. 3, 1961, 894c.00/6-2161, box 2902, State Department Central Decimal File, 1960–63, RG 59, NACP; Reischauer to George W. Ball, Aug. 5, 1961, ibid.; Reischauer to Rusk, Aug. 7, 1961, ibid.

29. Howard B. Schaffer, *Chester Bowles: New Dealer in the Cold War*, 202–31; Reischauer to Department of State, Sept. 21, 1962, Japan folder, box 217, Policy Planning Staff Files, 1962, RG 59, NACP; "Guidelines for Policy and Operations—Japan," Mar., 1962, ibid.

30. *The New York Times*, Nov. 20, 1960; *The New York World–Telegram and Sun*, May 8, 1958; MacArthur to Robertson, Apr. 15, 1958, *FRUS, 1958–1960*, 18:19–20; MacArthur to Dulles, Feb. 1, 1958, ibid., vol. 17/18 microfiche supplement.

31. *The Wall Street Journal*, July 15, 1963; Senate Armed Services Committee,

Development of the Ryukyu Islands. 89th Cong., 2nd sess., 13–14; House Committee on Appropriations, Foreign Assistance and Related Agencies Appropriations for 1967, 28.

32. House Subcommittee on Foreign Operations Appropriations, Mutual Security Appropriations for 1961, 86th Cong., 2nd sess., 96–97; Senate Committee on Armed Services, Nomination of John T. McNaughton and Development of the Ryukyu Islands, 87th Cong., 2nd sess., 30.

33. Ross to Geren, Aug. 25, 1961, box 2176, State Department Central Decimal File, 1960–63, RG 59, NACP; Baxter to Kitchen, Aug. 25, 1961, ibid.; Reynolds to Koren, Sept. 6, 1961, ibid.

34. *The New York Times,* Sept. 4, 1961; *Ryukyu Shimpo,* Oct. 5, 1961; *Okinawa Taimusu,* Oct. 5, 1961.

35. House Appropriations Committee, Foreign Operations Appropriations for 1965, Hearings before a Subcommittee of the Committee on Appropriations, 88th Cong., 2nd sess., 165–67; Caraway to Theimer, Apr. 4, 1962, DCSOPS Files–Civil Affairs-1960 box, Ryukyu Papers, USAMHI; Shriver to Haugerud, May 21, 1962, ibid.; Caraway oral history, vol. 3, sect. 8, pt. 2, 18, 62.

36. Memorandum for the record, Sept. 14, 1961, box 287, High Commissioner–Chief Executive Meetings subseries, Liaison Department Series, USCAR, RG 260, NACP; Caraway oral history, vol. 3, sect. 8, pt. 2, 56; Reischauer, *My Life,* 204.

37. Risher to Booth, Jan. 12, 1959, 147/8920-(59), box 136, Central Decimal File, JCS Files, RG 218, NACP; "Okinawa—Preliminary Conclusions from Task Force Visit," n.d., Karl Kaysen (9/7/61–11/30/61) folder, box 320, National Security File–Meetings and Memorandum, Kennedy Papers.

38. Swayne to Steeves, Nov. 24, 1961, box 2176, State Department Central Decimal File, 1960–63, RG 59, NACP; Swayne to Steeves, Dec. 5, 1961, ibid.; "Report and Recommendations of the Task Force Ryukyus," Dec., 1961, box 123B, Ryukyu Island Country File, President's Office File, Kennedy Papers.

39. Stahr to McNamara, Feb. 12, 1962, High Commissioner Policy File folder, box 12, Papers of James Lampert, USAMHI; Johnson to Rusk, Feb. 27, 1962, 794c.0221/1362, box 2176, State Department Central Decimal File, 1960–63, Record Group 59, NACP.

40. National Security Action Memorandum No. 133, Mar. 5, 1962, box 335, National Security File–Meeting and Memorandum, Kennedy Papers.

41. "Statement by the President upon Signing Order Relating to the Administration of the Ryukyu Islands," Mar. 19, 1962, John F. Kennedy, *Public Papers of the President: John F. Kennedy, 1962,* 247–48.

42. Editorial note in U.S. State Department, *FRUS, 1961–1963,* 22:773.

43. *Newsweek,* Mar. 19, 1962, 48; *The New York Times,* Apr. 23, 26, 1962; *Washington Evening Star,* Mar. 21, 1962.

44. Reischauer to Rusk, Apr. 17, 1962, 794c.00/1-462, box 2175, State Department Central Decimal File, 1960–63; Reischauer to Rusk, Mar. 20, 21, 1962, 794c.0221/1-362, ibid.

45. *Ryukyu Shimpo*, Mar. 21, 1962; *Okinawa Taimusu*, Mar. 21, 1962; High Commissioner to Department of the Army, Mar. 21, 1962, DCSOPS Files–Civil Affairs-1960s box, Ryukyu Papers; Lt. Col. George M. Bush, "Okinawa: A Study in Overseas Base Requirements," Mar. 14, 1963, ibid.

46. House Armed Services Committee, Subcommittee No. 2 Consideration of H.R. 10937, to Amend the Act Providing for the Economic and Social Development of the Ryukyu Islands, 5210.

47. *Ryukyu Shimpo*, May 21, 1962; *Okinawa Taimusu*, May 21, 23, 1962.

48. Memorandum for the Secretary of State by Kennedy, Mar. 5, 1962, 794c.0221/1-362, box 2176, State Department Central Decimal File, 1960–63; memorandum for the record, Mar. 8, 1962, ibid.

49. *The New York Times*, June 24, 1962; Johnson to Warner, enclosed in Swayne to Fearey and Bacon, Mar. 26, 1962, 794c.0221/1-362, box 2176, State Department Central Decimal File, 1960–63; Stahr to McNamara, May 24, 1962, 794c.0221/4362, box 2177, ibid.; memorandum for the record, June 19, 1962, box 287, High Commissioner–Chief Executive Meetings subseries, Liaison Department Series, USCAR Records, RG 260, NACP; Gillies oral history, Ryukyu Papers; Caraway oral history, vol. 3, sect. 8, pt. 2, 21.

50. Harriman to Johnson, May 29, 1962, 794c.0221/4362, box 2177, State Department Central Decimal File, 1960–63; Reischauer to Rusk, May 9, 1962, ibid.; Reischauer to Caraway, June 11, 1962, 794c.0221/6-162, ibid.; Gilpatric to Johnson, Mar. 22, 1962, box 2176, 794c.0221/1-362, ibid.

51. Harriman to Johnson, Apr. 6, 1962, 794c.0221/4362, box 2177, State Department Central Decimal File, 1960–63; Senate Committee on Armed Services, Development of the Ryukyu Islands, 11, 19, 32.

52. Reischauer to Rusk, Sept. 17, 1962, 794c.0221/7-362, box 2177, State Department Central Decimal File, 1960–63; Reischauer to Rusk, July 7, 1964, Ryukyu Islands folder, box 281, Ryukyu Islands Country File, National Security File, Papers of Lyndon Johnson, LBJL.

53. *The Washington Post*, May 3–7, 1964, Dec. 26, 1965. I would like to thank Leonard Downie, executive editor of *The Washington Post*, for his assistance in finding these articles.

Chapter 7. The Road to Reversion, 1964–67

1. Seizaburo Sato, Kenichi Koyama, and Shunpei Kumon, *Postwar Politician: The Life of Former Prime Minister Masayoshi Ohira*, trans. William R. Carter, 229–34; Masumi, *Contemporary Politics in Japan*, 8591; Masayoshi Ohira, *Brush Strokes: Moments from My Life*, 104.

2. Gerald L. Curtis, *The Japanese Way of Politics*, 27–30.

3. J. A. A. Stockwin, *The Japanese Socialist Party and Neutralism: A Study of a Political Party and its Foreign Policy*, 17, 118, 128; Watanabe, *Okinawa Problem*, 128.

4. Dan Kurzman, *Kishi and Japan: The Search for the Sun*, 47, 76–77.

5. John Welfield interview with Sato in Welfield, *Empire in Eclipse*, 127–30.

6. Curtis, *Japanese Way of Politics*, 6–7.

7. Ibid.; Fukui Haruhiro, *Party in Power: The Japanese Liberal-Democrats and Policymaking*, 124; Masumi, *Postwar Politics in Japan*, 279, 297–98.

8. Dower, *Empire and Aftermath*, 338; Curtis, *Japanese Way of Politics*, 161.

9. Sato, Koyama, and Kumon, *Postwar Politician*, 154, 158–59.

10. Ibid., 341; Fukui, *Party in Power*, 109.

11. Masumi Junnosuke, *Contemporary Politics in Japan*, trans. Lonny E. Carlile, 79–83; Sato, Koyama, and Kumon, *Postwar Politician*, 195–97, 206.

12. Sato, Koyama, and Kumon, *Postwar Politician*, 229–34; Masumi, *Contemporary Politics in Japan*, 85–91; Ohira, *Brush Strokes*, 104.

13. "Intelligence Note," n.d., Japan Memos folder, box 250, Japan Country File, National Security File, Lyndon Johnson Papers.

14. Masumi, *Contemporary Politics in Japan*, 91; Sato, Koyama, and Kumon, *Postwar Politician*, 238.

15. John Dower, "Yoshida in the Scales of History," in *Japan in War and Peace*, ed. John Dower, 212–13, 216–17, 230–38.

16. Thomas R. H. Havens, *Fire across the Sea: The Vietnam War and Japan, 1965–1975*, 133–35.

17. Jones to LBJ, Nov. 4, 1967, White House Central Files folder, box 1, Ryukyu Papers, USAMHI.

18. *The New York Times*, Sept. 3, 1967, Jan. 30, June 20, July 14, 1969; Masumi, *Contemporary Politics in Japan*, 100.

19. "Address by Prime Minister Sato in New York," *Japan Report*, Nov. 20, 1967; *The New York Times*, July 14, 1968.

20. Hasegawa Sukehiro, *Japanese Foreign Aid: Policy and Practice*, 3–21.

21. "Prime Minister Sato's Speech at Opening of 47th Extraordinary Session of National Diet," Nov. 27, 1964, CO 141 folder, box 46, Japan Country File, White House Central Files, Lyndon Johnson Papers; "Address of Eisaku Sato, prime minister of Japan, at the National Press Club," Jan. 12, 1965, CO 141 folder; Havens, *Fire across the Sea*, 26, 109.

22. *U.S. News and World Report*, Nov. 24, 1969, 84–85; *The New York Times*, July 14, 1968; Welfield, *Empire in Eclipse*, 129.

23. *The Washington Post*, Jan. 12, 1965; Washington *Evening Star*, Jan. 12, 1965; Masumi, *Contemporary Politics in Japan*, 100. American documents made available since the publication of these books show that Sato initiated diplomatic talks on Okinawa during the first days of his administration. In his memoirs Reischauer claimed that once Caraway retired, he got the military to allow more Japanese economic aid and carefully guided the two countries toward reversion. Reischauer, *My Life*. Material now available offers a different picture: reversion started to move forward because of Sato.

24. Reischauer to Rusk, Nov. 10, 1964, Cables (vol. 2) folder, box 250, Japan Country File, National Security File, Lyndon Johnson Papers.

25. *Visit to U.S. by the Prime Minister of Japan* (film), Jan. 12, 1965, Audio-Visual

Collection, LBJL; photo contact book, Jan. 12, 1965, Audio-Visual Collection.

26. *The Washington Post*, Jan. 13, 1965; memorandum of conversation, Jan. 12, 1965, Sato's Visit folder, box 253, Japan Country File, National Security File, Lyndon Johnson Papers; memorandum of conversation, Jan. 13, 1965, Japan Memos folder, box 250, ibid.; CIA intelligence memorandum, June 16, 1966, Japan Memos (vol. 2) folder, box 251, ibid.

27. *Okinawa Taimusu*, Aug. 19, 1965; *Japan Times*, Aug. 20, 1965; *Tokyo Shimbun*, Aug. 18, 1965; Masumi, *Contemporary Politics in Japan*, 101; U.S. Embassy–Tokyo to Rusk, Aug. 21, 1965, Press Visit–Prime Minister Sato folder, box 1795, International Activities subseries, Liaison Department Series, USCAR Records, RG 260, NACP.

28. *The New York Times*, Aug. 22, 1965; *Stars and Stripes*, Aug. 21, 1965; *Tokyo Shimbun*, Aug. 20, 1965.

29. *Nihon Keizai*, Aug. 22, 1965; *Ryukyu Shimpo*, Aug. 22, 1965; *Okinawa Taimusu*, Aug. 22, 1965; *Stars and Stripes*, Aug. 21, 1965.

30. Watson to Department of the Army, Aug. 19, 1965, Ryukyu Island folder, box 281, Ryukyu Country File, National Security File, Lyndon Johnson Papers.

31. Ibid.; "After-action Report, Visit of Prime Minister of Japan," Aug. 27, 1965, Sub-Committee on Public Affairs folder, box 2786, Public Affairs Department series, USCAR Records; *The New York Times*, Aug. 20, 1965; *Japan Times*, Aug. 22, 1965; *Stars and Stripes*, Aug. 21, 1965.

32. Watson to Department of the Army, Aug. 19, 1965, Ryukyu Island folder, box 281, Ryukyu Country File, National Security File, Lyndon Johnson Papers; *Stars and Stripes*, Aug. 21, 1965; "After-action Report, Visit of Prime Minister of Japan," Aug. 27, 1965; *Japan Times*, Aug. 22, 1965; *Mainichi Shimbun*, Aug. 20, 1965; *Asahi Shimbun*, Aug. 21, 1965.

33. *Stars and Stripes*, Aug. 21, 1965; *Newsweek*, Aug. 30, 1965, 35–36; *The New York Times*, Aug. 20, 1965.

34. Masumi, *Contemporary Politics in Japan*, 101; *Japan Times*, Aug. 27, 1965; *Mainichi Shimbun*, Aug. 20–21, 1965; *Ryukyu Shimpo*, Aug. 22, 1965.

35. Edwin Reischauer, *My Life*, 276; House Committee on Appropriations, Foreign Assistance and Related Agencies Appropriations for 1967, 2; House Committee on Appropriations, Foreign Assistance and Related Agencies Appropriations for 1969, 27; House Committee on Appropriations, Foreign Assistance and Related Agencies Appropriations for 1970, 452; CIA intelligence memorandum, June 16, 1966; Okinawa *Morning Star*, Dec. 24, 1966; Lt. Gen. Albert Watson II oral history, Senior Officers Debriefing Program, USAMHI, 4; Masumi, *Contemporary Politics in Japan*, 101; *Tokyo Shimbun*, Aug. 13, 1966.

36. Havens, *Fire across the Sea*, 176–78; CIA special report, "The Okinawan Issue in Japanese Politics," Japan Memos (vol. 4) folder, box 252, Japan Country File, National Security File, Lyndon Johnson Papers.

37. A poll taken by the staff of the *Mainichi Shimbun* a year later showed that

over 60 percent of the public supported functional revision. *Mainichi Shimbun*, Oct. 3, 1967.

38. *The New York Times*, Aug. 27, 1965; *Mainichi Shimbun*, Aug. 24, 1966.

39. Memorandum for record, Aug. 29, 1966, box 286, High Commissioner–Chief Executive Meetings subseries, Liaison Department Series, USCAR Records; memorandum for record, Dec. 22, 1966, ibid.; memorandum for record, Sept. 8, 1966, ibid.; *Mainichi Shimbun*, Aug. 24, 1966

40. *Asahi Shimbun*, Jan. 19, 1967.

41. Ibid.; *Tokyo Shimbun*, Jan. 22, 1967; *Mainichi Shimbun*, Jan. 22, 1967; *Sankei*, Jan. 21, 1967.

42. Watson oral history, 18–20; Reischauer, *My Life*, 276, 299.

43. CIA intelligence memorandum, June 16, 1966; Adam Yarmolinsky to Thaddeus Holt, Apr. 28, 1966, 1957–73 folder, Ryukyuan Affairs Division box, Directorate of International Affairs–DCSOPS, Ryukyu Papers.

44. *The New York Times*, Sept. 17, 1961, Nov. 8, 1965; Unger oral history, 27; Watson oral history, 26; *Army*, Oct. 1969, 52.

45. Conversation between General of the Army MacArthur and Mr. George F. Kennan, Mar. 5, 1948, attached to "Recommendations with Respect to U.S. Policy toward Japan" (PPS 28), Mar. 25, 1948, *FRUS, 1948*, 6:700–702; George Barrett, "Report on Okinawa: A Rampart We Built," *The New York Times Magazine*, Sept. 21, 1952, 9; *U.S. News and World Report*, June 22, 1951, 26; *The New York Times*, Sept. 1, 1965, Feb. 2, 10, 1969; Embassy to Secretary of State, Aug. 2, 1965, Cables folder (vol. 3), box 250, Japan Country File, National Security File, Lyndon Johnson Papers; Emmerson to Rusk, July 30, 31, Aug. 2, 3, 1965, ibid.; telcon with William Bundy, July 31, 1965, Japan folder, box 4, Papers of George W. Ball, LBJL; telcon with William Bundy, Aug. 8, 1965, ibid.; Watson oral history, 27.

46. Memorandum for the record, Dec. 7, 1965, box 287, High Commissioner–Chief Executive Meetings subseries, Liaison Department Series, USCAR Records; MacArthur to Schultze, Nov. 4, 1965, ST 51-3 Ryukyu folder, box 90, Confidential File, White House Central Files, Lyndon Johnson Papers; Vance to Schultze, Nov. 2, 1965, ibid.; White to Johnson, Dec. 17, 1965, ibid.

47. *Weekly Okinawa Times*, Dec. 25, 1965; Watson oral history, 7–11, 60.

48. JCS to Secretary of Defense, Dec. 23, 1965, Ryukyuan Affairs Division box, Directorate of International Affairs–DCSOPS, Ryukyu Papers. In his study of triangular relations between the United States, the Soviet Union, and China, Gordon Chang explained that American leaders focused on the harsh tone of Chinese rhetoric and thought that China intended to export Communist revolution to other nations. American policymakers misread Chinese intentions: the militant language was a cover. Chang shows with a careful, in-depth analysis that Chinese leaders were actually informing foreign communist movements that they would have to achieve their revolutions on their own. Nevertheless, American leaders believed China was responsible for the communist uprising in Vietnam and planned for a Chinese intervention in that

country. The Cultural Revolution did nothing to change the thinking in Washington. Gordon Chang, *Friends and Enemies: The United States, China, and the Soviet Union, 1948–1972*, 269–76.

49. Deborah Shapley, *Promise and Power: The Life and Times of Robert McNamara*, 128, 630; Yarmolinsky to Holt, Apr. 28, 1966, Ryukyuan Affairs Division box, Directorate of International Affairs–DCSOPS, Ryukyu Papers; memorandum of conversation, Nov. 28, 1967, Sato Visit folder, box 253, Japan Country File, National Security File, Lyndon Johnson Papers.

50. Reischauer to Rusk, May 24, June 28, 1966, Japan Cables folder, box 251, Japan Country File, National Security File; State-Embassy draft, n.d., enclosure to Barnett to Read, June 1, 1966, Ryukyu folder, box 82, Files of Bill Moyers, Aide Files, Lyndon Johnson Papers.

51. John T. McNaughton to Chairman, Interdepartmental Regional Group for the Far East, n.d., 1957–73 folder, Ryukyuan Affairs Division box, Directorate of International Affairs–DCSOPS, Ryukyu Papers.

52. Bundy to Johnson, May 23, 1966, Ryukyu folder, box 82, Bill Moyers files; Rostow to Johnson, May 30, 1966, ibid.

53. McGeorge Bundy to U. Alexis Johnson, Dec. 15, 1965, U. Alexis Johnson File, box 135, Name File, White House Central File, Lyndon Johnson Papers; Senate Committee on Armed Services. Development of the Ryukyu Islands, 15; Norman Mailer, *Harlot's Ghost*, 1298.

54. U. Alexis Johnson, *Right Hand*, 396, 402–403, 441; *The Washington Post*, Mar. 31, 1966; *The New York Times*, Mar. 31, 1966.

55. *Washington Daily News*, July 27, 1966; *Christian Science Monitor*, July 29, 30, Aug. 1 1966; *Los Angeles Times*, July 31, Aug. 7, 1966; *Time*, Aug. 5, 1966, 23; *Newsweek*, Aug. 8, 1966, 20; *U.S. News and World Report*, Aug. 8, 1966, 58–62; *Honolulu Advertiser*, Aug. 1, 1966; Baltimore *Sun*, July 27, Aug. 11, 1966; Senate Committee on Foreign Relations, Nominations of Robert R. Bowie and U. Alexis Johnson, 89th Cong., 2nd sess.; *Chuo Koron*, Feb., 1967.

56. Unger oral history, 29, 30, 39; U. Alexis Johnson, *Right Hand*, 456–57.

57. Unger oral history, 30.

58. Ibid., 4, 20.

59. A Harvard graduate, Steinberg lived in Tokyo and had a Japanese wife. *The Washington Post*, May 3, 6, 7, 1964; *Yomuri Shimbun*, Apr. 11–13, 1963.

60. The citations in this footnote are to a later edition of Oshiro's book. Oshiro Tatsuhiro, *Kakuteru paatii* (the cocktail party), 183–82, 188–99, 255; Kerr, *Okinawa;* The review also ran in the English-language version of the paper: *Weekly Okinawa Times*, Feb.18, 1967.

61. This short story has been published in several different venues. The citations here are to a 1972 compilation of Higashi's work: Higashi Mineo, *Okinawa no shonen* (Child of Okinawa), 9–10, 16.

62. USCAR, *The Newspapers of the Ryukyu Islands*, 1–3.

63. Caraway oral history, vol. 3, sect. 8, pt. 2, 15, 61; Watson oral history, 36.

64. *United States v. Ushi Shiroma*, Cr. No. 10841.123, *Federal Supplement*, 145.

65. Notes by Judd, box 85, Congressional File, Papers of Walter Judd, HISU.

66. U. Alexis Johnson, *Right Hand*, 474; "Report on Follow-Up Actions on Kishi Visit," *FRUS, 1955–1957*, vol. 23, pt. 1, 444–48; MacArthur to Herter, July 27, 1960, *FRUS, 1958–1960*, vol. 17/18 microfiche supplement; memorandum of conversation, June 21, 1962, 794c.0221/1-361, box 2176, State Department Central Decimal File, 1960–63.

67. *Stars and Stripes*, May 26, 1967; Okinawa *Morning Star*, May 26, 1966, May 25, 1967; "News Conference of U. Alexis Johnson," Mar. 3, 1967, Visitor–U.S. & Other folder, box 1797, International Political Activity subseries, Liaison Department Series, USCAR Records; Unger oral history, interview two, 27–28.

68. U. Alexis Johnson, *Right Hand*, 474; *New York Herald Tribune*, June 17, 1962; *Stars and Stripes*, Aug. 2, 1966; *The Washington Post*, Dec. 27, 1965; McGiffet to Unger, Sept. 26, 1967, Ryukyuan Affairs Division–Directorate of International and Civic Affairs folder, Ryukyus Internal and Civic Affairs box, Ryukyu Papers; Unger oral history, interview number two, 24; Johnson to Rusk, Dec. 20, 1967, Japan Cables (vol. 7) folder, box 252, Japan Country File, National Security File, Lyndon Johnson Papers; Rostow to LBJ, Jan. 29, 1968, ST 51-3 Ryukyu folder, box 90, Confidential File, White House Central Files, Lyndon Johnson Papers; memorandum of record, June 22, 1965, box 287, High Commissioner–Chief Executive Meetings subseries, Liaison Department Series, USCAR Records.

69. McGiffet to Unger, Sept. 26, 1967; Unger oral history, interview ten, 16.

Chapter 8. Reversion, 1967–69

1. Undersecretary Johnson's back grounder, Nov. 21, 1969, in Senate Committee on Foreign Relations, United States Security Agreements and Commitments Abroad, Japan and Okinawa: Hearings before the Subcommittee on United States Security Agreements and Commitments Abroad, 91st Cong., 2d sess., (Jan. 26–29, 1970), pt. 5:1439–45.

2. Previous writers working on this topic have focused only on the changes brought about by Okinawa reversion. Two scholars have examined U.S.-Japanese relations in light of the war in Vietnam. According to Walter LaFeber, Okinawa, trade, China, and the war wrecked relations between the United States and Japan, invoking a new era that resembled the 1920s more than the time between 1945 and 1960. Thomas R. H. Havens, however, argued that the war forced the United States to return Okinawa but also induced Japan to expand its defense commitments to include South Korea. Havens gives too much credit to the war. Even if there had been no Vietnam War, the Americans still would have returned Okinawa. In a doctoral dissertation later published as a book in 1970, Watanabe Akio called the return of the islands a sign that America accepted Japan's equality. Roger Buckley contended that U.S. diplomats mishandled the Okinawa issue, getting noth-

ing of value for the island. In a collective work, I. M. Destler, Haruhiro Fukui, and Hideo Sato argued that textiles, rather than Okinawa, was "the most severe crisis in U.S.-Japanese relations since the postwar occupation." However, my argument is that while Japan was strong, it was hardly interested in pursuing a course totally independent of the United States *because* of Okinawan reversion. Watanabe, *Okinawa Problem;* Roger Buckley, *U.S.-Japan Alliance Diplomacy;* Havens, *Fire across the Sea;* Walter LaFeber, "Decline of Relations during the Vietnam War," in *The United States and Japan in the Postwar World,* ed. Akira Iriye and Warren I. Cohen, 96–113; I. M. Destler, Haruhiro Fukui, and Hideo Sato, *The Textile Wrangle: Conflict in Japanese-American Relations, 1969–1971,* 7–8, 121–39.

3. U. Alexis Johnson, *Right Hand,* 470.

4. U. Alexis Johnson diary, Aug. 13, 1967 (tape 15), Papers of U. Alexis Johnson, LBJL, 5, 7; Johnson to Rusk, Aug. 1, 1967, box 251, Japan Country File, National Security File, Lyndon Johnson Papers; Johnson to Rusk, Nov. 6, 1967, box 252, ibid.

5. Robert McNamara, interview by Wakazumi Kei, *Chuo Koron,* July 15, 1966; meeting with foreign policy advisors, Nov. 4, 1967, White House Central Files, box 1, Ryukyu Papers, USAMHI; National Security Council memorandum for the record, Aug. 31, 1967, box 2, NSC Meeting File, National Security File, Lyndon Johnson Papers; Jenkins to Rostow, June 14, 1968, Japan Memos (vol. 3) folder, box 252, Japan Country File, National Security File; U Alexis Johnson diary, Aug. 13, 1967 (tape 15), 5, 7; Walt W. Rostow, interview by author, Austin, Texas, Nov. 12, 1991.

6. Rostow to LBJ, Sept., 11, 1967, box 76, President's Appointment File, Lyndon Johnson Papers.

7. Meeting with foreign policy advisors, Nov. 4, 1967; McNamara to LBJ, Sept. 13, 1967, box 76, President's Appointment File, Lyndon Johnson Papers.

8. McNamara to LBJ, Sept. 13, 1967; National Security Council memorandum for the record, Aug. 31, 1967; U. Alexis Johnson, *Right Hand,* 472, 475; meeting with foreign policy advisors, Nov. 4, 1967; Shapley, *Promise and Power,* 237–41; Mark Perry, *Four Stars,* 172; Wheeler to McNamara, July 20, 1967, U.S.-Japan Project, National Security Archive, The George Washington University, Washington D.C.

9. U. Alexis Johnson, *Right Hand,* 441, 443.

10. National Security Council memorandum for the record, Aug. 31, 1967; U. Alexis Johnson, *Right Hand,* 457, 452.

11. Dean Rusk oral history, LBJL, 22; National Security Council memorandum for the record, Aug. 31, 1967; Dean Rusk, letter to the author, Oct. 9, 1991; U. Alexis Johnson, *Right Hand,* 475–76; Meeting with foreign policy advisors, Nov. 4, 1967.

12. Rostow, interview.

13. U. Alexis Johnson, *Right Hand,* 483–86; Johnson to Rusk, Oct. 6, 1967, box 253, Japan Country File, National Security File, Lyndon Johnson Papers.

14. Johnson to Rusk, Nov. 1, 1967, enclosed in Rostow to LBJ, Nov. 1, 1967, box 251, Japan Country File, National Security File; Tower to Johnson, Nov. 8, 1967, box 1114, Papers of John Tower, Southwestern University.

15. U. Alexis Johnson, *Right Hand*, 478–86; Johnson to Rusk, Oct. 11, 1967, box 251, Japan Country File, National Security File; Johnson to Rusk, Oct. 28, 1967, ibid.; Johnson to Rusk, Nov. 6, 1967, box 252, ibid.; Rusk to Johnson, Dec. 28, 1967, ibid.

16. Rostow, interview; Sato to Rostow, Nov. 9, 1967, box 252, Japan Country File, National Security File; memo of conversation, Nov. 11, 1967, Non-Vietnam folder, box 16, Files of Walt Rostow, National Security File, Lyndon Johnson Papers.

17. Osborn to Rusk, Nov. 14, 1967, box 253, Japan Country File, National Security File; memorandum of conversation, Oct. 27, 1967, Japan memos (vol. 6) folder, box 252, ibid.; memo of conversation, Nov. 11, 1967; memorandum of conversation, Nov. [12], 1967, box 25, Memos to the President File, National Security File, Lyndon Johnson Papers; U. Alexis Johnson, *Right Hand*, 478–79.

18. Memorandum of conversation, Nov. 11, 1967; U. Alexis Johnson diary, May 5, 1968 (tape 16), 4–5.

19. Memorandum for the President, Nov. 13, 1967, box 25, Memos to the President File, National Security File; Mansfield speech enclosed in Johnson to Rusk, Sept. 14, 1967, box 251, Japan Country File, National Security File.

20. Welfield, *Empire in Eclipse*, 239–43; Rostow to LBJ, Nov. 14, 1967, box 82, President's Appointment File, National Security File; Bundy to Rostow, Nov. 15, 1967, box 252, Japan Country File, National Security File; "Joint Statement Following Discussion with Prime Minister Sato of Japan," Nov. 15, 1967, in Lyndon B. Johnson, *Public Papers of the Presidents: Lyndon B. Johnson, 1967*, 2:1036–37; notes for Nov. 14, 1967, box 3, Intra-Office series II, Papers of Richard Russell, University of Georgia.

21. U. Alexis Johnson oral history, 37–38, LBJL.

22. U. Alexis Johnson, *Right Hand*, 481–82.

23. Speech of Prime Minister Sato Eisaku of Japan, Nov. 15, 1967, box 253, Japan Country File, National Security File; *St. Louis Post Dispatch*, Nov. 16, 1967; *The Washington Post*, Nov. 16, 1967.

24. Washington *Evening Star*, Nov. 23, 1967; *The New York Times*, Nov. 17, 1967; *Pittsburgh Post-Gazette*, Nov. 16, 1967; *Asahi Shimbun*, Nov. 16, 1967; *Mainichi Shimbun*, Nov. 17, 1967; *Stars and Strips*, Nov. 18, 1967.

25. Report of Ad Hoc Committee on Control of Okinawa Teachers' Association, Feb. 3, 1966, Ad Hoc Committee–OTA folder, box 110, USCAR Records, RG 260, NACP; memorandum for High Commissioner, May 21, 1968, OTA (1966–67) folder, ibid.; agent report, July 10, 1967, ibid.; agent report, Nov. 12, 1968, ibid.; Department of Defense intelligence initial report, Aug. 2, 1968, ibid.

26. Unger to Department of the Army, Nov. 9, 11, 1968, Ryukyu Islands folder,

box 281, Ryukyu Islands Country File, National Security File, Lyndon
Johnson Papers.

27. Unger oral history, interview two, 24–28; memorandum of conversation,
Nov. 11, 1967; Jenkins to Rostow, Nov. 11, 1968, Ryukyu Islands folder, box
281, Ryukyu Islands Country File, National Security File; *Mainichi Shimbun*,
Nov. 12, 1968.

28. Manchester *Union Leader*, Jan. 5, 1968.

29. *The Progressive*, Nov., 1969; *The Reporter*, Nov. 2, 1967; *Army*, Nov. 1969; *Saturday Review*, Dec. 6, 1969; *Atlantic Monthly*, Oct., 1969; *The New Republic*,
June 14, 1969; *The Nation*, Feb. 3, 1969; *National Geographic*, Sept., 1969;
Travel, Mar., 1969; *The Wall Street Journal*, June 5, 1969; *The Reader's Digest*,
Nov., 1969; *U.S. News and World Report*, Sept. 22, 1969; *Time*, June 13, 1969;
The Christian Science Monitor, May 2, 31, 1969.

30. U. Alexis Johnson, *Right Hand*, 542; *Chuo Koron*, Oct., 1969; Edwin
Reischauer oral history, LBJL, 5–6; Armin H. Meyer, *Assignment Tokyo: An
Ambassador's Journal*, 27.

31. Richard Nixon, "Asia after Viet Nam," *Foreign Affairs* 46 (Oct., 1967): 121;
Stephen E. Ambrose, *Nixon: The Education of a Politician, 1913–1962*, 324;
idem, *Nixon: The Triumph of a Politician, 1962–1972*, 115–16; Jonathan
Aitken, *Nixon: A Life*, 2; *Asahi Shimbun*, Oct. 22, 1968.

32. Richard Nixon, *RN: The Memoirs of Richard Nixon*, 560–67; Schaller, *Altered
States*, 244.

33. Welfield, *Empire in Eclipse*, 243.

34. H. R. Haldeman, Jan. 11, 1972, *The Haldeman Diaries: Inside the Nixon White
House, the Complete Multimedia Edition*.

35. U. Alexis Johnson diary, Jan. 12, 1969 (tape 16), 22; U. Alexis Johnson, *Right
Hand*, 511; Emmerson to Johnson, Oct. 22, 1968, box 7, Papers of John K.
Emmerson, HISU.

36. LaFeber, *The Clash*, 348; Reischauer to Kissinger, Jan. 6, 1969, box 40, Correspondence and Other Papers 1966–81, Papers of Edwin Reischauer, Harvard
University; Henry A. Kissinger, *White House Years*, 325.

37. Kissinger, *White House Years*, 326–27; National Security Study Memorandum 5, Jan. 21, 1969, box 1, National Security Council Records, RG 273,
NACP; Memorandum for Dr. Kissinger, Jan. 22, 1969, Memoranda-
Declassified folder, box 1, Papers of Morton Halperin, LBJL. For U. Alexis
Johnson's later views of Kissinger, see *Right Hand*, 514, 516–18, (and especially) 521–24.

38. U. Alexis Johnson, *Right Hand*, 541, 544; Kissinger, *White House Years*,
327–28.

39. "U.S.-Japanese Relationship: Summary," Apr. 29, 1969, U.S.-Japan Project,
National Security Archive; NSSM-5: Japan, U.S.-Japan Project; U. Alexis
Johnson, *Right Hand*, 541, 544; Kissinger, *White House Years*, 327–28.

40. National Security Decision Memorandum 13, May 28, 1969, box 1, National
Security Council Records, RG 273, NACP; Kissinger, *White House Years*, 329;

The New York Times, June 3, 1969; Haldeman, June 3, 1969, *Haldeman Diaries*; Nixon, *RN*, 389; U. Alexis Johnson, *Right Hand*, 545; Haldeman meeting notes, June 4–5, 1969, box 40, Files of H. R. Haldeman, Nixon Presidential Project, NACP; National Security Decision Memorandum 13, May 28, 1969; Schaller, *Altered States*, 214, 290 n. 12.

41. Record of Chief of Staff Fonecom with Gen. Wheeler and Gen. Chapman, Nov. 21, 1969, Fonecoms (Oct.–Dec., 1969) folder, box 21, Papers of William Westmoreland, USAMHI.

42. Central Intelligence Agency information cable, Nov. 14, 1968, Ryukyu Islands folder, box 281, Ryukyu Islands Country File, National Security File, Lyndon Johnson Papers; Masumi, *Contemporary Politics in Japan*, 102–103.

43. U. Alexis Johnson, *Right Hand*, 521, 542–43; Kissinger, *White House Years*, 328–29; LaFeber, *The Clash*, 349.

44. U. Alexis Johnson, letter to the author, Oct. 8, 1991; Wakaizumi Kei, "Japan beyond 1970," *Foreign Affairs* 47 (Apr., 1969): 512–19.

45. Kissinger, *White House Years*, 335; U. Alexis Johnson, *Right Hand*, 543–44; *The New York Times*, Sept. 21, 1969.

46. Wakaizumi Kei, *Tasaku nakarishi o shinzemu to hossu* (Just the four of us—I want to believe there was no other alternative), 410–11; Kissinger, *White House Years*, 329–35; National Security Decision Memorandum 13, May 28, 1969.

47. *The New York Times*, Nov. 17, 1969; Havens, *Fire across the Sea*, 197; *Asahi Shimbun*, Nov. 18, 1969; "Exchange of Greetings, Nov. 19, 1971," *Department of State Bulletin* 61 (Dec. 15, 1969): 551.

48. Sato Eisaku, Nov. 19,1969, *Sato Eisaku nikki* (Sato Eisaku diary), 3:536; memorandum of conversation by James J. Wickel, Nov. 19, 1967, U.S.-Japan Project, National Security Archive.

49. "Text of Joint Communiqué, Nov. 21, 1969," *Department of State Bulletin* 61 (Dec. 15, 1969): 555–56; Kissinger, *White House Years*, 335; Meyer, *Assignment*, 45.

50. Undersecretary Johnson's back grounder, Nov. 21, 1969, in Senate Committee on Foreign Relations, United States Security Agreements and Commitments Abroad, Japan and Okinawa: Hearings before the Subcommittee on United States Security Agreements and Commitments Abroad, 91st Cong., 2d sess., (Jan. 26–29, 1970), pt. 5:1439–45.

51. Prime Minister Sato Eisaku's speech before the National Press Club, Nov. 21, 1969, ibid., pt. 5:1429–30, 1432.

52. U. Alexis Johnson testimony, ibid., pt. 5:1162.

53. *The Atlanta Constitution*, Nov. 22, 1969; *The Christian Science Monitor*, Nov. 29–30, 1969; *Chicago Tribune*, Nov. 22, 1969; Cleveland *Plain Dealer*, Nov. 22, 1969; *St. Louis Post Dispatch*, Nov. 21, 1969; *The New York Times*, Nov. 23, 1969; *Los Angeles Times*, Nov. 22, 1969; *Time*, Nov. 28, 1969. A neutral assessment came from *The Houston Post*, Dec. 2, 1969, with a dissenting voice from the Columbia *State*, Nov. 28, 1969.

54. *Kansas City Star,* Nov. 22, 1969; *The Boston Globe,* Nov. 22, 1969.

55. "First Annual Report to Congress on the United States Foreign Policy for the 1970s," in Richard Nixon, *Public Papers of the Presidents: Richard Nixon, 1970,* 142; Haldeman, Apr. 27, 1970, *Haldeman Diaries.*

Chapter 9. Aftermath, 1969–72

1. "Statement Delivered by High Commissioner James B. Lampert over Radio and Television Stations on Okinawa," USCAR, *Report for Period 1 July 1970 to 30 June 1971,* 264–65; *The Washington Post,* Dec. 21, 1970.

2. *The New York Times,* Mar. 24, 1962; *Congressional Quarterly,* Dec. 5, 1969.

3. Article 3 of the peace treaty, not Act 3, granted Japan residual sovereignty over the Ryukyu Islands. Caraway to Wedemeyer, n.d., box 1970, Caraway Papers.

4. *The New York Times,* Apr. 4, 1970; Okinawa *Morning Star,* May 14, 1972; Schless to Altman, Apr. 18, 1972, Ryukyus Internal and Civic Affairs box, Ryukyus Papers, USAMHI; McClellan to Holt, Apr. 24, 1972, ibid.; Holt to Rhatican, May 4, 1972, ibid.; Cashen to Belieu, May 12, 1972, ibid.; Belieu to Cashen, n.d., ibid.; Lt. Gen. James B. Lampert, Senior Officers Debriefing Program, USAMHI; *CR* (1969), 11955.

5. *The New York Times,* May 11, 1969; *The Wall Street Journal,* Nov. 12, 1969; Nelson to Caraway, Dec. 3, 1969, Okinawa *Morning Star* Correspondence folder, box 1969, Caraway Papers; Nelson to Caraway, Oct. 29, 1969, box 1970, ibid.

6. Nelson to Caraway, Oct. 29, 1969, box 1970, ibid.

7. *CR* (1969), 34682–83; *The New York Times,* Oct. 18, 1969.

8. Washington *Evening Star,* Nov. 4, 1970; "Staff Memorandum: Okinawa Reversion Treaty," Oct. 26, 1971, Okinawa Reversion Treaty Files, box 40, Senate Foreign Relations Committee Records, RG 46, NADC; Okinawa Business Advisory Group, summary of 4th meeting, Jan. 22, 1971,: Ryukyu folder, box 21, Subject File–States-Territories, White House Central Files, Nixon Presidential Project.

9. Memorandum for record, Mar. 22, 1971, box 11, Personal X File 1971–72, Lampert Papers; Stolle to Fong, Sept. 30, 1971, in Senate Committee on Foreign Relations, The Agreement between the United States of America and Japan Concerning the Ryukyu Islands and the Daito Islands, 92nd Cong., 1st sess., 129; Gale McGee to Nixon, Apr. 28, 1971, Ryukyu folder, box 21, Subject File–States-Territories; Thurmond to Nixon, Apr. 27, 1971, ibid.; Jackson to Nixon, Apr. 26, 1971, ibid.; Wolf to Nixon, Apr. 27, 1971, ibid.; Ford to Kissinger, Apr. 26, 1971, Japan folder, box 44, Subject File–Japan Country File, White House Central Files, Nixon Project; Dole to Kissinger, Apr. 27, 1971, ibid.; Kissinger to Ford, May 15, 1971, ibid.; Kissinger to Dole, May 15, 1971, ibid.

10. Aichi to Meyer, June 17, 1971, USCAR, *Report for Period 1 July 1970 to 30 June*

1971, 365–59; Senate Committee on Foreign Relations, Agreement between the United States of America and Japan, 85–89; USCAR, *The Final Civil Affairs Report, 30 June 1971–15 May 1972*, 6–7.

11. *CR* (1969), 14355–56; *The Arizona Republic*, Aug. 18, 1969.

12. *CR* (1969), 32866, 33051.

13. *The New York Times*, Nov. 6, 1969; Washington *Evening Star*, Nov. 13, 1969.

14. Sneider to Kissinger, May 29, 1969, Ryukyu folder, box 21, Subject File–States-Territories, White House Central Files, Nixon Project; Larry A. Niksch, "Congress and the Reversion of Okinawa," Aug. 13, 1970, Legislative Reference Service, Library of Congress; *The Shreveport Journal*, May 30, 1969; *The Birmingham News*, May 30, 1969; *The Hartford Courant*, May 30, 1969; *The Arizona Republic*, June 4, 1969; *Chicago Tribune*, June 4; Sept. 10, 1969.

15. *Mainichi Daily News*, Nov. 15, 1969

16. *CR* (1969), 35759–60.

17. Ibid., 35760–61; Hollings to Nixon, Nov. 25, 1969, box 43, Subject File–Japan Country File, White House Central Files, Nixon Project; Nixon to Hollings, Jan. 9, 1970, ibid.; Kissinger to Nixon, Jan. 1, 1970, ibid.; *CR* (1970), 4796, 10474.

18. Haldeman, "Appointment Log," Nov. 21, 1969, *Haldeman Diaries*; Alexander to Haig, Nov. 20, 1969, Ryukyu folder, box 21, Subject File–States-Territories, White House Central Files, Nixon project; *CR* (1971) 40159.

19. Fulbright to Rogers, Feb. 25, 1971, box 23, subseries 5, series 48, Papers of J. William Fulbright, University of Arkansas; Rogers to Fulbright, Mar. 3, 1971, ibid.; Green, Abshire, and Stevenson to Rogers, Jan. 29, 1971, Reversion Correspondence folder, box 12, Lampert Papers; John R. Stevenson, "Congressional Participation in the Reversion of the Ryukyus," Jan. 20, 1971, ibid.; Rogers to Nixon, Feb. 2, 1971, ibid.

20. Bergsten to Kissinger, Mar. 18, 1971, Japan folder, box 44, Subject File–Japan Country File, White House Central Files, Nixon Project; Flanigan to Kissinger, Mar. 31, 1971, ibid.; *CR* (1971), 13239; *The New York Times*, Apr. 19, 1971.

21. *The New York Times*, Apr. 29, 1971; *CR* (1971), 11684; Byrd to Fulbright, May 3, 1971, box 23, subseries 5, Series 48, Fulbright Papers.

22. *The New York Times*, May 3, June 10, 24, 1971; notation to Fulbright on May 3 clipping, Fulbright to Mansfield, May 4, 1971, box 23, subseries 5, Series 48, Fulbright Papers.

23. *CR* (1969), 32620; *CR* (1970), 10470–78, 10831; Belieu to Thurmond, Nov. 3, 1969, Ryukyu folder, box 21, Subject File–State-Territories, White House Central File, Nixon Project.

24. Destler, Fukui, and Sato, *Textile Wrangle*, 283, 290.

25. *The Washington Post*, Dec. 22, 1970; *Asahi Evening News*, Mar. 15, 1971.

26. George Gallup, *The Gallup Poll: Public Opinion, 1935–1971*, 3:2104–2105; idem, *The Gallup Poll: Public Opinion, 1972–1977*, 1:39.

27. "Message to the Senate Transmitting Agreement between the United States and Japan Concerning the Ryukyu and Daito Islands," Sept. 21, 1971, in Nixon, *Public Papers,* 962; Senate Foreign Relations Committee, *Agreement between the United States of America and Japan,* 39; *CR* (1971), 40147, 40158, 40388.

28. Lampert oral history, 2; *The Boston Globe,* July 11, 1978; House Committee on Appropriations, Subcommittee on Foreign Operations and Related Agencies Appropriations: Foreign Operations and Related Agencies Appropriations for 1970, *CR* (1970), pt. 1:164; "Biographical Sketch," Ryukyu Island Miscellaneous folder, box 17, Lampert Papers.

29. Lampert oral history, 6.

30. Ibid., 26, 30. Unger used the same notes for his oral history, making it essentially the same document as his briefing for Lampert. Unger oral history, Senior Officers Debriefing Program.

31. Ibid., 8–9, 17–18; Lampert to Siena, n.d., Outgoing Backchannel Messages (1969–72) folder, box 7, Lampert Papers.

32. Lampert to Department of the Army, Dec. 1, 1969, Bbx 286, High Commissioner–Chief Executive Meetings subseries, Liaison Department Series, USCAR Records RG 260, NACP; *The Wall Street Journal,* Dec. 24, 1969; *The New York Times,* May 6, 1972; *U.S. News and World Report,* May 22, 1972, 30, 32; *Time,* May 22, 1972; *San Francisco Examiner & Chronicle,* May 18, 1969; *Los Angeles Times,* Nov. 23, 1969.

33. *Los Angeles Times,* Nov. 23, 1969; USCAR, *The Final Civil Affairs Report,* 9.

34. USCAR, *The Final Civil Affairs Report,* 9.

35. "Remarks by Civil Administrator Robert A. Fearey at the Dining-Out of the 824th Combat Support Group," Feb. 27, 1971, USCAR, *Report for Period 1 July 1970 to 30 June 1971,* 271.

36. *The Wall Street Journal,* July 18, 1969; oral history, 36–43.

37. "Statement Delivered by High Commissioner James B. Lampert over Radio and Television Stations on Okinawa," USCAR, *Report for Period 1 July 1970 to 30 June 1971,* 264–65; *The Washington Post,* Dec. 21, 1970; Col. William G. Schless oral history, Senior Officers Debriefing Program, USAMHI, pt. 2, 3–4.

38. *The Honolulu Advertiser,* Jan. 14, 1971; "Remarks by High Commissioner James B. Lampert before the Fort Buckner Officer's Wives Club," Sept. 10, 1971, in USCAR, *The Final Civil Affairs Report.* 152.

39. Lampert to CINPAC, Jan. 11, 1971, Chemical Weapons folder, box 3, Lampert Papers; Lampert to Department of the Army, Jan. 11, 1971, ibid.

40. Lampert to Department of the Army, Jan. 12, 1971, Chemical Weapons folder, box 3, Lampert Papers.

41. Lampert to Department of the Army, Jan. 13, 1971, Chemical Weapons folder, box 3, Lampert Papers.

42. Johnson to Lampert, Jan. 20, 1971, Chemical Weapons folder, box 3, Lampert Papers; *The Japan Times,* Jan. 14, 17, 1971.

43. Schless oral history, pt. 2, 6.

44. American Embassy to Lampert, Jan. 4, 1971, Yamanaka File, Lampert Papers; Lampert to Department of the Army, Jan. 18, 1971, ibid.; Lampert to CINCUSARPAC, May 13, 1971, Chemical Weapons folder, box 3, Lampert Papers Lampert to Secretary of Defense, Sept. 10, 1971, ibid.

45. Okinawa Teachers' Association, "Sato Ho-Bei ni mukete no taisaku" (Countermeasures against Sato's visit to the United States), Sept. 8, 1969, Okinawa Teachers' Association folder, box 110, USCAR Records.

46. Sato, Koyama, and Kumon, *Postwar Politician*, 258.

47. *Chuo Koron*, Oct. 1969; *The Christian Science Monitor*, Feb. 19, 1969; Meyer, *Assignment Tokyo*, 46; Havens, *Fire across the Sea*, 204; Senate Committee on Foreign Relations, United States Security Agreements and Commitments Abroad, Japan and Okinawa: Hearings before the Subcommittee on United States Security Agreements and Commitments Abroad, 91st Cong., 2nd sess., (Jan. 26, 27, 28, and 29, 1970), pt. 5:1184.

48. *Asahi Evening News*, Nov. 27, 1969; Baltimore *Sun*, Nov. 22, 1969; Sato, Nov. 19, 1969, *Sato nikki*, 536.

49. Masumi, *Contemporary Politics in Japan*, 111–13.

50. Ibid.

51. Hori Shigeru, *Sengo seiji no oboegaki* (Memorandum of postwar politics), 134–36.

52. Lampert oral history, 3.

Bibliography

Archives

Air Force Historical Research Agency, Maxwell Air Force Base, Montgomery, Alabama. Pamphlets. Papers of Ralph Stearley. Unit Histories: History of the Twentieth Air Force.

Eisenhower Presidential Library, Abilene, Kansas. Papers of Simon B. Buckner, Jr.: Diary. Papers of John Foster Dulles: JFD-JMA Series; White House Memorandum Series. Papers of Dwight D. Eisenhower: Diary Series; International Series, Office of the Staff Secretary; Special Assistant Series. U.S. Army Unit Records: 7th Infantry Division. White House Office Files: Office of the Staff Secretary.

Harvard University, Cambridge, Massachusetts. Papers of Edwin Reischauer.

Hoover Institute, Stanford University, Palo Alto, California. Papers of John Caldwell. Papers of John K. Emmerson. Papers of Walter Judd. Papers of Paul Skuse. Papers of Joseph W. Stilwell. Papers of James T. Watkins IV.

Johnson Presidential Library, Austin, Texas. Audio-Visual Collection. Papers of George W. Ball. Papers of Morton Halperin. Papers of Lyndon Johnson: Aide Files, Files of Bill Moyers; National Security File, Country File (Japan) (Ryukyu Islands), Files of Walt Rostow, Memos to the President File, NSC Meeting File; President's Appointment File; White House Central File, Confidential File, Country File, Name File. Papers of U. Alexis Johnson: Diary.

Kennedy Presidential Library, Boston, Massachusetts. Papers of John F. Kennedy: President's Office File; National Security File.

MacArthur Memorial, Norfolk, Virginia. Record Group 5. Record Group 6. Record Group 8. Record Group 9. Record Group 10.

National Security Archive, The George Washington University, Washington D.C. U.S.-Japan Project.

Princeton University, Princeton, New Jersey. Papers of John Foster Dulles.

Southwestern University, Georgetown, Texas. Papers of John Tower.

Truman Presidential Library, Independence, Missouri. Papers of Dean Acheson. Papers of George Elsey. Papers of Robert Denninson. Papers of Harry S. Truman: President's Secretary's File.

U.S. Marine Corps Historical Center, Washington Navy Yard, Washington, D.C. Command Chronology Archives. Papers of Marius L. Bressoud, Jr. Papers of Charles I. Murray. Record Group 127: U.S. Marine Corps Records.

U.S. Army Military History Institute, Carlisle Barracks, Carlisle, Pennsylvania. Papers of James and William Belote. Papers of Simon B. Buckner, Jr. Papers of Paul Caraway. Papers of Rupert D. Graves: Diary. Papers of James Lampert. Papers of Matthew B. Ridgway. Papers of Fred C. Wallace. Papers of William Westmoreland. Ryukyu Papers.

U.S. Naval Academy, Annapolis, Maryland. Papers of William J. Sebald.

U.S. National Archives Washington, D.C. and College Park, Maryland. Nixon Presidential Project: Files of H. R. Haldeman; White House Central Files, Subject File (Country File, Japan; State-Territories). Record Group 46 (Senate Foreign Relations Committee Records). Record Group 59 (State Department Central Files). Record Group 218 (Joint Chiefs of Staff Files). Record Group 260 (U.S. Civil Administration of the Ryukyu Islands Records). Record Group 273 (National Security Council Records).

University of Arkansas, Fayetteville. Papers of J. William Fulbright.

University of California, Los Angeles. Film and Television Archive Research and Study Center: Hearst Newsreel Collection.

University of Georgia, Athens. Papers of Richard Russell.

University of Southern California, Los Angeles. Film Library: Film Script Collection.

Oral Histories

Author's Collection

Walt W. Rostow

Eisenhower Presidential Library

Walter Robertson

Georgetown University Library
Foreign Service Oral History Program

Olcott H. Deming
Douglas MacArthur II
Ulrich Straus
Philip Tresise

Johnson Presidential Library

U. Alexis Johnson
Edwin Reischauer
Dean Rusk

Kennedy Presidential Library

Edwin Reischauer

Princeton University
John Foster Dulles Oral History Collection

Maj. Gen. C. Stanton Babcock
Sir Howard Beale
Sir Carl Berendsen
W. Walton Butterworth
Sir Walter Nash
William J. Sebald

Truman Presidential Library

Lucius D. Battle
U. Alexis Johnson

U.S. Marine Corps Historical Center

Col. James R. Aichele
Maj. Gen. William P. Battell
Brig. Gen. Fred Beans
Maj. Gen. August Larson
Lt. Gen. Alan Shapley
Lt. Gen. Merwin Silverthorn
Lt. Gen. Ormond Simpson
Gen. Oliver P. Smith

U.S. Military History Institute
James and William Belote Papers

Col. Shimura Tsuneo

Ryukyu Papers

Capt. Lowe Bibby
Roderick Gillies
T/3 Ralph Saito
PFC Takejiro Higa

Senior Officers Debriefing Program

Lt. Gen. Paul W. Caraway
Lt. Gen. James B. Lampert
Col. William G. Schless
Lt. Gen. Ferdinand Unger
Lt. Gen. Albert Watson II

U.S. Naval Academy

William J. Sebald

Books

Acheson, Dean. *Present at the Creation: My Years in the State Department.* New York: W. W. Norton, 1969.

Aitken, Jonathan. *Nixon: A Life.* Washington: Regnery, 1993.

Allison, John. *Ambassador from the Prairie, or Allison in Wonderland.* Boston: Houghton, Mifflin, 1973.

Ambrose, Stephen E. *Nixon: The Education of a Politician, 1913–1962.* New York: Simon and Schuster, 1987.

———. *Nixon: The Triumph of a Politician, 1962–1972.* New York: Simon and Schuster, 1990.

Appleman, Roy, James M. Burns, Russell A. Gugeler, and John Stevens. *Okinawa: The Last Battle.* Washington, D.C.: U.S. GPO, 1948.

Astor, Gerald. *Operation Iceberg: The Invasion and Conquest of Okinawa in World War II, An Oral History.* New York: D. I. Fine, 1995.

Barclay, Glen St. J. *Friends in High Places: Australian-American Diplomatic Relations since 1945.* Melbourne, Australia: Oxford University Press, 1985.

Belote, James H., and William Belote. *Typhoon of Steel: The Battle for Okinawa.* New York: Harper and Row, 1970.

Berry, Henry. *Semper Fi, Mac: Living Memories of the U.S. Marines in World War II.* New York: Arbor House, 1982.

Blum, Robert M. *Drawing the Line: The Origin of American Containment Policy in East Asia.* New York: W. W. Norton, 1982.

Bradley, Omar N. *A General's Life.* New York: Simon and Schuster, 1983.

Buckley, Roger. *Occupation Diplomacy: Britain, the United States, and Japan, 1945–1952.* New York: Cambridge University Press, 1982.

———. *US-Japan Alliance Diplomacy, 1945–1990.* Cambridge, England: Cambridge University Press, 1992.

Buell, Thomas B. *The Quiet Warrior: A Biography of Admiral Raymond A. Spruance.* Boston: Little, Brown, 1974.

Burkman, Thomas, ed. *The Occupation of Japan: The International Context.* Norfolk, Va.: MacArthur Memorial, 1984.

Chang, Gordon. *Friends and Enemies: The United States, China, and the Soviet Union, 1948–1972.* Stanford: Stanford University Press, 1990.

Cohen, Theodore. *Remaking Japan: The American Occupation as New Deal.* New York: Free Press, 1987.

Cook, Haruko Taya, and Theodore F. Cook. *Japan at War: An Oral History.* New York: The New Press, 1992.

Curtis, Gerald L. *The Japanese Way of Politics.* New York: Columbia University Press, 1988.

Department of Internal Affairs. *Documents on New Zealand External Relations.* Vol. 3,

The ANZUS Pact and the Treaty of Peace with Japan. Wellington, New Zealand: Government printer, 1985.

D'Este, Carlo. *Patton: A Genius for War.* New York: HarperCollins, 1995.

Destler, I. M., Haruhiro Fukui, and Hideo Sato. *The Textile Wrangle: Conflict in Japanese-American Relations, 1969–1971.* Ithaca, N.Y.: Cornell University Press, 1979.

Dingman, Roger. *Ghost of War: The Sinking of the* Awa maru *and Japanese-American Relations, 1945–1995.* Annapolis: Naval Institute Press, 1997.

Dower, John. *Empire and Aftermath: Yoshida Shigeru and the Japanese Experience, 1878–1945.* Cambridge: Harvard University Press, 1978.

———. *Embracing Defeat: Japan in the Wake of World War II.* New York: W. W. Norton/The New Press, 1999.

Eisenhower, Dwight D. *Public Papers of the Presidents of the United States: Dwight D. Eisenhower, 1954.* Washington, D.C.: GPO, 1960.

———. *Public Papers of the Presidents of the United States: Dwight D. Eisenhower, 196061.* Washington, D.C., GPO, 1961.

———. *The Papers of Dwight David Eisenhower.* Vol. 7, *Chief of Staff.* Baltimore: Johns Hopkins University Press, 1978.

Federal Supplement.

Feifer, George. *Tennozan: The Battle of Okinawa and the Atomic Bomb.* New York: Ticknor and Fields, 1992.

Finn, Richard B. *Winners in Peace: MacArthur, Yoshida, and Postwar Japan.* Berkeley and Los Angeles: University of California Press, 1992.

Fisch, Jr., Arnold G. *Military Government in the Ryukyus Islands, 1945–50.* Washington, D.C.: GPO, 1987.

Frank, Benis M., and Henry I. Shaw. *Victory and Occupation.* Washington, D.C.: GPO, 1968.

Fuchaku, Isamu, Mitsugu Miyagi, Gasei Higa, and Zenkichi Toyama. *Tours of Okinawa.* Tokyo: Bridgeway Press, 1959.

Fuchaku, Isamu, and Mitsugu Miyagi. *Okinawa at Work.* Rutland, Vt.: C. E. Tuttle Co., 1965.

Fujiyama, Aiichiro. *Seiji waga michi* (Politics, my way). Tokyo: Asahi Shinbunsha, 1976.

Fukui, Haruhiro. *Party in Power: The Japanese Liberal-Democrats and Policymaking.* Berkeley and Los Angeles: University of California Press, 1970.

Gaddis, John Lewis. *Strategies of Containment: A Critical Appraisal of Postwar American National Security Policy.* New York: Oxford University Press, 1982.

Gallicchio, Marc S. *The Cold War Begins in Asia: American East Asian Policy and the Fall of the Japanese Empire.* New York: Columbia University Press, 1988.

Gallup, George. *The Gallup Poll: Public Opinion, 1935–1971.* New York: Random House, 1972.

———. *The Gallup Poll: Public Opinion, 1972–1977.* Wilmington, Del.: Scholarly Resources, 1978

Hasegawa, Sukehiro. *Japanese Foreign Aid: Policy and Practice.* New York: Praeger, 1975.

Havens, Thomas R. H. *Fire across the Sea: The Vietnam War and Japan, 1965–1975.*
    Princeton: Princeton University Press, 1987.
Higa, Mikio. *Politics and Parties in Postwar Okinawa.* Vancouver: Publications
    Centere, University of British Columbia, 1963.
Higashi, Mineo. *Okinawa no shonen* (Child of Okinawa). Tokyo: n.p., 1972.
Hoopes, Townsend, and Douglas Brinkley. *Driven Patriot: The Life and Times of James
    Forrestal.* New York: Knopf, 1992.
Hori, Shigeru. *Sengo seiji no oboegaki* (Memorandum of postwar politics). Tokyo:
    Mainichi Shinbunsha, 1975.
Huber, Thomas M. *Japan's Battle for Okinawa, April–June, 1945.* Leavenworth Papers
    No. 18. Ft. Leavenworth, Kans.: Combat Studies Institute, Command and
    General Staff College, 1990.
Immerman, Richard H. *John Foster Dulles and the Diplomacy of the Cold War.*
    Princeton: Princeton University Press, 1990.
Iriye, Akira. *The Cold War in Asia: A Historical Introduction.* Englewood Cliffs, N.J.:
    Prentice-Hall, 1974.
Isaacson, Walter, and Evan Thomas. *The Wise Men: Six Friends and the World They
    Made—Acheson, Bohlen, Harriman, Kennan, Lovett, McCloy.* New York: Simon
    and Schuster, 1986.
James, D. Clayton. *The Years of MacArthur, 1880–1964.* 3 vols. Boston: Houghton
    Mifflin, 1970–85.
Japan Report. New York: Consulate General of Japan, n.d.
Johnson, Lyndon B. *Public Papers of the Presidents of the United States: Lyndon B.
    Johnson, 1967.* Vol. 2. Washington, D.C.: GPO, 1968.
Johnson, U. Alexis. *The Right Hand of Power: The Memoirs of an American Diplomat.*
    Englewood Cliffs, N.J.: Prentice Hall, 1984.
Kennan, George F. *Memoirs, 1925–1950.* Boston: Little, Brown, 1967.
———. *Memoirs, 1950–1963.* Boston: Little, Brown, 1969.
Kennedy, John F. *Public Papers of the Presidents of the United States: John F. Kennedy,
    1962.* Washington, D.C.: GPO, 1963.
Kerr, George. *Okinawa: The History of an Island People.* Rutland, Vt.: C. E. Tuttle Co.,
    1958.
Kincade, Diane D., ed. *Silent Hattie Speaks: The Personal Journal of Senator Hattie
    Caraway.* Westport, Conn.: Greenwood Press, 1979.
Kissinger, Henry A. *White House Years.* Boston: Little, Brown, 1979.
Kluger, Richard. *The Paper: The Life and Death of the New York Herald Tribune.* New
    York: Knopf, 1986.
Kolko, Joyce, and Gabriel Kolko. *The Limits of Power: The World and United States
    Foreign Policy, 1945–1954.* New York: Harper and Row, 1972.
Krulak, Victor H. *First to Fight: An Inside View of the U.S. Marine Corps.* Annapolis:
    Naval Institute Press, 1984.
Kurzman, Dan. *Kishi and Japan: The Search of the Sun.* New York: Obolensky, 1960.
LaFeber, Walter. *The Clash: U.S.-Japanese Relations throughout History.* New York:
    W. W. Norton, 1997.

Linn, Brian McAllister. *Guardians of Empire: The U.S. Army in the Pacific, 1902–1940*. Chapel Hill: University of North Carolina Press, 1997.

MacArthur, Douglas. *Reminiscences*. New York: McGraw-Hill, 1964.

McPherson, James M. *Battle Cry of Freedom: The Civil War Era*. New York: Oxford University Press, 1988.

Malone, David. *Hattie and Huey: An Arkansas Tour*. Fayetteville: University of Arkansas Press, 1989.

McGibbon, Ian, ed. *Undiplomatic Dialogue: Letters between Carl Berendsen and Alister McIntosh, 1943–1952*. Auckland, New Zealand: Auckland University Press, 1993.

McGlothlen, Ronald. *Controlling the Waves: Dean Acheson and U.S. Foreign Policy in Asia*. New York: W. W. Norton, 1993.

McIntyre, W. David. *Background to the Anzus Pact: Policy-Making, Strategy, and Diplomacy, 1945–55*. Christchurch, New Zealand: Canterbury University Press, 1995.

Mailer, Norman. *Harlot's Ghost*. New York: Random House, 1991.

Manchester, William. *American Caesar: Douglas MacArthur, 1880–1964*. New York: Little, Brown, 1978.

———. *Goodbye, Darkness: A Memoir of the Pacific War*. Boston: Little, Brown, 1980.

Masayoshi, Ohira. *Brush Strokes: Moments from My Life*. Tokyo: Foreign Press Center, 1978.

Masumi, Junnosuke. *Postwar Politics in Japan, 1945–1955*. Translated by Lonny E. Carlile. Berkeley: Center for Japenese Studies, Institute of East Asian Studies, University of California, 1985.

———. *Contemporary Politics in Japan*. Translated by Lonny E. Carlile. Berkeley and Los Angeles: University of California Press, 1995.

Mayers, David Allan. *Cracking the Monolith: U.S. Policy against the Sino-Soviet Alliance*. Baton Rouge: Louisiana State University, 1986.

Menzies, Sir Robert Gordon. *The Measure of the Years*. London: Cassell, 1970.

Merritt, Marian Chapple. *Is Like Typhoon: Okinawa and the Far East*. Tokyo: Tokyo World News and Publishing, n.d.

Meyer, Armin H. *Assignment Tokyo: An Ambassador's Journal*. Indianapolis: n.p., 1974.

Millett, Allan R. *Semper Fidelis: The History of the United States Marine Corps*. New York: Macmillan, 1980.

Moon, Katharine H. S. *Sex among Allies: Military Prostitution in U.S.-Korean Relations*. New York: Columbia University Press, 1997.

Morris, Morton D. *Okinawa: A Tiger by the Tail*. New York: Hawthorn Books, 1968.

Morrison, Samuel Eliot. *Victory in the Pacific, 1945*. Vol. 14 of *History of United States Naval Operations in World War II*. Boston: Little, Brown, 1960.

Mosley, Leonard. *Dulles: A Biography of Eleanor, Allen, and John Foster Dulles and their Family Network*. New York: Dial Press, 1978.

Nelson, Anna Kasten, ed. *The State Department Policy Planning Staff Papers, 1948*. Vol. 2. New York: n.p., 1983.

Nichols, David, ed. *Ernie's War: The Best of Ernie Pyle's World War II Dispatches*. New York: Random House, 1986.

Nixon, Richard. *Public Papers of the Presidents of the United States: Richard Nixon, 1970.* Washington, D.C.: GPO, 1971.

———. *RN: The Memoirs of Richard Nixon.* New York: Grosset and Dunlap, 1978.

Oppler, Alfred C. *Legal Reform in Occupied Japan: A Participant Looks Back.* Princeton: Princeton University Press, 1976.

O'Sheel, Patrick, and Gene Cook, eds. *Semper Fidelis: The U.S. Marines in the Pacific, 1942–1945.* New York: William Sloane Associates, 1947.

Oshiro, Tatsuhiro. *Kakuteru paatii* (The cocktail party). Tokyo: n.p., 1982.

Packard, George R., III. *Protest in Tokyo: The Security Treaty Crisis of 1960.* Princeton: Princeton University Press, 1966.

Patrick, John. *The Teahouse of the August Moon, a Play by John Patrick.* New York: Putnam, 1954.

Patrick, John, Stan Freeman, and Franklin Underwood. *Lovely Ladies, Kind Gentlemen.* New York: S. French, 1971.

Perry, Mark. *Four Stars.* Boston: Houghton Mifflin, 1989.

Potter, E. B. *Nimitz.* Annapolis: Naval Institute Press, 1976.

Pruessen, Ronald. *John Foster Dulles: The Road to Power.* New York: Free Press, 1982.

Reischauer, Edwin O. *Japan Past and Present.* 1946. Reprint, New York: Knopf, 1953.

———. *The United States and Japan.* Cambridge: Harvard University Press, 1950, 1957, 1965.

Reischauer, Edwin O., and Joseph Yamagiwa, *Translations from Early Japanese Literature.* Cambridge: Harvard University Press, 1951.

Reischauer, Edwin O. *Wanted: an Asian Policy.* New York: Knopf, 1955.

———. *Ennin's Travels in T'ang China.* New York: Ronald Press Company, 1955.

———, ed. *Ennin's Diary: The Record of a Pilgrimage to China in Search of the Law.* New York: Ronald Press Company, 1955.

Reischauer, Edwin O., and John K. Fairbank. *A History of East Asian Civilization.* 1960. Reprint, Boston: Houghton Mifflin, 1965.

Reischauer, Edwin O. *Beyond Vietnam: The United States and Asia.* New York: Knopf: 1967.

———. *My Life between Japan and America.* New York: Harper and Row, 1986.

Reischauer, Haru Matsukata. *Samurai and Silk: A Japanese and American Heritage.* Cambridge: Belknap Press of Harvard University Press, 1986.

Reynolds, David. *Rich Relations: The American Occupation of Britain, 1942–1945.* New York: Random House, 1995.

Rhodes, Richard. *Dark Sun: The Making of the Hydrogen Bomb.* New York: Simon and Schuster, 1995.

Sato, Eisaku. *Sato Eisaku nikki* (Sato Eisaku diary). Vol. 3. Tokyo: Asahi Shinbunsha, 1998.

Sato, Seizaburo, Kenichi Koyama, and Shunpei Kumon. *Postwar Politician: The Life of Former Prime Minister Masayoshi Ohira.* Translated by William R. Carter. New York: Kodansha International, 1990.

Schaffer, Howard B. *Chester Bowles: New Dealer in the Cold War.* Cambridge: Harvard University Press, 1993.

Schaller, Michael. *The American Occupation of Japan: The Origins of the Cold War in Asia.* New York: Oxford University Press, 1985.

———. *Douglas MacArthur: The Far Eastern General.* New York: Oxford University Press, 1988.

———. *Altered States: The United States and Japan since the Occupation.* New York: Oxford University Press, 1997.

Schonberger, Howard B. *Aftermath of War: Americans and the Remaking of Japan, 1945–1952.* Kent, Ohio: Kent State University Press, 1989.

Sebald, William J. *With MacArthur in Japan: A Personal History of the Occupation.* New York: W. W. Norton, 1965.

Shapley, Deborah. *Promise and Power: The Life and Times of Robert McNamara.* Boston: Little, Brown, 1993.

Shiels, Frederick L. *America, Okinawa, and Japan: Case Studies for Foreign Policy Theory.* Washington, D.C.: University Press of America, 1980.

Skates, John Ray. *The Invasion of Japan: Alternative to the Bomb.* Columbia: University of South Carolina Press, 1994.

Sledge, E. B. *With the Old Breed at Peleliu and Okinawa.* New York: Oxford University Press, 1990.

Sneider, Vern. *The Teahouse of the August Moon.* New York: Putnam, 1951.

———. *The King from Ashtabula.* New York: Putnam, 1960.

Spector, Ronald H. *Eagle against the Sun: The American War with Japan.* New York: The Free Press, 1984.

Spender, Jean. *The Charge Is Murder!* Sydney: Dy Mock's Book Arcade, 1933.

Spender, Percy. *Exercises in Diplomacy: The ANZUS Treaty and the Colombo Plan.* New York: New York University Press, 1969.

Stockwin, J. A. A. *The Japanese Socialist Party and Neutraliam: A Study of a Political Party and its Foreign Policy.* Melbourne, Australia: Melobourne University Press, 1968.

Toulouse, Mark. *The Transformation of John Foster Dulles: From Prophet of Realism to Priest of Nationalism.* Macon, Ga.: Mercer University Press, 1985.

Truman, Harry S. *Memoirs.* 2 vols. Garden City, N.Y.: Doubleday, 1955–56.

Tuchman, Barbara. *Stilwell and the American Experience in China, 1911–45.* New York: Macmillan, 1970.

Ugaki, Matome. *Fading Victory: The Diary of Admiral Matome Ugaki, 1941–1945.* Pittsburgh: University of Pittsburgh Press, 1992.

U.S. Civil Administration of the Ryukyu Islands. *Civil Affairs Activities in the Ryukyu Islands for the Period Ending 31 March 1957.* Vol. 5, no. 1. Washington, D.C.: GPO, 1957.

———. *Civil Administration of the Ryukyu Islands, Report for Period 1 July 1962 to 30 June 1963.* Washington, D.C.: GPO, 1963.

———. *The Newspapers of the Ryukyu Islands.* San Francisco, 1964.

———. *Civil Administration of the Ryukyu Islands, Report for Period 1 July 1964 to 30 June 1965.* Washington, D.C.: GPO, 1965.

———. *Civil Administration of the Ryukyu Islands, Report for Period 1 July 1966 to 30 June 1967.* Washington, D.C.: GPO, 1967.

————. *Civil Administration of the Ryukyu Islands, Report for Period 1 July 1967 to 30 June 1968.* Washington, D.C.: GPO, 1968.

————. *Civil Administration of the Ryukyu Islands, Report for Period 1 July 1968 to 30 June 1969.* Washington, D.C.: GPO, 1969.

————. *Civil Administration of the Ryukyu Islands, Report for Period 1 July 1970 to 30 June 1971.* Washington, D.C.: GPO, 1971.

————. *The Final Civil Affairs Report, 30 June 1971–15 May 1972.* Washington, D.C.: GPO, 1972.

U.S. Congress, House of Representatives. Committee on Appropriations: *Foreign Aid Appropriation Bill for 1950, Hearings before the Subcommittee of the Committee on Appropriations.* 81st Cong., 1st sess.

————. Committee on Appropriations: *The Supplemental Appropriation Bill for 1955, Hearings before Subcommittees of the Committee on Appropriations.* 83rd Cong., 2nd sess., pt. 2. Washington, D.C.: GPO, 1954.

————. Committee on Appropriations: *The Supplemental Appropriation Bill for 1956, Hearings before Subcommittees of the Committee on Appropriations.* 84th Cong., 1st sess. Washington, D.C.: GPO, 1955.

————. Committee on Appropriations: *The Supplemental Appropriation Bill for 1957, Hearings before Subcommittees of the Committee on Appropriations.* 84th Cong., 2nd sess. Washington, D.C.: GPO, 1956.

————. Subcommittee on Foreign Operations Appropriations, *Mutual Security Appropriations for 1961.* 86th Cong., 2nd sess. Washington, D.C.: GPO, 1960.

————. Committee on Appropriations, *Subcommittee No. 2: Consideration of H.R. 10937, to Amend the Act Providing for the Economic and Social Development of the Ryukyu Islands.* Washington, D.C.: GPO, 1962.

————. Committee on Appropriations, *Foreign Operations Appropriations for 1965, Hearings before a Subcommittee of the Committee on Appropriations.* 88th Cong., 2nd sess. Washington, D.C.: GPO, 1965.

————. Committee on Appropriations: *Foreign Assistance and Related Agencies Appropriations for 1967.* Washington, D.C.: GPO, 1966.

————. Committee on Appropriations: *Foreign Assistance and Related Agencies Appropriations for 1969.* Washington, D.C.: GPO, 1968.

————. Committee on Appropriations: *Foreign Assistance and Related Agencies Appropriations for 1970.* Washington, D.C.: GPO, 1969.

————. Committee on Appropriations, Subcommittee on Foreign Operations and Related Agencies Appropriations: *Foreign Operations and Related Agencies Appropriations for 1970,* pt. 1. Washington, D.C.: GPO, 1970.

————. Committee on Armed Services: *Report of a Special Committee of the Armed Services Committee, Following an Inspection Tour October 14–November 23, 1955.* Washington, D.C.: GPO, 1956.

————. Committee on Armed Services: *Okinawan Lands, Hearings before a Subcommittee of the Committee on Armed Services.* 84th Cong., 1st sess. Washington, D.C.: GPO, 1957.

U.S. Congress, Senate. Committee on Appropriations: *The Supplemental Appropriation Bill for 1955, Hearings before the Committee on Appropriations.* 83rd Cong., 2nd sess., pt. 2. Washington, D.C.: GPO, 1954.

————. Committee on Appropriations: *The Supplemental Appropriation Bill for 1957, Hearings before the Committee on Appropriations.* 84th Cong., 2nd sess. Washington, D.C.: GPO, 1956.

————. Committee on Appropriations: *Foreign Assistance and Related Agencies Appropriations for 1964.* 88th Cong., 1st sess. Washington, D.C.: GPO, 1963.

————. Committee on Armed Services: *Nomination of John T. McNaughton and Development of the Ryukyu Islands.* 87th Cong., 2nd sess. Washington, D.C.: GPO, 1962.

————. Committee on Armed Services: *Development of the Ryukyu Islands.* 89th Cong., 2nd sess. Washington, D.C.: GPO, 1966.

————. Committee on Foreign Relations: *Nominations of Robert R. Bowie and U. Alexis Johnson.* 89th Cong., 2nd sess. Washington, D.C.: GPO, 1966.

————. Committee on Foreign Relations: *United States Security Agreements and Commitments Abroad, Japan and Okinawa, Hearings before the Subcommittee on United States Security Agreements and Commitments Abroad.* 91st Cong., 2nd sess., pt. 5. (January 26–29, 1970). Washington, D.C.: GPO, 1970.

————. Committee on Foreign Relations: *The Agreement between the United States of America and Japan Concerning the Ryukyu Islands and the Daito Islands.* 92nd Cong., 1st sess. Washington, D.C.: GPO, 1971.

U.S. Department of State. *Conference for the Conclusion and Signature of the Treaty of Peace with Japan, San Francisco, California, September 4–8, 1951: Record of Proceedings.* Washington, D.C.: GPO, 1951.

————. *Foreign Relations of the United States, 1947.* Vol. 6, *The Far East.*

————. *Foreign Relations of the United States, 1949.* Vol. 7, pt. 2, *The Far East and Australasia.*

————. *Foreign Relations of the United States: Memoranda of the Secretary of State, 1949–1951, and Meetings and Visits of Foreign Dignitaries, 1949–1952* (microfiche supplement).

————. *Foreign Relations of the United States, 1950.* Vol. 6, *East Asia and the Pacific.*

————. *Foreign Relations of the United States, 1951.* Vol. 6, part 1, *Asia and the Pacific.*

————. *Foreign Relations of the United States, 1952–1954.* Vol. 14, pt. 2, *China and Japan.*

————. *Foreign Relations of the United States, 1955–1957.* Vol. 23, pt. 1, *Japan.*

————. *Foreign Relations of the United States, 1958–1960.* Vol. 18, *Japan, Korea.*

————. *Foreign Relations of the United States, 1958–1960.* Vol. 17/18 (microfiche supplement).

————. *Foreign Relations of the United States, 1961–1963.* Vol. 22, *Northeast Asia.*

————. *Department of State Bulletin,* 945–72.

Wakaizumi, Kei. *Tasaku nakarishi o shinzemu to hossu* (Just the four of us—I want to believe there was no other alternative). Tokyo: Bungei Shun Ju, 1994.

Watanabe, Akio. *The Okinawa Problem: A Chapter in Japan-U.S. Relations.* Melbourne, Australia: Melbourne University Press, 1970.

Watt, Sir Alan. *Australian Diplomat: Memoirs of Sir Alan Watt.* Sydney: Angus and Robertson, 1972.

Weigley, Russell. *The American Way of War: A History of United States Military Strategy and Policy.* New York: Macmillan, 1973.

———. *Eisenhower's Lieutenants: The Campaign of France and Germany, 1944–1945.* Bloomington: Indiana University Press, 1981.

Weinstein, Martin E. *Japan's Postwar Defense Policy, 1957–1968.* New York: Columbia University Press, 1971.

Welfield, John. *An Empire in Eclipse: Japan in the Postwar American Alliance System— A Study in the Interaction of Domestic Politics and Foreign Policy.* Atlantic Highlands, N.J.: Athlone Press, 1988.

Whitney, Courtney. *MacArthur: His Rendezvous with History.* New York: Knopf, 1956.

Williams, Justin, Sr. *Japan's Political Revolution under MacArthur: A Participant's Account.* Athens: University of Georgia Press, 1979.

Willoughby, Charles A., and John Chamberlain, *MacArthur, 1941–1951.* New York: McGraw-Hill, 1954.

Yahara, Hiromichi. *The Battle for Okinawa.* New York: J. Wiley, 1995.

Yoshida, Shigeru. *Kaiso junen.* Vol. 3. Tokyo: Shinchosha, 1958.

———. *The Yoshida Memoirs: The Story of Japan in Crisis.* Translated by Yoshida Kenichi. London: Heinemann, 1963.

Zabilka, Gladys. *Customs and Culture of Okinawa.* Rev. ed. Rutland, Vt.: Bridgeway Press, 1959.

Articles and Chapters

Ballantine, Joseph W. "The Future of the Ryukyus." *Foreign Affairs* 31, no. 4 (July, 1953): 663–74.

Bennett, Henry Stanley. "The Impact of Invasion and Occupation on the Civilians of Okinawa." *U.S. Naval Institute Proceedings* 72 (February, 1946): 263–76.

Biggs, Barton M. "The Outraged Okinawans." *Harper's Magazine,* December, 1958, 56–60.

Cohen, Yehudi A. "The Sociology of Commercialized Prostitution in Okinawa." *Social Forces* 37, no. 2 (December, 1958): 160–71.

Dingman, Roger. "Alliance in Crisis: The Lucky Dragon Incident and Japanese-American Relations." In *The Great Powers in East Asia, 1953–1960,* edited by Warren I. Cohen and Akira Iriye, 187–214. New York: Columbia University Press, 1990.

Dower, John. "Occupied Japan in the American Lake, 1945–1950." In *America's Asia: Dissenting Essays on Asian-American Relations,* edited by Edward Friedman and Mark Selden, 187–206. New York: Pantheon Books, 1971.

———. "Reform and Reconsolidation." In *Japan Examined: Perspectives on Modern Japanese History,* edited by Harry Wray and Kilary Conroy, 343–51. Honolulu: University of Hawaii Press, 1983.

———. "Yoshida in the Scales of History." In *Japan in War and Peace: Selected Essays,* edited by John Dawer, 208–41. New York: New Press, 1993.

Dulles, John Foster. "Policy for Security and Peace." *Foreign Affairs* 32, no. 3 (April, 1954): 353–64.

Ford, Clelland S. "Occupation Experiences on Okinawa." *The Annals of the American Academy of Political and Social Sciences* 267 (January, 1950): 175–92.

Foltos, Lester J. "The New Pacific Barrier: America's Search for Security in the Pacific, 1945–47." *Diplomatic History* 13 (summer, 1989): 317–42.

Graybar, Lloyd J. "The Buckners of Kentucky." *The Filson Club Quarterly* 58, no. 2 (1984): 202–18.

Haley, J. Fred. "The Death of Gen. Simon Bolivar Buckner." *Marine Corps Gazette,* November, 1982.

Ito, Takashi. "Shigemitsu Mamoru and the 1955 System." In *Creating Single-Party Democracy: Japan's Postwar Political System,* edited by Katakoa Tetsuya, 100–18. Stanford: Stanford University Press, 1992.

Karasik, Daniel D. "Okinawa: A Problem in Administration and Reconstruction." *Far East Quarterly* 7, no. 3 (May, 1948): 254–67.

LaFeber, Walter. "Decline of Relations during the Vietnam War." In *The United States and Japan in the Postwar World,* edited by Akira Iriye and Warren I. Cohen, 96–113. Lexington, Ky.: University Press of Kentucky, 1989.

Ma, L. Eve Armentrout. "The Explosive Nature of Okinawa's 'Land Issue' or 'Base Issue,' 1945–1977: A Dilemma of United States Military Policy." *Journal of American–East Asian Relations* 1, no. 4 (winter, 1992).

Menzies, Sir Robert Gordon. "The Pacific Settlement Seen from Australia." *Foreign Affairs* 30, no. 2 (January, 1952): 188–96.

Nimitz, Chester W. Foreword to *Brave Ship, Brave Men,* by Arnold S. Lott. Annapolis: Naval Institute Press, 1986.

Nixon, Richard. "Asia after Viet Nam." *Foreign Affairs* 46, no. 1 (October, 1967): 111–25.

Reischauer, Edwin. "The Broken Dialogue with Japan." *Foreign Affairs* 39, no. 1 (October, 1960): 11–26.

Schaller, Michael. "Securing the Great Crescent: Occupied Japan and the Origins of Containment in Southeast Asia." *Journal of American History* 69, no. 2 (September, 1982): 392–414.

———. "MacArthur's Japan: The View from Washington." *Diplomatic History* 10, no. 1 (winter, 1986): 1–24.

Selden, Mark. "Okinawa and American Security Imperialism." In *Remaking Asia: Essays on the American Uses of Power,* edited by Mark Selden, 279–304. New York: Pantheon Books, 1974.

Wakaizumi, Kei. "Japan beyond 1970." *Foreign Affairs* 47, no. 3 (April, 1969): 509–20.

Unpublished Material

Foltos, Lester. "The Bulwark of Freedom: American Security Policy for East Asia, 1945–1950." Ph.D. diss., University of Illinois, 1980.
Niksch, Larry A. "Congress and the Reversion of Okinawa." August 13, 1970. Legislative Reference Service, Library of Congress.

CD-ROM

Haldeman, H. R. *The Haldeman Diaries: Inside the Nixon White House, the Complete Multimedia Edition.* Santa Monica, Calif.: Sony Imagesoft, 1994.

Motion Pictures and Television

The Teahouse of the August Moon. Directed by Daniel Mann, screenplay by John Patrick. MGM studios, 1956.
"The Teahouse of the August Moon." Television adaptation by John Patrick. Broadcast date: November 26, 1962, NBC television network.

Index